The Rise of Cable Programming in the United States

TEXAS FILM AND MEDIA STUDIES SERIES
THOMAS SCHATZ, EDITOR

THE RISE OF
CABLE PROGRAMMING
IN THE UNITED STATES

REVOLUTION OR EVOLUTION?

MEGAN MULLEN

UNIVERSITY OF TEXAS PRESS, AUSTIN

First edition, 2003

Requests for permission to reproduce material
from this work should be sent to Permissions,
University of Texas Press, Box 7819, Austin, TX
78713-7819.

∞ The paper used in this book meets the minimum
requirements of ANSI/NISO Z39.48-1992
(R1997) (Permanence of Paper).

Library of Congress
Cataloging-in-Publication Data

Mullen, Megan Gwynne, 1964–
    The rise of cable programming in the
United States: revolution or evolution? /
Megan Gwynne Mullen.
        p.   cm. — (Texas film and media
studies series)
    Includes bibliographical references and index.
    ISBN 0-292-75272-5 (cloth) —
    ISBN 0-292-75273-3 (paper)
    1. Cable television—United States.
2. Television programs—United States.
I. Title.   II. Series.
HE8700.72.U6M85   2003
384.55′532′0973—dc21
2002011029

In memory of my grandmother,
Sara Bailey Jones

Between 1948 and 1995, cable television in the United States grew from a form of basic antenna service for isolated, rural communities into a nationwide entertainment and information medium, capable of providing hundreds of diverse channels of programming. Cable changed in terms of the technology it uses, its regulatory status, its industrial structure, people's uses for it, and many other factors. This study focuses specifically on the history of cable *programming,* though it has become evident in the course of researching and analyzing this topic that the actual program selections and program texts available on cable have been shaped by a broad range of cultural forces. Thus, the study examines various regulatory and economic constraints that the cable industry experienced over the years, and considers the types of programming innovation that took place under those conditions. It looks at the incentives and expectations that have been formulated for the cable industry at certain stages of its history. And it discusses the ways in which these have been negotiated and rearticulated by the parties concerned—the cable industry, policymakers, the public—to produce the standards and practices of modern, satellite-era cable programming.

One goal of this study is to outline the history of cable programming—particularly its early years—chronologically. To date, few comprehensive histories of cable television have been written, and none have dealt with programming specifically. A complementary goal is to develop a theory that uses historical developments in economics, policy, and technology to explain formal attributes of cable programming. A number of studies have examined modern cable's narrowcast program services. Other research has looked at cable's formal innovations, including the music video and home shopping formats. But few studies have considered the importance of cable's complex relationship with, and persistent reliance on, broadcast television—the historical imperative that drives modern cable programming practices.

A wide and, perhaps, eclectic variety of primary sources contributed to the research in this book. Several trade publications were used. *Broadcasting and Cable* magazine (earlier called *Broadcasting-Telecasting* and *Broadcasting*) was used extensively. Although this publication historically has reflected the views and interests of the broadcast industries (radio and television), it is also true that it provides the most consistent coverage of the developing cable industry during the period covered by this book. Moreover, the centrality of information from *Broadcasting*, particularly in discussion of cable's early years, supports a key premise of this book: that cable's fortunes have been inextricably linked to broadcast television and its programming. Information about the community antenna television (CATV)/cable industry specifically was also drawn from such publications as *NCTA Membership Bulletin, TV Communications, Cablevision,* and *Multichannel News.* While none of these publications boasts the longevity of *Broadcasting,* they do provide more specific details about cable programming strategies. More general periodicals— including the *New York Times, Variety,* and *TV Guide*—supplied additional information, particularly as relates to popular and critical responses to the medium and its potential. Other primary material includes promotional materials provided directly by cable networks.

Government publications, particularly *FCC Record,* were used for specific details about industry regulations. Furthermore, the transcribed hearings and testimony that preceded the enactment of those regulations shed light upon contentious issues that long since have been resolved. They indicate—often in minute detail—what was at stake for the parties concerned. Various studies, commissioned by government bodies as well as private interests, also were consulted. In addition to providing well-researched historical background, they offer important insights into cable policy-making processes.

The resources of the National Cable Television Center and Museum, Penn State University (most of which are now archived at the center's new facility in Denver), were invaluable. The documents (primarily corporate records) from the Irving Kahn collection proved useful in tracking critical developments in the early years of satellite cable. Other documents and artifacts (including an early local origination time-and-temperature device)—whether or not they are mentioned specifically in the book—offered better understanding of the topics discussed. Most notably, the oral history transcripts from the Cable Pioneers collection provided critical insights about U.S. cable's early development. Several are cited directly.

The interviews used in writing this book include those conducted personally, as well as a number of oral history interviews archived at the National Cable Center. Personal interviews reflect both people involved with early cable and people currently involved in cable programming. The Cable Center maintains audiotapes and transcriptions of interviews with cable television's founders, conducted by members of the Cable Pioneers association during the 1980s and 1990s. Both completed and incomplete oral histories were consulted.

These interviews represent firsthand accounts of events—an extremely valuable source of information. People working in the modern cable industry can offer insights about cable programming practices from within a corporate environment that is very unfamiliar to an academic researcher. And the cable industry is young enough that many of its founders are still living and are eager to share their recollections, as well. Surely some of the most valuable and original resources informing this book were the various individuals who shared their personal recollections. It should be noted, of course, that much of this information cannot be verified either in other primary sources or in more comprehensive secondary sources. But with no comprehensive histories of U.S. cable television to refer to, the people who helped me "piece together the puzzle" were indispensable.

Textual analysis in this book is limited to cable programming of the early 1990s. Virtually no original cable programming remains from the early cable (CATV) era. To analyze cable's predominant program source from those years—broadcast television—would merely overstate the point that cable was extremely dependent on its predecessor medium. Although local cable access programming from the 1970s is available at various facilities around the country, other researchers already have taken on the task of discussing this material.[1]

Many of the television programs discussed herein were running on cable during the research for this book, either as first-run episodes or as reruns. Indeed, a large portion of the text-based analysis in this study derives from many hours spent in front of the television. Videotapes of continuous cable programming also were analyzed to identify scheduling patterns. Programs and program schedules not currently available for viewing have been described in more general terms such as genre. Where necessary, television listings in regional newspapers and *TV Guide* were consulted.

A large portion of the research for this project was done at the National Cable Television Center and Museum, Penn State University. I am extremely indebted to the center's director, E. Stratford Smith, for sharing invaluable recollections from his five-decade involvement with the cable industry. In addition to spending many hours answering my questions, Strat was extremely generous both in giving me access to his personal research and in helping me find my way through the extensive holdings of the Cable Center. Pamela Czapla, director of the center's library program, also gave me a great deal of assistance with my research.

I also am grateful to Bill Arnold of the Texas Cable TV Association for sharing his knowledge of cable television's history and for putting me in touch with numerous contacts in the cable industry.

Others in the cable industry who shared time, information, and insights include: Leslie Reed and David Baldwin, Home Box Office; David Coe, Bainbridge (New York) Cable; Mary Cotter, NewChannels Corporation; Robert Miron, Newhouse Broadcasting; Jerry Henry, Ron Lindsley, and Bruce Tompkins, Oneonta NewChannels; Walt Rasmussen and Raymond Bermond, EMI Communications; Albert Bagnardi, (formerly) Oneonta Video; Mark Solow, The Family Channel; Beverly Hermann, Lifetime Television; Reese Schonfeld, Television Food Network; Meg LaVigne and Lee Kinberg, WSBK-Boston; Marie Jacobson, Comedy Central; Lisa Turner, TCI of Cumberland, Maryland; and Andrea Hood, United Video.[2]

A scholarship from the Texas Cable TV Association helped me complete a substantial portion of my early research. Additional assistance at the early stage came from Shell Oil Foundation grants for graduate travel-related research at the University of Texas. Later travel support came from the University of New Hampshire's Center for the Humanities. The University of Wisconsin–Parkside offered support in the form of course release time during the final preparation of the manuscript.

My parents, Sally Jones Mullen and James Mullen, have given me support of many sorts—ranging from financial assistance to research contacts in my hometown of Oneonta, New York (a town that turned out to be strikingly significant to this study).

I would like to acknowledge the support and encouragement of colleagues both at the University of New Hampshire and at the University of Wisconsin–Parkside.

Finally, I would like to recognize the efforts of my dissertation supervisors, Sharon Strover and Tom Schatz, for their enthusiastic support of this project in its earliest manifestation at the University of Texas at Austin. Tom continued this important involvement as my editor through the lengthy revising and updating process that finally produced this book.

The Rise of Cable Programming in the United States

Cable History and Television Theory

In an important 1971 policy proposal, The Sloan Commission on Cable Communications likened the ongoing developments in cable television to the first uses of movable type and the invention of the telephone. They urged a complete overhaul of existing cable policy, referring to such a measure as "the revolution now in sight" (2). The Sloan Commission was not the only party to hold high expectations for cable during the late 1960s and early 1970s—years that have become known as cable's "Blue Sky" period. In fact, a number of similar proposals were forwarded, suggesting that cable could provide services ranging from coverage of local politics to specialized professional programming to home security. It eventually could remedy all the perceived ills of broadcast television, including lowest-common-denominator programming, inability to serve the needs of local audiences, and failure to recognize the needs of cultural minorities.

Were these expectations met when satellite cable finally arrived in the late 1970s and 1980s? Many analysts, particularly those advocating minimal government intervention in the telecommunications industries, would readily agree that they were. By the early 1990s cable did offer a variety of specialized satellite-carried program services or "networks." Many communities provided programming of local interest—even if this programming drew a minuscule audience share. And some cable networks had tried using some sort of interactivity as a programming strategy. Nevertheless, during U.S. satellite cable's early years it maintained, above all, a strong resemblance to and dependence on broadcast television—featuring a large number of broadcast reruns, old movies, and other inexpensive fare. This precedent still stands in many respects. Understanding why this has been the case is a primary purpose for this study, in which I trace U.S. cable programming back to the late 1940s, well before cable's first trials with satellite technology.

The history of cable television in the United States is both longer and more eventful than many people realize. Those who subscribe to cable today, in order to receive a larger number of channel options than broadcast television alone can offer, have little reason to think about the uses for cable prior to 1980, or about the policy battles surrounding the medium during those earlier decades. Conversely, few of those who relied on cable for basic television service from the 1950s through the 1970s could have foreseen a future in which hundreds of commercial cable networks would compete with broadcast television networks to capture and define the interests of America's television viewers. Nevertheless, the history of U.S. cable is a continuous one, and this is especially apparent when one looks into the historical forces that have shaped today's cable programming. The fascinating blend of caution, controversy, and optimism that defined U.S. cable's early decades greatly influenced the direction of modern cable and related broadband technologies.

It is only in considering the precedents and expectations inherited by those working in the modern cable industries that we can begin to understand the programming choices that have been made. This book thus has two main goals. The first is to survey the historical circumstances that led to cable's reliance on broadcast-type programming. The second is to look critically at the strategies that were developed to make cable programming seem like something new and innovative. Above all, I wish to demonstrate the important connections between these two seemingly unrelated goals.

The parameters of my study are guided by historical events. I begin with cable's own beginning in the late 1940s and end with 1995, the approximate point at which I believe the U.S. cable industry had reached maturity and cable had begun to merge with other technologies. The significance of the starting point should seem clear: cable technology brought with it the earliest cable programming—even if, initially, that meant nothing more than retransmitted broadcast programming.

My reasons for selecting the end point might seem less clear. By the mid-1990s most early cable networks had recovered their start-up costs and had the ability to acquire or produce original programming if they chose to do so. Also the provisions of the 1992 Cable Act had moved beyond discussion to implementation. This act was the second major piece of legislation to amend the 1934 Communications Act in response to cable specifically and, much more than its 1984 predecessor, addressed the viability of cable as a competitor for broadcast television. Finally, around 1995 several events transpired that foretold a future in which cable alone would provide neither the specialization nor the inter-activity that consumers desire. First, 1995 saw the rise of Netscape as both a popular Internet browser and a set of standards for networked computer communication. As the Internet has grown more sophisti-cated and commercialized, we have seen increasing efforts to link its ca-pabilities to services traditionally provided by television. By 2000 most television networks—broadcast and cable—had their own interactive and coordinated websites. Second, since the mid-1990s multichannel television options have been provided by more technologies than cable alone; in fact, the multiplicity of networks in operation today is due in large part to the competition between cable and direct broadcast satel-lite. And the 1996 Telecommunications Act clearly dealt with cable as only one component of an increasingly multimediated communication environment. A main emphasis of this important and controversial piece of legislation was to foster the growth and convergence of new me-dia technologies by removing obstacles to their development by private enterprise.

Half a century of cable history is more than enough to fill a book, and the development of cable as a distinct medium is an area that has re-ceived little attention from scholars. The post-1995 telecommunications environment surely merits consideration on its own terms—a project that is under way on several fronts. This important work has begun to consider cable television and related technologies in their role as con-tent providers, not simply as delivery systems. A study demonstrating that cable has, in fact, been a content provider and innovator for decades seems an essential link between this newer work and existing work in television history. That is the project I have undertaken in this book.

A Brief (and Personalized) History of Cable Television in the United States

My television-viewing experiences while growing up in Oneonta, New York, during the 1960s and 1970s were the primary inspiration for this study. Oneonta is a small city, located some 150 miles northwest of New York City. The nearest broadcast television stations are located in Utica, Binghamton, Albany/Schenectady, and Syracuse. Each of these cities is at least 45 miles away, and all are separated from Oneonta by moun-tains. People in Oneonta have tried using rooftop antennas, but even the most elaborate of these can pick up nothing more substantial than a static-filled picture from Binghamton's one VHF station. So for Oneonta residents, cable television has seemed almost as essential as garbage collection or telephone service. Without cable, we would have had no television service at all. In fact, Oneonta was one of the earliest communities in the United States to have cable service—starting in 1954.

Cable television, first known as "community antenna television" (or CATV), emerged in the late 1940s, only a few years after the founding of commercial broadcast television, on which cable has been extremely dependent over the years. The earliest CATV systems consisted of very tall antennas erected by small-town entrepreneurs as a way to bring the closest available broadcast signals into their communities. The need for CATV had arisen in towns like Oneonta that were too small to sustain broadcast stations of their own and too remote or mountainous for their residents to receive signals using home antennas. Upon reaching the towering community antennas, the desired signals were "cleaned up" (i.e., interfering signals and other kinds of distortion were eliminated), amplified to their original strength, and then transmitted to subscribers' homes by wire. CATV operators charged monthly fees for the service. At this point, cable programming consisted of nothing more than a collection of the nearest available broadcast signals. This early form of cable was, in effect, nothing more than a retransmission medium. However, community antennas had been in use for only a few years before this began to change. By the early 1950s a distinct CATV industry had emerged, and there were indications that it would develop as a supplement to, rather than simply a retransmission of, broadcast television.

As detailed in Chapter 2, the 1950s were a decade of entrepreneurship and technological innovation for the new medium—as well as a period of very rapid growth. Terrestrial microwave relays, which were introduced to the industry in the early 1950s, not only increased the distances over which television signals could be carried, but also allowed operators some choice as to which broadcast signals they would offer on their systems. A few CATV operators also experimented with program origination, efforts ranging from primitive local newscasts to Hollywood movies and kinescoped television programs.

In a few places, community antenna service was combined with pay-TV, a concurrently developing industry that had been started by some Hollywood studios and other established media corporations. Of course the full convergence of CATV and pay-TV in the form of pay-cable networks remained years in the future. By themselves, the various wired and broadcast forms of pay-TV were perceived as a viable threat to the existing system of advertiser-supported broadcast network television.

Indeed, in spite of pay-TV's promise, organized opposition and regulatory debate prevented most systems from moving beyond early experimentation; the fledgling CATV industry naturally was reluctant to become involved with such an uncertain enterprise. Still, the simple fact that pay-TV existed and was discussed at this early stage tells us quite a lot about society's expectations for television and the degree to which they were being met by the existing system.

Throughout the 1950s the CATV industry itself remained largely unfettered by government regulations. But the 1960s proved to be a dramatically different stage in its development. By 1960 CATV had become a viable presence in the television industry, serving 650,000 television households. Many of the small-town, mom-and-pop CATV systems begun in the 1950s were being bought out by multiple system operators (MSOs)—corporations that, in some cases, had ties to other entertainment industries. This new class of cable operators wanted to expand their business into markets already served by broadcast television. Thus, the medium no longer could be dismissed by either government regulators or the general public as some sort of temporary measure or cottage industry that would disappear after enough broadcast television stations had been launched.

During the 1960s the Federal Communications Commission grew extremely concerned about protecting the interests of broadcasters. The Commission felt that CATV service might jeopardize its cherished doctrine of localism in television service—a concern prompted in large part by complaints registered by several small broadcasters during the late 1950s. What ensued was a series of strict regulatory pronouncements by the FCC, including the 1965 *First Report and Order,* 1966 *Second Report and Order,* and 1968 freeze on the development of cable systems in the top 100 broadcast markets. These measures severely hindered the industry's expansion—particularly with regard to its entering communities already served by one or more broadcast television stations. Additionally, a number of landmark court cases were tried during the 1960s. At issue in these cases were CATV systems' rights: to use microwave relays to bypass local signals, to use copyrighted program material, and to operate in or near broadcast markets.

By the later part of the decade the industry was in a state of confusion and frustration. The changing climate of this time is the focus of Chapter 3. The "cable" industry, as it was called by that point, had developed new programming capabilities, had increased channel capacity, and was ready to expand into larger communities. However, the overbearing regulatory climate made it virtually impossible for cable companies to pursue any of these areas of expansion. Then, around 1968, attitudes toward cable began a sharp reversal; suddenly it was being hailed as the medium that would expand and improve television service. Idealistic "Blue Sky" planners—including government policymakers, consumer advocates, and academics—envisioned cable becoming "an electronic highway" (Ralph Lee Smith) or "the television of abundance" (Sloan Commission). For the most part, these visionaries did not advocate specific services for cable to provide. Instead they outlined plans by which the medium and its users might be encouraged to develop new and beneficial applications as needs arose. The parties engaging in Blue Sky discourses represented a surprising array of interests. As Thomas Streeter explains, regardless of whether people expressed optimism about cable's capabilities and wished to tap into its benefits or were more concerned that without guidance cable would grow into a negative social force, most were united in a sense of urgency about establishing effective policy for the medium (1987, 176).

There were several factors fueling this new interest in cable's potential. First, the debates and hearings surrounding the mid-1960s regulations had put cable in the public spotlight. Simply having an awareness of the medium and its function caused many people to begin contemplating its potential. Also, the space race was at its peak by this point, and communications satellites were very much on the public agenda. Cable presented itself as a terrestrially based distribution technology that could complement satellites. Finally, it was becoming an accepted reality that broadcast television never would be able to provide local service to the entire nation. Cable instead began to be perceived as the medium that would accomplish this, as well as eliminate channel scarcity and provide special-interest programming.

In an effort to follow the tide of popular optimism the FCC, in 1969, required systems with 3,500 or more subscribers to begin offering local programming. The cable trade press immediately filled with programming suggestions and success stories. In 1972 the FCC passed yet another *Cable Television Report and Order*—this time buttressing the program origination requirement with a mandate for all medium and large cable systems to provide production facilities for public, educational, and government (PEG) access programming. To compensate for the additional financial burden imposed by this requirement, the FCC also included several regulatory provisions allowing cable operators to enter broadcast markets and to expand the number and types of broadcast signals they carried. The 1972 rules represented an attempt to bring about implementation of the optimistic Blue Sky plans without creating economic hardship for the cable systems that were affected.

Nonetheless, many cable operators still claimed the program origination and access provisions presented an unreasonable financial and technological burden; and over the course of the next several years, either the FCC or the federal courts lifted them, one by one. Thus, it was the leniency provisions that were to remain in place, rather than those promoting public service. No federal program origination or PEG access requirements remained in effect as of 1980. In fact, the regulatory stance toward cable grew progressively more lenient throughout this decade. So, in spite of the resolute public service intent of the 1972 rule-making, it actually had the effect of initiating a *deregulatory* trend in cable—a trend that was complemented by the concurrent deregulation of the domestic communications satellite industry under an FCC policy called "Open Skies."

This was the environment in which the earliest satellite-carried cable networks were started. The first of these was Time Inc.'s Home Box Office (HBO), a pay-cable service that had been transmitting movies and sports programming by microwave to cable systems throughout Pennsylvania and upstate New York (including the cable system in Oneonta) since 1972. In 1975 HBO leased a transponder on RCA's recently launched *Satcom 1* satellite, and very quickly became a cable network with the potential for nationwide viewership. HBO's satellite debut created an entirely new market for cable service among television viewers already well served by broadcast stations—a market that would grow exponentially as more satellite services launched and more cable operators gave their subscribers access to this programming.

In 1976 Ted Turner's Atlanta independent station, WTBS, became the second satellite network and the first cable "superstation." Pat Robertson's Christian Broadcasting Network launched its CBN-Cable service in 1977. Several other satellite-carried cable networks were launched prior to 1980, including two additional superstations, WGN-Chicago and WOR–New York; Jim and Tammy Faye Bakker's PTL; Univision/ Galavision, the Spanish-language service; ESPN, the sports service; Nickelodeon for children; C-SPAN, the public affairs service; The Movie Channel; and Showtime. The rise of U.S. cable's first wave of satellite networks is covered in Chapter 4. Chapter 5 then follows the fortunes of these early satellite networks, as well as those of the many new entrants in the cable programming marketplace, into the 1980s and early 1990s.

Chapter 6 takes a different turn in that its focus is not a specific time period. Rather, the goal of this chapter is to discuss and analyze the programming, promotion, and scheduling strategies that emerged with satellite cable and that have distinguished it from broadcast television. Most of cable's early satellite networks relied heavily on program genres—often actual programs—already proven successful on broadcast television. Uplinking to satellite was a major expense, and the additional cost of instituting major new programming infrastructures would have put most of them out of business. While numerous additional satellite cable networks have been launched since 1980, most similarly have adopted programming and scheduling strategies that either rely on actual broadcast television programming (syndicated movies or off-network reruns) or imitated broadcast formats. Off-network reruns and old movies already have established popularity with audiences, and often these types of syndicated programming can be acquired at a low cost. Even original cable programming has been most successful when it has fit within established television genres—such as news and sports—and drawn from the conventions of those genres.

There have been exceptions to this pattern—notably the music video and home shopping formats, as I will discuss in later chapters—but these new programming formats are extremely amenable to the imperatives of commercial television. Consequently they have been absorbed by the program-recycling strategies more than they have supplanted them. While cable has been hailed repeatedly as having the potential to reach cultural minorities and niche audiences, the commercial imperative to program inclusively has counterbalanced most attempts at specialization. Regardless of the extensive variety of cable programming outlets in existence by the 1990s, each continues to be shaped by the same imperative that has always driven commercial television: to draw the largest possible audience within a self-defined market niche.

A term like "revolution" or even "fundamental change" hardly seems appropriate for such a situation. Still, there have been a number of innovations in modern cable that cannot be dismissed as mere imitation. They must be considered instead as responses to the bifurcated demand that has always characterized television: a demand for programming that is innovative while nonetheless adhering to long-established standards. In other words, in the process of trying to differentiate their schedules from those of both broadcast and cable competitors, while also offering audiences what is familiar and builds cultural cohesion, cable networks have introduced some captivating and influential programming strategies. Indeed, innovations first observed on cable in the 1980s can now be seen on broadcast networks and stations as well.

To a large extent, modern cable became an aftermarket for broadcast television programs and theatrical films. A 1991 study found that more than 95 percent of "dramatic" (i.e., fiction) programming on basic cable and 91 percent on premium cable consisted of material that already had appeared either on broadcast television or in movie theaters in the United States (or, in a few instances, abroad). Since their production costs already have been recovered in earlier exhibition windows, these kinds of programs are available from syndicators for much less money than it would cost to produce new programs. Furthermore, broadcast-type programming has shown itself, time and again, to be popular with audiences. Even much of cable's original programming has shown a strong resemblance to what is available on broadcast television. This was evident as of 2000, when most cable networks were no longer struggling to find resources for original programming; certainly it had been evident a decade earlier when they were struggling. While the 1991 study found a large percentage of "informational" and "performance/event" programming to have been produced originally for cable, a more detailed breakdown of these categories would show that they consist primarily of news, sports, children's programs, and other established broadcast genres.[1]

Economic information such as this does not, by itself, explain the failure of satellite cable to emerge as an entertainment and information medium significantly different from broadcast television. Since the introduction of satellites, we have witnessed cable networks either fail because their programming was too specialized or succeed only after adjusting their program schedules to accommodate a balance of the familiar and the new. It should not be surprising that cable networks' survival often has meant drawing from a large stockpile of syndicated broadcast programming or producing low-budget imitations of familiar broadcast genres. But the fact that cable networks economize on production and acquisition expenditures by using broadcast-type programming offers only a partial explanation of common programming practices. And it does very little to explain why established networks continue to draw from the same sources of familiar programming long after they have accumulated the resources to afford newer and more innovative fare.

Such a programming strategy would not succeed if the audience were not willing to watch—and pay for—programming that is extremely familiar. Thus, it is necessary to examine why broadcast-type programs have continued to draw large numbers of viewers, even when rerun or produced on lower budgets, and therefore have generated substantial advertising and subscriber-fee revenue. It is necessary to consider the role of television as a cultural mediator and source of shared knowledge—to ask, in other words, how television programming both reflects and shapes viewers' tastes and expectations. Such a mode of inquiry not only provides an explanation for the cable programming strategies that emerged under open-entry competition; it also gives insights into why various policy initiatives instituted in response to Blue Sky quickly gave way to open-entry competition in cable in the first place.

Background and Relevant Literature

Dating back to the late 1940s, each successive stage of cable programming development has represented an extension of what already was available and succeeding on television at the time of a particular innovation. Thus, the first principal objective of this study is to establish how and why cable, from its earliest days as CATV, has depended on broadcast television in essential ways—even while forging its own distinct path. Some of the most successful early strategies for enhancing CATV/cable service involved the "importation" of distant broadcast signals, particularly those of major-market independent stations that scheduled many reruns and old movies. Groundbreaking modern cable networks continued the tradition by promoting themselves as "homes" for old movies and television reruns (some of the more obvious examples being American Movie Classics, Turner Classic Movies, Nick at Nite, and TV Land). Moreover, the audience-targeting strategies of individual cable networks often have resembled the daypart segmentation of broadcast networks, indicating that the reliance goes beyond simply imitating broadcast television's programming selection.

The second principal objective of this study is to survey and analyze the characteristic programming types and programming strategies used by modern cable networks. Exhibiting cable programming so as to make it appealing to viewers who might otherwise turn to the newer and higher-budget programming of broadcast networks presented both a creative and a financial challenge to fledgling cable networks. They had to plan program contexts at least as carefully as they chose program content. In other words, they had to make what was old—or cheap, or overused—seem new again. So, rather than simply showing broadcast reruns or old movies, as most independent broadcast stations have done, many cable networks devised strategies to recontextualize, reinvigorate, and occasionally, reconfigure that programming. This study ultimately will suggest that what constituted cable programming in the presatellite era was both expanded and reshaped—though by no means replaced—by the programming of modern cable.

A look at television history is the necessary starting point for this project, since it allows us to see how deeply established the American audience's expectations for television programming were by the time of Blue Sky. It also allows us to see how great a role cable already played in providing television programming by that stage. Cable's reliance on broadcast-type programming has a lengthy history; indeed cable technology came to exist exclusively for the purpose of retransmitting broadcast signals. In cable's early decades, improvements in technology increased the number of channels per system, and the additional channels nearly always were employed to carry additional broadcast signals. Even various strategies that cable entrepreneurs devised over the years to distinguish their service constituted supplements to, not replacements for, the broadcast programming carried on their systems. And the lengthy government policy-making processes designed to steer cable away from its reliance on broadcast programming usually resulted, instead, in reinforcing the existing relationship between cable and broadcast television.

Documenting cable's place within television history

While much of this study deals with modern, satellite-served cable, the beginning of which I attribute to events in the late 1960s and early 1970s, it is necessary first to establish a historical context for those events. The fact that cable has received relatively little consideration in existing television histories obscures the integral role it has played in providing virtually universal television service in the United States for nearly half a century. Since the 1950s basic cable has been vital to television service for much of the country, and pay-TV has been on the public agenda at least as long. The few standard television histories that mention either cable or pay-TV at all give them very little attention.

Various Blue Sky articles and policy proposals include details of cable history as background to arguments about cable's future. There is some useful detail in these, but the information tends to be anecdotal and sometimes is poorly substantiated. At the present time, comprehensive historical accounts of cable and pay-TV are scarce. The most informative discussion of early cable is Mary Alice Mayer Phillips's *CATV: A His-*

tory of Community Antenna Television (1972). Though long out of date and primarily a regulatory history in the first place, the first 45 pages provide a detailed and interesting account of the invention and growth of CATV. In fact, many of the more detailed histories of early cable focus on regulatory and economic aspects of the medium. Among these are *Cable Television and the FCC: A Crisis in Media Control* by Don R. LeDuc (1973) and *Cable Television U.S.A.* by Martin Seiden (1972). A much more recent book, Stephen Keating's *Cutthroat: High Stakes and Killer Moves on the Electronic Frontier* (1999), discusses the business history of U.S. cable in the context of chronicling the battle between the cable and direct broadcast satellite industries that took place during the 1990s.

A few sources look at early forms of pay-TV separately from cable. Early pay-TV is discussed by Timothy R. White in "Hollywood's Attempt at Appropriating Television: The Case of Paramount Pictures." A more comprehensive resource, *The Electronic Box Office: Humanities and the Arts on the Cable* (1974), edited by Richard Adler and Walter S. Baer, provides overviews and analyses of various pay-cable systems proposed during the early 1970s, as well as consideration of the overall role it was believed pay-cable would play in providing entertainment, information, education, and other services. Also, *Subscription Television: History, Current Status, and Economic Projections* (1980), a research study completed by H. H. Howard and S. L. Carroll, provides detailed information about both cable and over-the-air forms of pay television from the 1940s through the late 1970s.

A handful of histories on specific modern cable networks have been written, including *Inside HBO* (1988) by George Mair, *Inside MTV* (1988) by R. Serge Denisoff, *CNN: The Inside Story* (1990) by Hank Whittemore, *ESPN: The Uncensored History* (2000) by Michael Freeman, and a number of accounts of Ted Turner's rise to prominence in cable programming.[2]

The cable industry's historical relationship with the Hollywood film industry, an important consideration in understanding cable programming, has been discussed by two writers: Thomas Whiteside in his lengthy, three-part *New Yorker* magazine series, "Onward and Upward with the Arts" (1985); and Michele Hilmes in *Hollywood and Broadcasting* (1990). Whiteside's piece provides important details about both cable and pay-TV history. It offers a thorough consideration of the industrial connections between these two industries. Hilmes's more scholarly work discusses pay-TV ventures in the 1950s, noting briefly their significance to the emerging CATV industry. Also, Hilmes's final chapter,

"Film/Television/Cable," details the involvement of Hollywood studios with cable programming during the late 1970s and early 1980s.

Furthermore, while none of the historical works described so far adequately theorizes of how economic, regulatory, and technological developments in cable history have affected modern cable programming, Hilmes's *Hollywood and Broadcasting* suggests a model for such an undertaking. Hilmes draws from a wide range of primary sources, including trade press articles, corporate records, government publications, and radio program texts. She also builds a cultural studies–based theory of textual production. Hilmes combines textual analysis with a chronological history of the relationships among the film, broadcasting, and cable industries.

Similarly, I will use archival resources, including periodical articles, government documents, and oral history transcripts, to build a historically grounded consideration of modern U.S. cable's programming, scheduling, and promotion practices. For my study, the pivotal decade is 1965–1975, for it is during these years that a future path for cable was articulated, plans for its realization were implemented, and then its direction was almost completely reversed. Understanding this surprising and ironic turn of events—as well as the cable programming climates that preceded and followed it—involves examining primary documents from the time, as well as considering scholarly work that deals with textual production, audience behavior, and industry structure and economics.

Understanding Blue Sky

As discussed above, the various Blue Sky documents have proven somewhat useful as secondary historical sources; however, their greater significance here lies in their role as primary documentation of an era in which cable's future was perceived as both promising and uncertain. In this book I am situating cable's Blue Sky period (1968–1974) as the immediate predecessor to, and foundation for, modern cable in the United States. As I will demonstrate, there were important programming precedents set during cable's early (CATV) decades. But it was not until the late 1960s that policymakers and the general public began operating under the assumption that cable would, and should, function as more than a retransmitter of broadcast programming. Idealistic wired television scenarios were laid out in such documents as the Sloan Commission report, *On the Cable: The Television of Abundance* (1971); Ralph Lee

Smith's *The Wired Nation* (1972); "The Rostow Report," prepared by President Johnson's Task Force on Telecommunications Policy (1968); various Rand Corporation studies; and a host of other reports and popular press articles.

While various economists and policy analysts have examined the failure of Blue Sky policy initiatives, only one scholar has dealt in depth with the sociopolitical climate that generated the Blue Sky documents. Thomas Streeter (1987) offers a unique and illuminating perspective on the relationships between government policymakers and the general public by analyzing the discourses of the Blue Sky era. He suggests that the optimism surrounding cable technology—optimism that brought about dramatic policy changes—derived much less from debate among divergent factions than from an uncritical faith in the ameliorative powers of new technology. This supports the notion that modern cable represents a set of compromises between the expectations of Blue Sky and the preexisting practices and imperatives of the television industry overall.

In a comprehensive study that includes a brief discussion of cable, Streeter (1996) critiques commercial broadcasting policy in the United States over the course of the twentieth century. Among various other insights, this book lends a new insight to an old problem: how to account for the repeated triumph of private interests over government policy—an issue critical to explaining the outcomes of the Blue Sky era. One tendency in explaining this outcome has been (as in Don R. LeDuc's *Beyond Broadcasting*, 1987) to attribute it to the greater power and influence of media corporations vis-à-vis government agencies. Theoretical discussions range from blaming structural failures (often due to limited staff and financial resources) within government agencies to perceiving the agencies to have been taken over or "captured" by corporate interests.[3] What many of these theories seem to overlook is the process of negotiation between society's idealistic uses for communication media and people's real-life relationships with, and expectations for, those media and their content. Streeter tries to sort through this problem using an interdisciplinary methodology that ranges from critical legal studies to feminist theory.

Streeter's work also makes us aware that the Blue Sky reports, while a new phenomenon in cable specifically, represented only the latest set of public service initiatives in electronic media generally. The larger issue of how to provide comprehensive and varied broadcasting service in the United States has been examined with regard to earlier media. For example, both Susan Douglas (1987) and Robert McChesney (1993) have written detailed accounts of the popular and political discussions that preceded passage of the Radio Act of 1927 and the 1934 Communications Act. Though their interpretations differ, both Douglas and McChesney consider the effects of industrial precedent and competing business agendas on the development of radio and its programming. Also some writers recently have turned their focus to how policy issues involving media of the past are resurfacing with the Internet.[4] In all of this work, a major focus has been reconciling the economic imperatives and the public service goals of commercial media.

It is particularly worth noting here that, during the 1980s and 1990s, cable television was part of a larger U.S. media environment that was becoming more and more consolidated. Growing numbers of local cable systems were being bought out by MSOs. The MSOs, in turn, were part of larger corporations that typically held a stake in cable network ownership. The large parent corporations or media conglomerates—entities such as Time-Warner, TCI, Disney, and Viacom—were increasingly driven by "synergy," the desire to control a diverse, yet nonetheless coordinated, collection of smaller companies. Synergy serves as the vehicle for cross-promotion of a media product or "event" (such as a blockbuster movie or a major music CD release) and distribution of that product through different media outlets or "windows." Thus, a cable network might help promote a theatrical film by running publicity programs for it (e.g., "The Making of . . .") and later receive first television rights to exhibit that film.

The goals of conglomerate formation and synergy hardly have been compatible with those articulated by most Blue Sky visionaries. Certainly any local programming efforts would have been antithetical to the synergistic goal of coordinating programming and distribution operations from national headquarters. And moves toward producing original niche-interest programming would have been countered by budget-minded corporate executives wishing to channel existing media products through as many windows as possible before investing in new production. Furthermore, the neoconservative political climate of the 1980s did nothing to hinder consolidation in the media and other industries—and everything to promote it. Federal policymakers repeatedly asserted a need to remove obstacles to private enterprise and thereby foster economic growth and development of new products. McChesney, Edward Herman, Norman Solomon, and Patricia Aufderheide are some of the scholars who have harshly critiqued the effects of free enterprise on media content in the United States.[5] None of these scholars deals with cable exclusively, but clearly the effect of free enterprise on cable programming—as a long-heralded alternative to commercial broadcast television—has been a particular source of concern for them and many others.

What economics can (and cannot) explain

In the United States a long-standing and contentious policy issue has been how to foster the goals of democratic communication with minimal government intervention in actual program content. Most scholars readily agree that, with the commercial broadcast network system so firmly entrenched and the supply of broadcast-type programming so plentiful, it would take a monumental policy effort to steer any form of television toward a new programming model. There is less agreement about whether or not open-entry competition can lead, through consumer mandate, to a program selection that proportionately reflects the interests of the American public and provides maximum benefit to all viewers. Neoclassical economic programming models advocate open-entry competition as the most efficacious path to programming diversity. On the surface, open-entry competition indeed does seem to have resolved any technological limitation to providing a wide variety of programming, and therefore seems well suited to demonstrating the validity of neoclassical models. But a counterargument to this notion is that, without the necessary regulatory catalyst, cable generally has fallen back on long-established broadcast programming patterns. As Streeter explains, it is not that modern cable lacks diversity of perspectives or fails to serve a variety of interests; rather, the limitation lies in cable programmers' overreliance on syndication libraries and other sources of familiar programming. This is a matter of economics, not a matter of technological capability (1996, 236–237). Rather than introducing new content types into the larger pool of television programs, as would be expected in a neoclassical model, satellite cable has fed the demand for existing categories of syndicated product. In the open-entry environment of modern cable, reruns, old movies, and other recycled programs are the dominant programming fare. This material quite simply is the cheapest and most readily available.

Public goods such as media products are inherently recyclable since one person's consumption of a particular product does not limit the possibility for other people to consume the same product simultaneously or in the future. Television programming outlets, whether broadcast or cable, can maximize their production investments through both widespread circulation of the same programs and reuse of older programs, provided adequate means of distribution are in place. The supply of high-budget television programming has increased over the years, particularly as new distribution and exhibition windows such as cable, VCRs, and independent broadcast stations have become available. The larger the potential audience for a program, and the greater the possible number of exhibition outlets, the more likely are the chances of recovering an investment and ultimately making money from that program. Thus, the main incentives to finance and produce new programming also are guided by the proliferation of syndication.

This helps us to understand why both niche-interest and locally oriented programming are at a considerable disadvantage when no subsidies are available. LeDuc explains that locally produced programming did not come to dominate broadcast television because both economics and viewer expectations would have made it unfeasible. Without network feeds, independently owned stations could not afford the high-budget productions that draw audiences. The affiliation process has been sanctioned by the FCC because it helps the survival of local stations, even if the degree of local service is compromised (1987, 13–14). This also explains why most modern cable programming has been made available by nationwide satellite services rather than by locally based producers. LeDuc does not go into much detail about the combined effect of economics and viewer expectations, but such an inquiry seems critical to understanding why modern cable networks have been as successful as they have.

LeDuc's political economy–based theory differs dramatically from the neoclassical models mentioned above; he advocates greater regulatory intervention while the neoclassical theorists generally oppose any regulatory constraints. Yet both approaches seem to presume a much less nuanced cable programming environment than the one that has evolved under open-entry competition. When applied to television, economic models tend to relegate programs to functional categories based on length, genre, etc.[6] In many instances, economists do not go beyond the use of the term *imperfect substitute* when accounting for content variations in television programs or schedules. Certainly economic models provide a starting point for understanding the constraints of the television marketplace, but the fact that there is necessarily variation among individual programs must be taken into account in any practical applications of the models (a point that usually receives at least a footnote in economic theories). In order to understand the strategies cable networks have employed to compete within these constraints, it is essential to analyze the texts of individual programs as well as the strategies for positioning those programs within larger schedules. As discussed below and in Chapter 6, strikingly innovative strategies of intertextuality and self-promotion were devised as a means of distinguishing schedules of routine broadcast-type fare while fledgling cable networks gained financial stability. In turn, these short-term strategies became distinctive characteristics of programming in a mature cable industry; many networks continue to rely on familiar program types long after the practice ceased to be necessary for recovering start-up costs. Obviously, the economics of public goods are complemented by television viewers' persistent willingness to watch rerun material.

Public sphere versus cultural forum

In order to understand why television programs remain meaningful over time, it is necessary to consider the degree to which television viewing has supplanted traditional community-building activities. Does television provide a central place in which a society's interests and concerns can be shared? Does it provide common points of discussion? Or does it, instead, offer only an illusory sense of community? The simple fact that this is a topic of discussion for scholars and policymakers is evidence of the enduring and pervasive presence of television. That it has been a matter of concern indicates that people have not accepted passively and uncritically the notion that an entirely commercial medium can promote cultural cohesion and foster dialogue among citizens. This is the tension that fueled the Blue Sky discourse, but its origins correspond to the rise of commercial media—well before the advent of cable.

The work of the Frankfurt School, for instance, speaks to a scholarly dissatisfaction with the impacts of industrialization on traditional forms of cultural expression. Many criticisms of early mass media—as laid out, to give just one example, in Theodor Adorno and Max Horkheimer's seminal 1944 essay, "The Culture Industry: Enlightenment as Mass Deception"—addressed a perceived dulling of thought and homogenization of cultural expression. While Adorno and Horkheimer wrote this particular piece too early to consider television specifically, their sentiments were echoed by television reformers of the 1960s.

In his provocative 1961 "Vast Wasteland" speech, FCC commissioner Newton Minow called for extensive reform of U.S. broadcast television. Similar ideas were expressed later by Ralph Lee Smith in *The Wired Nation,* where he called upon U.S. regulators and citizens in general to reform cable policy before it became too late to accomplish such a goal.

The debates carried on during cable's pivotal Blue Sky years, by Smith and many others, helped Americans articulate the terms of their frustration with commercial television. The debates also encouraged people to believe that cable could reintegrate communities and turn passive viewers into active participants. One of the benefits of cable most highly promoted in the various Blue Sky documents was its potential for interactivity—ranging from participation in town meetings to at-home schooling for bedridden children to church services for distant or disabled parishioners. While services such as these were used primarily as examples of new functions cable *might* take on, their selection clearly points to an expectation that cable would allow many functions associated with public spaces to be relocated to the domestic sphere. Even the discussion of various potential cable program services—ballet, theater, classical music performances—alludes to scenarios in which the small screen could beneficially supplant traditional public gatherings.

Jürgen Habermas's argument in *The Structural Transformation of the Public Sphere* (1989) is relevant here. He, similar to most Blue Sky visionaries, believes that a mass-mediated public sphere is possible, but can be achieved only with an intervention of massive proportions (222–235). According to Habermas, the function of the Enlightenment's "public sphere of letters," which he characterizes as the ideal, began to shift as industrialized consumer society began to flourish, and critical debate among the literate public was curtailed. The need for shared experience itself was not diminished; rather, it has continued in the false consensus engineered by the public relations industry to give consumer products the credibility typically reserved for public authority—a trend magnified by the rapidity of electronic media. With the entrenchment of private interests in the political process, citizens have become more subjects of publicity than members of participatory publics (194–195).

Habermas offers a point of departure for understanding the limitations of mass media in promoting public debate and fostering the circulation of ideas, and his work reveals a great deal about the goals of Blue Sky. Still, some scholarship has suggested that his notion is unrealistic in today's society. Nicholas Garnham (1992) notes that recent scholars, including Habermas, "fail to start from the position that the institutions and processes of public communication are themselves a central and integral part of the political structure and process" (361).

In fact, many scholars see the connections among individuals in postindustrial society as too complex and too widespread to allow the sorts of discourse Habermas attributes to the bourgeois public sphere. But they do not all lament this or see it as a limitation to the terms of public discourse in the ways Habermas does. Implicit in the work of scholars like Marshall McLuhan is the idea that more rapid means of transportation and communication in the postindustrial era have replaced the bourgeois public sphere of letters with a more widespread and inclusive forum. Drawing in part from the ideas of McLuhan, Joshua Meyrowitz (1985) discusses how mass media (particularly television) actually have broken down many of the boundaries that once separated categories of individuals and excluded many from the public sphere. The public sphere in the postindustrial era, his argument suggests, is more inclusive than it was previously, largely because of the role mass media have played in challenging traditional power structures and hierarchies.

It is important to consider James Carey's (1989) ritual view of communication in this regard, for this view challenges the idea that communication necessarily is used by central authorities to exercise control (18). In the ritual view, communication is seen as a consensual process of cultural meaning-making—or, as Carey puts it, "a symbolic process whereby reality is produced, maintained, repaired, and transformed" (23). This idea has been discussed with regard to television specifically. John Fiske and John Hartley (1978) refer to television's "bardic" function. They explain that "television functions as a social ritual, overriding individual distinctions, in which our culture engages in order to communicate with its collective self" (85). Horace Newcomb and Paul M. Hirsch (1983) similarly describe television as a "cultural forum," a site in which societies negotiate meaning.

In one way or another all of these scholars implicitly address the reason why cable networks have been so successful in continuing to provide broadcast-type programming. Like any form of television, modern cable networks thrive on familiarity, repetition, and common experience and thus can be understood as engendering social discourse, not opposing it. Audiences state their preference for innovation, but gravitate toward what is familiar—a tendency of which those in the television industries are well aware. As much as people idealized the scenarios described by the Blue Sky writers, and as much as they initially appeared to support government policy aimed at bringing those scenarios to fruition, most actually used their television dials to "vote" in support of traditional broadcast fare—whether received over the air or by cable. Most people expected a steady supply of new programs and new episodes of existing programs, but they did not, at least in the short term, expect so much innovation that familiar genres and scheduling patterns would be disrupted.

The balance between familiar and new that is so essential to successful television programming posed a creative challenge for start-up cable networks. While they had no trouble supplying the familiar, most had difficulty finding the resources to balance it with the new. The dilemma led to a variety of strategies intended to address the audience's familiarity with older material and older programming conventions head-on, but also to suggest new ways of relating to them. So the most successful and enduring innovations in cable programming have been those that have recognized and exploited the textual complexity of television, combining traditionally discrete schedule components (programs, commercials, network IDs) into programming that is both old and new. An overview of theoretical work on television texts will shed more light on this idea.

The television text

In order to approach the extreme complexity of television texts in general and cable texts specifically, it is necessary to turn to more text-centered theoretical work. As the widespread use of empirical research (such as ratings data, demographics, and psychographics) by broadcast networks and cable networks clearly indicates, the television schedule is hardly a random juxtaposition of heterogeneous programs and commercials. Some of the most important contributions to television scholarship have been those that attempt to define or delimit the object of study by considering the interactions—both planned and coincidental—among program and commercial texts. Some theoretical work in the area of broadcast television programming written during the 1970s and 1980s suggests important ways of conceptualizing television texts that highlight the differences between them and other media texts (such as theatrical film).

In *Television: Technology and Cultural Form* (1974), Raymond Williams uses the term "flow" to stress that commercial television programming is "planned in discernible sequences which . . . override particular programme units." Williams identifies three sequences of television flow—programs, commercials, and self-promotional material—which are combined strategically to "capture" and "retain" viewers for a given period of time (91). Nick Browne expands upon the idea of flow in "The Political Economy of the Television (Super)Text" (1984), speaking more directly to the *nature* of the relationships among programs and "interstitial" material. What Browne calls the television "supertext" (i.e., the sequence of material during a period of viewing) both mirrors and constructs the daily schedule and work week of the general population (589).

The notion of television as a single unbounded text is critical to understanding how units of programming and commercials can be recombined in service of television's overriding commercial imperative. Yet these studies do not account for all of the historical factors shaping the development of broadcast television programming. Most notably, Williams and Browne assign more importance to the coherence of complete program schedules than they do to the coherence of individual programming units that comprise those schedules. In fact, though, nearly all television programs and commercials are designed so that they can fit a variety of different schedules—what John Ellis (1992) describes as the balance between "autonomy" and "contingency" that continues to characterize segments of programming after they have been positioned within particular schedules (117–118). Individual units of programming must be structured in ways that facilitate their inclusion in virtually any scheduling sequence without loss of relevance to viewers. For decades, television programmers have fragmented and rearranged programming units within television schedules—in "magazine format" commercials, syndicated reruns, spin-off programs and TV characters' "guest appearances."

In two important articles, Mimi White (1986, 1989) characterizes the television text that has been cultivated, both directly and indirectly, on American commercial television over a period of several decades as a single, endlessly self-referential diegesis. She explains that

> familiar categories and distinctions among programs, and between programs proper and commercials, are at once maintained in general and broken down in numerous individual instances. . . . [T]elevision offers coherent terms of address across and within its heterogeneous totality rather than in relation to individual episodes, programs, or even a given evening's programming. (1986, 60–62)

In other words, TV's idealized viewer—and its most highly valued con-sumer—is one who is extremely familiar with the medium's intertextual system of signification.

On an aesthetic level, White's theory is equipped to deal with broad-cast television programs, commercials, and most importantly, the rela-tionships among them. This sophisticated conceptualization of televi-sion programming also begins to suggest ways of considering the effects of satellite cable and related technologies, as well as the new viewing be-haviors that have accompanied them, on programming and scheduling strategies. Because of their heavy reliance on off-network reruns, cable networks in particular are known for foregrounding and exploiting the connections among different programs and various other schedul-ing components, and certain cable networks have built entire iden-tities around the intertextual relationships White describes. They invite viewers to revel in TV nostalgia. Cable networks have dissected and rearranged program texts far beyond anything seen on broadcast televi-sion (at least before it was influenced by cable's programming strate-gies), leading some to perceive cable as exemplary of the so-called post-modern condition.

Calling television the quintessential postmodern form of culture sometimes seems to have become a requisite throwaway line for critical study of the medium. Indeed, television is a purveyor of heterogeneous and randomly juxtaposed mass culture texts. It confuses commerce and art. It is relentlessly self-reflexive. And every day it seems to have grown more congested with the empty signification of pastiche. Television viewers have grown progressively more attuned to these attributes over the course of television history. We readily accept the fact that programs are placed alongside other programs within larger schedules in ways that are not necessarily meant to make sense. In fact, we now are en-couraged, through the availability of remote control devices and VCRs, to arrange programs in whichever sequences we desire. We also take it for granted that certain programs (or program components), such as syndicated off-network reruns or old movies, need to be understood or "read" with a camp sensibility that pokes fun at their overly familiar and outdated conventions.

As much as television programming in general embodies these post-modern attributes, cable programming specifically seems to epitomize them. Not only the schedules of cable networks, but even individual, self-contained cable programs often are composed of jumbled texts with little or no controlling logic. The most obvious example of this is the music video "block" on MTV. However, the programming of other cable networks—ranging from E! Entertainment Television to CNN Headline News—also is characterized by short program units that seem to be arranged arbitrarily. And as much as broadcast network programming refers to its own history and signifiers from elsewhere in the "world" of television, cable networks such as Nick at Nite build their entire schedules upon notions of reflexivity and the collapsing of history. Certain cable programming mocks itself, joking irreverently about television production conventions and audience behaviors. Pioneering cable programs like Comedy Central's *Mystery Science Theater 3000* laughed at the audiences who laugh at the low production values of B movies from previous decades. MTV's *Beavis and Butt-Head* built its reputation on mocking hokey music videos. Cartoon Network's *Space Ghost: Coast to Coast* recycles a classic superhero cartoon as a way to poke fun at the celebrity interviews of late-night talk shows.

First introduced in the 1980s, this hip programming strategy has proliferated on cable—as a cost-cutter initially, but later adapting itself to more lavish programming budgets. The symbiosis of the formal and the economic demonstrated here should remind us that aesthetics alone do not determine production outcomes. As Jim Collins (1992) explains:

> The problem for television studies, as it tries to come to terms with postmodernism, is how to reconcile the semiotic and economic dimensions of television. Stressing the semiotic to the exclusion of the economic produces only a formalist game of "let's count the intertexts," but privileging the economic to the point that semiotic complexity is reduced to a limited set of moves allowed by a master system is just as simplistic. (339)

Collins made this statement in an introductory essay, merely suggesting how other studies of television and the issues of postmodernism might proceed. But this area of cable programming theory has barely begun to be explored, in spite of the fact that the environment of modern cable programming represents television at its postmodern best.

Indeed, a few scholars who work under the rubric of postmodern theory, but who challenge purely formalist versions of that theory, have begun to suggest ways to interpret the fragmented and fragmentable texts of today's multichannel television environment. The most valuable of these studies attribute a postmodern production aesthetic to the economic and industrial circumstances within which texts are produced— studies, in other words, that delve into the commodity roots of so-called postmodern culture. Andreas Huyssen (1986) challenges ideas put forward by Jean-François Lyotard, Fredric Jameson, and others by explaining that "art's aspirations to autonomy, its uncoupling from church and state, became possible only when literature, painting and music were first organized according to the principles of a market economy" (17). In other words, the new master narratives—and, by extension, new forms of expression—are driven by multinational capital.

Most of the existing work that considers postmodern aesthetics in conjunction with economics has centered on music video. Andrew Goodwin's *Dancing in the Distraction Factory* (1992) offers the most comprehensive insight into music video's merging of television programs, television commercials, and pop singles. Goodwin challenges the work of scholars who discuss music video's formal attributes (in particular its visual stylization) without giving equal attention to the political economy of the genre and its medium. He asserts, for example, that there are clear commercial motivations behind music video's use of such supposedly postmodern devices as intertextuality and quotation. And this is a purpose ideally suited to the television supertext. Goodwin describes key cross-promotional relationships that run throughout the MTV schedule, encompassing "VJ/host presentational material, complementary star profiles and interviews, news and reviews of new tours, movies, videos and albums, and celebrity documentaries" (174).[7]

Aside from the work on music video, the text-based study of cable programming is an area that remains largely neglected by scholars. One place such an endeavor might begin is in the area of co-optation. Cable networks have demonstrated a remarkable awareness of television-viewing behaviors and attitudes—ranging from the camp and nostalgia with which many viewers interpret "classic" sitcoms and low-budget movies to the impatient channel-surfing that accompanies use of remote control devices. Many networks have reshaped or recontextualized their programming in ways that both accommodate these behaviors and breathe new life into the older, often overused programs.

Knowing the audience

Television fan culture has begun to be theorized by scholars including Henry Jenkins and Constance Penley. In *Textual Poachers* (1992), for example, Jenkins discusses ways in which organized groups of television "fans" manipulate (often physically) fictional television narratives so as to alter, perhaps subvert, their hegemonic meanings. Fans circulate these texts in the form of unauthorized videocassettes, photocopied novels, and other artifacts. Jenkins considers the circulation of fan texts to be an underground activity, of which original program producers are likely to disapprove. However, he does not account for the ways in which fan practices, like other subcultural activities, might actually be co-opted by producers as strategies for commercial program production. In fact, several popular cable networks do feature programs in which behaviors similar to those described by Jenkins have been incorporated into the production process—typically through voice-over/image-over techniques. These are programs about television viewing, a *mise-en-abyme* situation that redefines older programming according to the practices of camp viewership. In this way, trendy new programs can be produced at very low cost.

In *Subculture: The Meaning of Style* (1979), Dick Hebdige outlines a theory that could help explain how the fan culture discussed by Jenkins and others becomes commodified. Hebdige focuses on youth music subcultures, and explains that, as soon as subcultural signifiers become familiar within society at large, their incorporation into dominant hegemonic discourses renders them safe, controllable, and ultimately, profitable. Gerald Graff (1989) similarly suggests that new forms of resistance arise as hegemonic powers co-opt and disarm existing ones; thus co-optation fuels an ongoing process of cultural production. Therefore, audience appropriation of TV texts must be cultivated even while being channeled back into viewing patterns that support the medium's commercial structure—what Stephen Heath (1990) calls "determined consensuality."

Along with fan practices and camp viewing, other viewing patterns that have been accommodated within cable program texts and schedules include "surfing" or "grazing," the use of remote control devices to change channels quickly, and "zipping," the use of VCRs to skip commercials. As cable networks have developed strategies to distinguish their programming, they also have been aware that, like any contemporary television program outlets, they must adapt to new viewing behaviors in a way that is satisfactory to both audiences and advertisers. Both VCRs and remote control devices can affect viewers' attention spans, their preferred viewing times, and whether or not they watch commercials. Remote control in particular allows viewers to select from multiple television channels as a way to avoid commercials. With the widespread use of these technologies, then, program "flow" no longer involves the carefully planned sequences of programs and commercials that Williams described, and Browne's "supertext" is no longer as easily controlled by programmers. Consequently, in today's viewing environment successful television programming necessitates strategies for constantly recapturing viewer attention—even if only for minutes or seconds at a time.

A number of quantitative studies have attempted to uncover patterns of viewing behavior associated with the use of remote control.[8] However, there has been little analysis of the ways program texts and programming strategies accommodate the new technologies. As is discussed at length in Chapter 6, a major cable programming innovation has been devising short, self-contained programming units (the most prominent example being the music video) that can be viewed either individually or in clusters that comprise programs of more traditional lengths.

Assessing Modern Cable Programming within a Historical Context

Examining the impact of viewing behaviors on modern cable programming strategies contributes a great deal to an explanation for the failure of the various idealistic scenarios envisioned for cable. In the late 1960s and early 1970s, even while plans were being formulated for an array of specialty services, the cable programming actually being watched was not that different from what is available on cable today. By that stage of television history, certain program genres had established popularity with American audiences, and it would have taken a radical reconfiguration of existing policy to change that. While such a reconfiguration was tried briefly, cable regulators ultimately left the medium's program development to the forces of open-entry competition—a choice that favored continuity over radical change.

Thus, while new cable-related technologies ranging from satellites to remote control devices unquestionably affected modern cable programming, in most respects they did more to alter how broadcast-derived programming was delivered and presented than to introduce actual alternatives to that programming. Commercial broadcast television has depended on an ability to *include* as many potential viewers as possible. This is an inevitable attribute of any advertiser-supported medium. Since cable depends on some combination of advertising support and subscriber fees, it too must program as inclusively as possible. Naturally, this imperative opposes any attempts at niche targeting.

Still, the impacts of the Blue Sky discourses on modern cable programming were not negligible. Modern cable emerged as a compromise between the discourses of Blue Sky and the imperatives of open-entry competition. It seems unlikely that consumers would accept cable networks that pitched themselves simply as outlets for secondhand broadcast programming, since broadcast television provides a fairly comprehensive selection of its own recycled product. Although cable faced the same sorts of market constraints as broadcast television, it also had to live up to its reputation as a medium capable of much more specialization. In other words, pioneering satellite cable networks needed to strike a delicate balance between providing what is old, because it is both popular and affordable, and convincing their viewers that their schedules were new and specialized, because this is what people had come to expect from cable. The "revolution" of which the Sloan Commission and other Blue Sky visionaries wrote in the early 1970s might not have occurred. But cable networks nonetheless have remained keenly aware of the public's ongoing belief that cable can provide a far more complete entertainment and information service than broadcast television alone ever has. Viewed in retrospect, the evolution of U.S. cable television from the late 1940s through the mid-1990s represents adherence to tradition, strides toward innovation, and above all, compromise and negotiation.

Community Antenna Television, 1948–1968

In his influential 1964 book, *Understanding Media,* Marshall McLuhan observed that "the 'content' of any medium is always another medium." McLuhan's statement reminds us that new media do not enter society as *tabulae rasae;* instead they are introduced to improve upon the functions already performed by existing media. It is only after the newer media have been in use for a while that their own unique capabilities are discovered or revealed. An especially good demonstration of this point is the historical relationship between broadcast and cable television in the United States. As I argue throughout this book, although cable television was first used to improve the function and reach of broadcast television, cable also, over time, developed its own distinguishing attributes. The present chapter shows that cable already had begun to forge its own path during its first two decades of existence.

Cable's technological predecessor was broadcast television, and by the late 1940s that medium had become a noticeable presence in the United States. At the beginning of 1948, 19 stations were operating in 12 cities, and approximately 100 more had been licensed.[1] Also by that year, television programming had coalesced in the form of complete daily and weekly schedules with distinct genres and regularly scheduled programs. Four television networks were in operation at that point: NBC, CBS, DuMont, and ABC. And people with access to television had begun to watch such now-classic programs as *Kraft Television Theatre, Texaco Star Theatre, Toast of the Town,* and *Gillette Cavalcade of Sports.*

Broadcast television was well on its way to becoming America's dominant entertainment and information medium. During the 1950s and 1960s producers, sponsors, and audiences all began to develop certain expectations for the medium. By the early 1950s television had adapted most programming conventions of *its* corporate and technological predecessor, radio, to appeal to audiences visually as well as aurally. Familiar television genres, including the situation comedy and the quiz show, were in place. Production styles, such as the telefilm and proscenium styles, were becoming industry standards. And television networks were replacing radio's single-sponsor advertising format with the "magazine" format, in which interchangeable "spot" commercials (similar to the ads found in magazines) allow several advertisers to contribute to the production costs of a program.

The 1950s also saw the rise of both telefilm (as opposed to live) program production and its complement, program syndication (both first-run and off-network). The use of telefilm was advantageous to the networks because it allowed them to retain control of production and content while shifting the financial risk over to outside producers. Furthermore, telefilms benefited their producers since the filmed programs could be retained and rerun an indefinite number of times, generating revenues far into the future. This shelf-life was extended considerably by the introduction of videotape during the late 1950s. The degree of flexibility telefilm and videotape production techniques brought to television programming complemented the flexibility of magazine-format sponsorship. By the 1960s virtually every component of the television schedule was both interchangeable and recyclable—traits that have defined the economic fortunes of virtually every form of television since.

It must be noted that the early and rapid coalescence of broadcast television owes a great deal to that medium's ability to reach the majority of potential viewers throughout the country. It did not accomplish this alone. Operating alongside broadcast television during the 1950s and 1960s, though receiving much less fanfare, were some other new communication technologies that extended its reach. Most notable of these was community antenna television, or CATV, the retransmission medium that was to evolve into modern cable television. Many people do not even realize that cable existed before the 1970s; in fact, a number of important technological, business, regulatory, and programming developments occurred during that medium's first two decades. By the late 1960s and early 1970s cable already had various services and capabilities that distinguished it from broadcast television. These were the remarkable result of research and experimentation within an industry operating quietly in America's rural areas and dominated by small-town entrepreneurs. As this chapter will make apparent, familiarity with cable's community antenna years is essential to understanding cable programming in the modern satellite era.

This chapter traces how and why sociocultural factors leading to a demand for CATV in the first place also prompted various CATV operators to seek ways of enhancing the service they offered during the 1950s and 1960s. It details strategies initiated within the CATV industry itself, as well as key intersections between CATV and the concurrently developing industry known variously as "pay," "subscription," or "toll" television. During the 1950s and 1960s CATV and pay-TV promised much more than they actually delivered in terms of programming innovation, since only a few isolated communities actually had access to programming not derived from broadcast signals. Yet the plans, ambitions, and technological innovation that emerged in the CATV and pay-TV industries during these decades foreshadowed a great deal about the modern cable industry and its programming.

The 1950s were a decade of rapid growth and relatively unfettered expansion and experimentation for CATV. In fact, every significant development in modern cable programming can be linked to one or more programming strategies first tried in the 1950s. While most in the industry sensed that government regulations were not far off and might restrict their future growth, that did not prevent them from exploring new program sources and testing new technologies. The 1950s witnessed the coming together of scattered, independent businesspeople into a distinct industry, able to exchange ideas and plan for the future. These years also saw the first uses of microwave relays and other technologies to supplement what simple community antennas could provide. And at the same time the first efforts at locally originated programming and integrated pay-TV/CATV operations were taking place.

In contrast, the period from 1960 to 1968 witnessed the smallest number of innovations in CATV/cable programming. The regulatory climate surrounding CATV proved to be a major impediment to the medium's business and programming expansion, especially in the populous urban markets so highly coveted by CATV operators. The 1960s saw CATV move from a virtually unregulated industry to one governed by some very constricting bodies of rules. In addition, a major copyright case involving CATV systems was moving through the courts. CATV operators did not wish to venture beyond the simple retransmission of broadcast signals for fear that any new programming schemes in which they invested would be declared illegal. So in spite of the promising programming innovations initiated by the CATV industry during the 1950s, the stagnation in programming development during the 1960s helped ensure cable's future reliance on broadcast programming.

CATV is one of the two ancestors of modern cable that traces its origins to the late 1940s and 1950s. The other is pay-TV. From the time it was introduced in the late 1940s, the expectations for pay-TV were

high. Through a variety of technologies—both wired and broadcast—
pay-TV's promoters promised programming of a quality and degree of
specialization unmatched by commercial broadcast television. Several
experiments were conducted during the 1950s and 1960s, including
some designed to operate in conjunction with CATV. But, as with CATV,
pay-TV did not develop as quickly or as thoroughly during either the
1950s or the 1960s as its proponents had hoped. Throughout both
decades, the industry was plagued by public controversy and regulatory
uncertainty. This left the U.S. television agenda to be set mainly by the
broadcast network "cartel." Programming alternatives came from the
handful of independent commercial stations and educational stations—
most of which were, at best, marginally viable.

Ultimately, pay-TV—like CATV—did more to buttress the programming model of commercial broadcast television than to provide alternatives to it. In spite of loftier ambitions, the few pay-TV experiments
able to get off the ground at all inevitably ended their short-lived operations with program schedules remarkably similar to those of broadcast
networks. Whether this was cause or consequence of the FCC's reluctance to license pay-TV on a permanent basis is a subject for debate. In
any event, any productive long-term exchanges between the CATV and
pay-TV industries lay years in the future. CATV operators, cautioned by
pay-TV's economic and regulatory fortunes as well as uncertainty within
their own industry, generally contented themselves with providing as
many channels of broadcast television as they could.

For the most part, this chapter considers the CATV and pay-TV industries separately, noting the instances where the two converged in any
way. The greater emphasis here is on CATV. Though pay-TV certainly
merits in-depth consideration, such a project is beyond the scope of this
book. As many unrelated developments were taking place simultaneously, the approach in this chapter is topical rather than chronological.
Before discussing individual programming developments, it will be
helpful to look briefly at the "invention" of CATV and the formation of
the CATV industry.

The Beginning of Community Antenna Service

As discussed above, the 1950s were an important time in broadcast
television history. The medium was both reaching critical mass and
developing unique programming conventions. Nonetheless, at the start
of that decade, many areas of the United States remained unserved or
underserved by television. The Federal Communications Commission's

station-licensing freeze, which lasted from 1948 to 1952, had left only a few very large cities with extensive television coverage, a number of smaller cities with only one station apiece, and many communities with no television at all.[2] As Erik Barnouw (1990) points out, this proved to be an excellent opportunity to observe the immense popularity of the new medium, but it was equally clear that the demand for television far exceeded the coverage provided by existing stations (112–114). Therefore, a major impact of the freeze was to encourage experimentation in alternative ways of sending and receiving television signals—experiments initially perceived as mere stopgap measures, to last only until the FCC resumed station licensing. On the fringes of cities with television, enterprising technological amateurs (many with military training) devised methods for extending broadcast signals into communities not served by television. These included booster or translator stations,[3] as well as community antenna systems (CATV). While boosters and translators continued quietly as retransmitters of broadcast signals, CATV grew into much more.

The date usually cited for CATV's "invention" is 1948, the year in which L. E. (Ed) Parsons of Astoria, Oregon, built an antenna on top of the local hotel and was able to receive the signal of the nearest broadcast television station—from Seattle, 125 miles northeast of Astoria. Parsons was a local radio broadcaster with some electrical engineering background, and he built the antenna mostly out of curiosity. Still, Parsons's innovation received a great deal of attention from residents of Astoria, who clamored to the hotel for a glimpse of the new entertainment medium. Eventually, they encouraged Parsons to wire the rest of the town (Phillips 1972, 11–14).

In its earliest years, CATV systems, including that of Parsons and those of several others throughout the country, did nothing more than amplify and extend any broadcast signals that could be collected at the highest available points in or near towns being served.[4] Nonetheless, CATV service spread very rapidly, since people living outside major cities were well aware of television and were eager to gain access to its programming. And once basic CATV technology had been perfected, a system could be built by virtually anyone with the adequate investment capital—which, in many cases, was as little as a few thousand dollars. By the early 1950s dozens of systems were in operation throughout the country.

CATV entrepreneurs came from many different backgrounds. Some systems were begun by independent citizens as a community service. Other systems were started on a cooperative basis by groups of citizens. Still others were begun by experienced radio broadcasters. Many CATV systems were started by appliance dealers, eager to sell television sets in their communities. Within a remarkably short period of time, however, a commonality of interests had been perceived among this varied group, and a major trade organization was formed. The first meeting of the National Community Television Association (NCTA, initially known as the National Community Television Council) was held on 18 September 1951 in Pottsville, Pennsylvania. The main purpose of the meeting was to discuss a proposed federal tax on CATV systems, but it seems of greater significance, in retrospect, that this meeting was the first formal indication of a distinct CATV industry. At this and subsequent meetings, the expected rallying cries against unfavorable legislation and other regulatory issues were complemented by ideas about how to add channel options to CATV systems. News of the emerging industry tended to propagate and spread rapidly through both meetings and the weekly *NCTA Membership Bulletin*.[5]

Initially, reception via community antennas was limited to the nearest and most unobstructed broadcast signals. In many places other, weaker signals were available as well, but remained untapped at first. But as the capacity of CATV systems increased from three channels to five, operators began to explore additional sources of programming. Amplifying weaker signals was the simplest way to add channels. John Walson Sr. of Mahanoy City, Pennsylvania, provided New York City's WPIX and WNEW—both popular independent stations—to his subscribers at some point during the 1950s. In a 1987 interview, Walson described a system of stacked antennas that brought the two stations to his system over the air, and explained that the channels were added as a defensive measure against the efforts of a local competitor.[6] Similarly, in 1953, NCTA president Martin Malarkey's Pottsville, Pennsylvania, system announced plans to add four channels to its existing three—including WPIX for its baseball coverage.[7] The *Lansford Evening Record* noted that CATV subscribers in many towns were eager to have the station carried by their systems.[8]

Amplifying off-air signals from distant cities was not an option for all CATV systems, though. Beyond a certain distance, broadcast signals are simply too weak. Therefore, by themselves, community antennas could be used only in areas near broadcast television markets. The introduction of microwave technology changed this. Microwave relays made it possible to import signals over very great distances, making the technology a boon to isolated communities and communities desiring additional broadcast signals. The relays also allowed operators to be more selective about which broadcast signals they would make available to their subscribers. Through the use of microwave, CATV grew from a regional antenna service to a national information and entertainment medium.

Adding More Channels

Microwaves are a form of electromagnetic radiation with frequencies ranging from several hundred MHz to several hundred GHz and wavelengths ranging from approximately 1 to 20 centimeters. Because of their high frequencies, microwaves have the advantage of being able to carry more information than ordinary radio waves, and are capable of being beamed directly from one point to another. Since terrestrial microwave is limited to line-of-sight transmission, it uses a series of relay points, or "hops," for carrying information over long distances.[9] In addition to their use by the CATV/cable industry, microwave relays have been used for remote newscasts and by broadcast networks to transmit programs to affiliate stations.

Initially, the relays were used by the CATV industry simply to extend the nearest broadcast signals, as community antennas did. Within a few years, however, CATV operators throughout the country began to use this technology to *select* certain broadcast signals based on their potential popularity with subscribers. The new means of control over what a CATV system could offer its customers marked the beginning of what Martin Seiden calls the "second phase" of cable development.[10] Microwave allowed CATV operators to conceptualize and promote their service as something more than simply a haphazard collection of nearby broadcast signals. For instance, in September 1956 the CATV system in Pendleton, Oregon, became the first to use microwave relays to bring subscribers a complete package of broadcast networks—in this case, the three affiliate stations came from Spokane.[11] Other systems soon adopted this practice.

A somewhat different use of microwave relays was to import popular major-market independent stations—a practice started by Walson and Malarkey, as discussed above. When other CATV systems found themselves unable to draw the desired signals using basic antennas, microwave presented an alternative. For example, when it launched in 1954, Oneonta Video of Oneonta, New York, was seeking ways to program the fifth channel of its five-channel system. Initially there was some discussion of adding a channel that showed movies, and then a January 1956 newspaper article mentioned plans to add "a New York sports station" to Oneonta's lineup.[12] During the mid-1950s an Oneonta Video technician went to observe the operations of Western Microwave, a network in the eastern half of Montana that had been relaying the signals of the closest network affiliate stations to remote towns there. Upon his return, plans began for a similar operation to be called Eastern Microwave.[13] When the company started business in 1962, it carried three New York independent stations—WPIX, WNEW, and WOR—to the Oneonta area, where it served several CATV systems.[14]

Eastern Microwave was not the only company to use microwave to carry independent stations to cable systems. In 1962 H&B Microwave, a subsidiary of the large H&B Communications Corp. (which at the time owned microwave relays and CATV systems throughout the country), began carrying the signal of Chicago's WGN to the Dubuque, Iowa, CATV system.[15] Like the New York stations, WGN was an extremely popular early independent station, owing in large part to a schedule featuring many movies and local sports. Within the next few years, other CATV systems in the Midwest began to import WGN via microwave.

These early uses of microwave relays mark a significant milestone in CATV/cable history: they indicated that the demand for broadcast-type programming might exceed that which broadcast networks alone could provide. Major-market independent stations promised to provide large quantities of programs with known popularity, either because of previous showings (as was the case with movies and off-network reruns) or because of fan followings (as with sports). During the 1950s broadcast television producers and Hollywood studios were only beginning to realize the popularity of their products—not to mention their long-term profit potential—when recycled through syndication.[16] Yet at this early stage, representatives of the CATV industry already were showing an awareness of the television audience's affinity for repeat viewing. In addition to relieving CATV operators of the burden of producing original programs, which was hardly feasible for their small-scale operations, this practice helped lay the foundation for the modern cable industry.

Distant signal importation, by conventional antenna or by microwave, also began to supplement channel selections in broadcast television markets with one or more stations. In some cases the additional signals were carried over great distances, either giving CATV subscribers alternatives to the local stations or replacing them altogether. In markets with only one or two poorly funded UHF stations, CATV was almost as popular as it was where there were no broadcast stations at all.

Signal importation also was lucrative in situations where two or more broadcast markets existed in close enough proximity to make desirable signals from one city available off the air via a community antenna in another city or cities. For example, as of 1966, eight CATV systems had been franchised in greater San Diego, with four already operating (U.S. FCC 1966). San Diego itself was well served by broadcast television; three VHF stations provided coverage of the broadcast networks, and two independent UHF stations and one educational UHF station were in the planning stages. What made CATV marketable in San Diego, though, were Los Angeles stations—particularly the independent stations—that were just distant enough to make home-antenna reception in San Diego difficult.

For the most part, San Diego stations were included along with the Los Angeles stations in the channel packages of CATV systems operating there, but even so, CATV opponents there suggested that the availability of the distant stations would diminish the viewership of local stations. A survey found that viewership for local network affiliate stations (as opposed to those imported from Los Angeles) during prime time was approximately 33 percent higher among CATV nonsubscribers, and "of the cable subscribers, 49 percent reported that they viewed a San Diego channel most; 55 percent named a Los Angeles channel."[17]

Clearly the importation of distant signals gave CATV its ticket into broadcast markets—places where it never would have been marketable otherwise. By the mid-1960s this was the area of CATV's greatest and most promising expansion; larger communities offered the critical mass of subscribers needed to test new technologies and programming options. According to *Broadcasting,* as of early 1966, 15 community antenna systems were operating in 12 of the top 100 broadcast television markets, 4 were under construction, 22 franchises had been granted, and franchise applications were under consideration by local authorities in 70 more of those markets.[18] But CATV's growing presence in broadcast markets also brought on the first regulatory curbs on the expanding industry. Following a wave of aggressive regulation in the mid-1960s CATV's ambitions were far outweighed by restrictions on its geographic expansion and, consequently, its overall growth.

Resistance to the expansion of the CATV industry, and the regulatory measures that ensued, might seem very tangential to a consideration of early developments in cable programming. But reviewing this critical juncture in CATV/cable history is essential to understanding the obstacles that stood in the way of later efforts to reform the medium's programming structures.

CATV Regulation Begins

On the whole, broadcast station owners' views on CATV ranged from embracing the retransmission technology to outright contempt for it. Many broadcasters—particularly UHF broadcasters—were pleased with the additional viewership made possible by CATV. As Barry Litman explains, the FCC's "mixed bag" policy of licensing both VHF and UHF stations had relegated the latter to a weaker market position. This unfavorable situation was exacerbated by the technological inferiority of UHF: VHF covers a wider area and has a stronger signal. UHF stations were further handicapped by the fact that, until the 1960s, most television households used VHF-only receivers (Litman 1990, 131–133).[19]

Thus, many UHF broadcasters appreciated both CATV's extension of their signals and the ability of CATV systems to convert those signals to frequencies that could be tuned using the VHF dial. For example, in 1955, WHUM, the CBS affiliate in Reading, Pennsylvania, published a booklet titled "Television in Pennsylvania," in which it credited CATV for adding 66,000 TV homes to its audience and making the area a "UHF Heaven."[20] Another eastern Pennsylvania UHF station, Scranton's WDAU, employed a "community antenna liaison," whose job was to ensure that CATV systems continued to carry WDAU's signal.[21] Not all broadcasters were pleased with CATV, though. During the late 1950s a group of them (primarily in western states) filed complaints with the FCC charging that CATV's rapidly expanding programming capability threatened their economic success. Some of their complaints focused on issues of copyright and program exclusivity rights, but mostly the broadcasters were dissatisfied with CATV operators' use of microwave relays to bypass nearby broadcast signals. When CATV systems imported the signals of larger, better-funded stations, the station owners contended, it created unfair competition for local stations. In 1958 Montana multiple station owner Ed Craney went so far as to claim that "all tv can be obliterated except for two stations—one in New York and the other in Hollywood—brought to the populace of the United States via catv systems, boosters, translators and satellites."[22] Though this scenario may seem exaggerated, Craney's concerns echoed those of other broadcasters. And federal regulators, still concerned with the issue of localism in television service, paid close attention.

These complaints helped initiate a period of debate that ultimately led to strict regulatory guidelines for the entire CATV/cable industry. Government policymakers had been aware that the need to intervene in the development of CATV could arise at some point, but they had been holding off on efforts to begin such proceedings. During the early 1950s the FCC viewed CATV (as well as booster and translator stations) as harmless stopgap measures that would disappear as soon as a more effective license-allocation scheme was in place for broadcast television. As late as 1955, the Commission believed that terms set forth in the *Sixth Report and Order* would be met.[23] But by the end of the decade, it was clear that granting more station licenses would not solve the problem of providing television service to remote communities (particularly in large, sparsely populated western states).

Indeed, a variety of constituencies felt that CATV was harming local television audiences more than helping them. As the FCC concluded in a 1959 report:

> A CATV system cannot cater to local preferences in programming, cannot serve local merchants, cannot provide a local news and weather service, cannot promote local civic and charitable enterprises, and cannot furnish a forum for discussion of local problems. Instead, it repeats the local programming designed for another community, the advertising of businesses in that community and the news, public service announcements and political and other discussions aimed at the residents in that other community . . . result[ing] in a parody on local service.[24]

Nonetheless it took another five years, and several failed policy initiatives on the part of both Congress and the FCC, before comprehensive rules governing CATV were implemented. In the meantime, the CATV industry and its regulators grappled with a confusing practice of case-by-case regulation. This practice, which really only dealt with issues surrounding the use of microwave relays, continued for five years.

The first major CATV ruling the FCC made was in the *Carter Mountain Transmission Corp.* case.[25] At issue in this case was the potential for CATV to threaten the fortunes of a small local broadcaster if a microwave relay was used to import more popular stations from larger cities. In this case the microwave outfit, Carter Mountain Transmission Corp., refused both to protect the local station against program duplication on the imported stations and to require the CATV system to carry the station's signal. While other CATV and microwave operators undoubtedly were more accommodating to local stations, *Carter Mountain* made it clear that this could not be taken for granted. The FCC ultimately denied the microwave license and subsequently imposed must-carry and nonduplication programming provisions on all existing common carrier microwave licensees.

The decision-making process in *Carter Mountain*—a very lengthy and difficult one due to the virtual absence of judicial precedent—made it apparent that action needed to be taken toward regulating CATV in a uniform way. The hearings and testimony had addressed the various complaints broadcasters were making about CATV, and seemed to capture the essence of how the retransmission medium could threaten the FCC's cherished ideal of localism in television service. It also represented decisive action in a regulatory arena where none had been taken previously. This was seen as only a temporary solution to a much larger problem, though.[26]

In 1965 the FCC passed its *First Report and Order on Cable Television*. Largely drawing from the *Carter Mountain* decision, the major provision of this ruling was to require local signal carriage by any microwave-served CATV system operating within that station's predicted grade A contour. It also guaranteed local stations protection against program nonduplication on imported distant signals for a period of 15 days before and after a network broadcast. This provision applied to microwave-served CATV systems operating within stations' grade A or grade B contours.[27] At this stage, the concern remained only in the area of microwave use and its possible harm to local stations, but more restrictions awaited the CATV industry. The *First Report and Order* was, as Martin Seiden later characterized it, "a stopgap measure . . . to test the winds of opinion, as well as for the anti-CATV forces to consolidate" (Seiden 1972, 87).

The 1965 rules were amended substantially after less than a year, reflecting an awareness that the issues surrounding CATV involved much more than simply the microwave relays. Among various other revisions, the 1966 *Second Report and Order* expanded FCC jurisdiction to include all CATV systems, regardless of whether or not they were served by microwave, thus adding 1,200 systems to the 400 over which it had asserted jurisdiction in the previous year. The rules also restricted the growth of CATV in the top 100 broadcast markets by virtually banning distant signal importation there. This ostensibly was to protect UHF stations, as it was argued that those areas held the strongest potential for UHF development.

The 1966 rules reflected a great deal of regulatory uncertainty on the subject of CATV. On the one hand, the rules clearly were intended to protect broadcasters. On the other hand, the FCC also asserted that it did not wish to bring about the demise of the entire CATV industry, which, by this point, it had deemed an integral part of a national television service (U.S. FCC 1966). So the rules made a few concessions to existing CATV operations. For example, the "nonduplication" period established in the 1965 rules was changed from "15 days before and after" a local station's broadcast to a single 24-hour broadcast day. In fact, there were several loopholes in the rules, and the FCC generally was willing to let broadcast stations and CATV systems work out "private arrangements" in order to meet program protection requirements.[28] The industry did continue to expand wherever and whenever it was able. Only half a year after the 1966 rules were implemented, *Broadcasting* reported that CATV entry into the top broadcast markets was continuing, with powerful new multiple system operators (MSOs) in particular taking advantage of every available loophole in the restrictions. For example, as of October 1966, Charleston, West Virginia (market #45), had been franchised and Indianapolis (#18) was considering bids.[29] In effect, the rules allowed CATV to continue operating—as long as it preserved the status quo in broadcast television.

By the mid-1960s the status quo in broadcasting increasingly meant control of the industry by large media corporations. Small, independent broadcasters had decreased in number since the late 1950s, and rather than fighting against CATV, many of them—opting for the "if you can't beat 'em, join 'em" strategy—had become CATV operators themselves in order to stay in business. Lobbying efforts at this stage were carried out mostly by organizations such as the Association of Maximum Service Telecasters (AMST). AMST members typically were corporate-owned major-market VHF stations, most of which were affiliated with broadcast television's "big three" networks. They wanted to see UHF flourish and CATV disappear, since the signals of popular VHF stations from other markets, carried by CATV, provided much more competition for them than their weak local UHF counterparts did.

In retrospect, the strategy of AMST and the large station owners seems to have boosted the fortunes of the broadcast networks since it allowed them to continue setting the agenda for televised entertainment

and information in the United States. The 1966 ruling allowed broadcast station ownership to become more consolidated—and, ironically,
less locally grounded. It also relegated CATV to a position from which
it could only repeat and reinforce the programming strategies of broadcast television. CATV, by being denied entry into larger communities,
was unable to draw the subscriber revenues needed to develop any new
services that might have enhanced or even replaced its retransmission
function. CATV's presence in broadcast markets also might have helped
independent and educational stations, most of which were only marginally viable at this stage, by extending their viewership. Clearly CATV's
fortunes had far-reaching implications at this point.

In the meantime, of course, existing CATV entrepreneurs had continued to expand their reach as much as possible using microwave relays and other means of distant signal importation. Large microwave
networks like H&B, Eastern Microwave, and Walson's Service Electric
(which had grown to serve a large portion of eastern Pennsylvania) were
able to develop fairly extensive coverage areas and served growing numbers of CATV systems in locations where they posed no competition to
broadcast stations.[30] By 1964 there were 77 common-carrier microwave
companies operating in the United States, and many new relays were
under construction (Seiden 1965, map supplement). Some CATV systems also operated their own microwave relays (known as community
antenna relay service or CARS). All of these microwave businesses flour-
ished and helped set a programming precedent for the future cable industry: then as in more recent years, viewers looked to CATV for broadcast programming more than anything else. CATV operators in the 1960s
were well aware that restrictions on their industry might be tightened
even further, possibly banning the use of microwave relays entirely, so
they kept a cautious eye on Washington. But they did not refrain from
the practice of signal importation.

During the 1950s and 1960s, then, CATV remained, above all, a retransmission service for broadcast signals—whether by antenna or by
microwave relay—and from an economic standpoint nothing else really
merits consideration. But since a major purpose of this study is to identify programming *precedents* set during the medium's earliest years, it is
important to discuss the few pioneering efforts to offer CATV programming that did not derive from broadcast signals. For in these isolated instances one can see that some CATV operators had perceived demand
not being met by broadcast television and were trying, with whatever

resources were available to them, to meet that demand. The legacy of these efforts, in both policy and programming, should become apparent in later chapters.

Local Origination

Local origination (typically abbreviated as "l.o.") refers to programming—whether originally produced or acquired—that is made available by local CATV/cable systems exclusively for their subscribers. It does not derive from broadcast signals. The first documented CATV l.o. programming was done by Martin Malarkey, for his Pottsville, Pennsylvania, system. In 1951, shortly after this system had begun operation, Malarkey produced a local news program using a small Dage closed-circuit television camera in his office.[31] During the next two years, as reported by the *NCTA Membership Bulletin,* he conducted "interviews of city officials, heads of civic organizations, system personnel, visiting dignitaries, professional artists and most touching, an interview of the winner of the local Soap Box Derby and his family."[32]

Probably the earliest local CATV programming to be scheduled on a regular basis—a simple one-camera setup similar to that tested by Malarkey—was done by Port Video Corp. of Port Jervis, New York, beginning in 1957. The programming was described as "stills taken by a local cameraman, sports, school groups, news and local talent. A high school science class [put] on projects ranging from computers to skin-diving." By 1962 PJ Tv Inc., as the system's program service was called, was providing locally originated programs from 11 A.M. to 11 P.M., five nights a week. This operation was sustained by local advertising sales.[33] Several other systems began this type of local origination during the 1960s.

Another type of CATV/cable fare that was used in the 1960s was automated programming. In 1959 Lloyd Calhoun of Hobbs, New Mexico, became the first CATV operator to provide a time and temperature channel. This was nothing more than a camera continuously panning a row of weather gauges. Within the next several years other CATV weather channel equipment began to appear, including Ameco's "Weather-Matic," a direct-readout time-weather machine (for which an optional news display also was available), in 1965.[34] Also in 1965, the Associated Press subsidiary, Press Association, announced its "News Channel," which featured 24-hour visual text of Associated Press news items as they came off the wire. News Channel was in use on 76 systems within its first two years.[35] In January 1966 AP's news rival, United Press International, announced its comparable Video News Service. This system's equipment could be used for locally originated news along with the UPI feed. Another UPI news service, Alphamatic News, was launched in November 1967. In the late 1950s several companies—including Muzak, Alto Fonic, and Beam-Cast—had begun marketing background music packages for use with local and automated channels.[36]

CATV operators also were interested in the use of movies and other preexisting programming material. As early as the second annual meeting of the NCTA, in 1953, there was discussion about using films and kinescoped television programs on local channels. Some operators believed the programming could be financed by advertising sales.[37] The only CATV system actually known to carry out such a plan at this time was Potomac Valley Television Co. of Cumberland, Maryland. By his third year in business, 1954, Potomac Valley's owner, J. Holland Rannells, was showing films, news, and other programs of local interest on a vacant channel. He had acquired two film chains, film and slide projectors, and a multiplexer for this purpose.[38] At first, the costs of most of this programming were subsidized by community antenna operations, but in 1955 Rannells began to seek advertising, approaching local merchants as well as national advertisers. The advertiser-sponsored program origination quickly failed, though, and in 1958 Rannells filled his vacant channel with a combination of off-air programming from five Pennsylvania and Virginia stations.[39] Not surprisingly, the next programming innovation he introduced, in 1961, was the use of a microwave relay.[40]

Rannells's efforts were unique for the 1950s. For one thing, his was one of the few CATV businesses with enough subscriber income to support the experimental programming. Cumberland was a relatively large community, and it was isolated and mountainous enough to make CATV service essential to anyone wanting to watch television there. Also, he appears to have been less cautious than his fellow NCTA members about possible copyright infringement. In fact, the organization's official position on any use of copyrighted program material not deriving from broadcast signals was one of extreme wariness. E. Stratford Smith, NCTA general counsel at the time, recalls warning CATV operators repeatedly against ambitious program origination plans that might violate the copyrights of program owners and thereby jeopardize the legality of the CATV industry as a whole.[41]

The Copyright Issue

Smith's concern was warranted. With the exception of the rudimentary local news programming and the automated channels discussed above, virtually all CATV programming technically was copyrighted material, even though operators paid nothing for its use. If CATV had remained simply an antenna service, the legality of operators' use of programming produced by and for other parties probably would not have been questioned any more than home videotaping for personal use is today. However, importing distant signals and using old movies and taped reruns of commercial television programs to supplement those signals was a thornier legal issue. It threatened to become more complicated as CATV operators began trying to market their service in communities already served by broadcast stations that either owned or were paying for the copyrighted material.

At least a few CATV systems failed to heed the warnings of Smith and the NCTA, judging by the occasional documented use of pirated movies during the mid-1960s. In July 1967, for instance, *Broadcasting* reported that a Houston-based firm called International Artists was distributing some recent feature films on two-inch videotape to cable systems in the Pacific Northwest.[42] Most systems avoided this practice, though— and with good reason since by the mid-1960s copyright litigation was no longer a threat, but a reality. Throughout most of that decade, CATV operators nervously awaited the outcomes of two precedent-setting court cases.

The first of these was *Fortnightly v. United Artists*, 392 US 390 (1968). The Fortnightly Corporation owned two small West Virginia community antenna systems, neither of which actually used microwave relays or originated programming of any kind. Nonetheless, United Artists, a major television program syndicator, challenged Fortnightly's right to use any broadcast signals containing its copyrighted programs without permission and without providing financial compensation. *Fortnightly* went to trial in 1962, and the case finally was resolved in 1968. Initially the case was decided in favor of the plaintiff, but was reluctantly overturned in federal court because the wording of the archaic 1909 Copyright Act—the most recent body of copyright legislation at the time— could not adequately address issues involving electronic media.

Had the CATV industry lost this particular case, not only would operators have become liable to pay copyright fees on any programming they would use in the future, but also for programs used up to three years prior to the ruling. The final ruling in *Fortnightly* represented an important milestone for CATV, since it allowed the industry to begin promoting itself as a television programming operation, rather than simply an antenna service. Indeed, it was only after the final *Fortnightly* verdict that the NCTA felt confident in adopting the term "cable television" instead of "CATV."[43] Nonetheless, the need for copyright guidelines in the CATV/cable industry was never questioned—by policymakers or by those working in the industry—and few people believed the *Fortnightly* ruling would endure. The obsolescence of the 1909 statute clearly had been the main factor in the favorable court decision, and more than anything else, the ruling indicated a need for new legal guidelines in copyright matters.

Fortnightly was not the only copyright-related challenge CATV/cable was facing. As it became apparent that some operators wanted to offer channels of non-broadcast-derived programming, much of it in the form of copyrighted movies and television reruns, and even to seek advertising support or charge additional subscriber fees for that programming, the practices of the entire industry were questioned anew. Thus, in 1964 CBS filed a case against TelePrompTer Corporation, a rapidly growing MSO.[44] The case, *Teleprompter Corp. v. CBS, Inc.,* 415 US 395 (1974), remained in the courts for a decade, but as with *Fortnightly,* the cable industry ultimately won the case in the Supreme Court after defeats in lower courts. The ancient Copyright Act again was a major factor—although during the later years of *Teleprompter,* a copyright bill already was making its way through Congress. As discussed in the next chapter, the final version, called the Copyright Revision Act, was passed in 1976.

Still, with the copyright issue temporarily on hold, CATV/cable operators felt much more confident in pursuing different types of programming—making it one factor in the late-1960s/early-1970s discussions about how to maximize cable's potential as a form of television. This important shift in programming strategy will be discussed in much more detail in the next chapter. At this point it is important to consider the pay-TV industry of the 1950s and 1960s. For this concurrently developing form of television also had a powerful impact on expectations and programming strategies for modern cable. Microwave relays and various types of program origination equipment gave CATV operators a limited ability to distinguish their service from broadcast television, even while remaining entirely dependent on it. And fledgling local origination schemes suggested how CATV operators might have distinguished their service under more favorable conditions. But from its very inception the pay-TV industry was separate from the existing system of advertiser-supported broadcast television and thus offered a laboratory of sorts for alternative programming strategies.

Pay-Television: The 1950s

From its earliest days, pay-TV held a great deal of promise as a medium that would supplement commercial broadcast programming with both high-quality and niche-interest programs. This industry was founded on a belief that viewers would be willing to pay directly for more desirable programming. But pay-TV also was perceived as a threat to the system of advertiser-supported, "free" television in the United States, and therefore remained too deeply mired in regulatory controversy to demonstrate the full extent of its capability. As with CATV program origination efforts, early pay-TV systems are worth noting more because of the programming precedents they set than because of what they actually accomplished during their brief trials.

Pay-television was considered as early as 1949, when Zenith Radio Corp. filed a petition with the FCC to begin testing its Phonevision system. Phonevision used telephone lines both for taking program orders and for decoding a scrambled broadcast signal in a subscriber's home. A year after its license application, Zenith conducted a 90-day test of 300 Chicago households, and found that average weekly movie consumption of in-home movies was more than four times that of theatrical film consumption. Also in 1950, another broadcast pay-TV system, the Skiatron Electronics and Television Corporation's Subscriber-Vision, which used IBM punch cards for both program selection and billing, began tests. These were conducted on New York's WOR during otherwise off-air hours and, like Phonevision, seemed promising. Encouraged by their successful trials, the companies petitioned the FCC for permission to operate nationwide.[45] Both were denied permits, however, pending further investigation of the pay-TV concept in general.

Meanwhile, an experimental *wired* pay-TV system was being built. In 1953 the International Telemeter Corporation, a company founded in 1951 and partly owned by Paramount Pictures, launched a combination CATV and pay-TV operation in the wealthy desert community of Palm Springs, California. The Palm Springs system offered movies, sports, and special-event programming on a "pay-as-you-see" basis. Some Los Angeles sports events not broadcast by local stations were transmitted live to Palm Springs via microwave. And arrangements had been made with three local movie theaters to chain certain films they were showing (all Paramount productions) and then feed the films, in the form of scrambled signals, into CATV subscribers' homes. Subscribers paid for these programs individually through coin boxes attached to their television sets. In addition, a community antenna service provided Los Angeles television signals free of charge.[46]

In spite of the many offerings, though, the system was discontinued in 1955. Telemeter's vice president Paul MacNamara cited inability to secure rights to an adequate supply of Hollywood films as the primary reason for the experiment's discontinuation.[47] Nevertheless, International Telemeter spent the next five years actively promoting its wired pay-TV system, frequently pointing out attributes that would make it compatible with CATV. During various demonstrations, the system was said to have a strong potential for community-based programming; company representatives even suggested that it held the potential for local advertising support. As one spokesperson pointed out, "Many towns don't have tv stations in operation as a local ad medium and Telemeter [could] fill this void."[48]

There were stumbling blocks, though. By this early stage the legal status of pay-TV already was in limbo—brought about by loud protests against all forms of pay-TV, as well as by the FCC's concern that *broadcast* pay-TV specifically would constitute a use of the airwaves that was not in the public interest. Pay-television's opposition was dominated by broadcasters, broadcast networks, and movie theater owners—with the additional support of various labor unions, consumer groups, and women's organizations (Whiteside 1985; Hilmes 1990, 128–130). They argued that pay-TV would reduce movie theater attendance (already in decline since the rise of commercial broadcast television) and quite possibly destroy "free" television, which they claimed was a more democratic system. There was also a concern that the Hollywood movie studios might come to dominate pay-TV in the way they had dominated theatrical exhibition prior to the 1948 *Paramount* Decree (Hilmes 1990, 133–134). Those in favor of pay-TV countered that this form of television would strengthen the market position of UHF and other nonnetwork broadcast stations, enable the production of more specialized and higher-quality programming, and provide viewers with commercial-free television service.

From February 1955 through March 1959, the FCC held hearings on whether or not to allow broadcast pay-TV systems, deciding in the end to accept applications for experimental licenses only.[49] But since the FCC had asserted authority over broadcast pay-TV based solely on its station-licensing authority, wire-based forms of pay-TV such as Telemeter remained relatively unregulated, though they certainly were watched carefully (Howard and Carroll 1980, 9–19). This also encouraged a few individuals already in the CATV industry to begin exploring forms of pay-TV that would be compatible with their service. One of these was Milton Jerrold Shapp, president of Jerrold Electronics Corporation (at that time the principal developer, manufacturer, and supplier to the CATV industry). In 1955 Shapp began promoting CATV's coaxial cable networks as being superior to broadcast signals for the transmission of pay-TV programming.[50]

After several unrealized plans to test pay-TV on CATV systems around the country, Shapp's company equipped and helped launch a short-lived but groundbreaking trial. On 3 September 1957 Video Independent Theatres (VIT), an Oklahoma City–based chain of movie theaters, began a wired pay-TV service called Telemovies in Bartlesville, Oklahoma, about 50 miles north of Tulsa. The operation was run by a VIT subsidiary, Vumore Video, which at the time operated CATV systems in five other Oklahoma communities. The Telemovies system was capable of delivering five channels of programming, but initially it offered only two: a first-run movie channel and a rerun movie channel.[51] Newly released movies were screened in a downtown Bartlesville television studio and then transmitted by coaxial cable to subscribers' homes. The movies were shown concurrently in VIT's local movie theaters. As a result of negotiations by Shapp and his associate Zalmund Garfield, most Hollywood studio executives had agreed to allow Telemovies to use their new movie releases for the pay-TV experiment.[52]

Shapp's influence was only one factor that made Telemovies unique among pay-TV systems of the time. Another was that it charged subscribers a flat monthly rate of $9.50, rather than a per-program fee— prefiguring the payment system used by modern satellite-carried pay-cable networks such as Home Box Office and Showtime. Also, because Telemovies was owned by the same outfit that controlled all of the local movie houses, it faced none of the opposition from theater owners that plagued other pay-TV systems during the late 1950s and early 1960s. VIT president Henry Griffing explained that Telemovies supplied motion pictures to viewers who could not, or did not wish to, view them in theaters. This provided an additional source of revenue, rather than unwanted competition, for his theater chain.[53]

In spite of the factors weighing in favor of Telemovies, its subscriptions dropped by half, from 600 to 300, in the first few months of operation, and the venture lost more than $40,000 during the same period. Interestingly, the final strategies enlisted to keep the system afloat were the addition of community antenna service, along with one channel of movies and another with background music, time, and temperature. The monthly fee was reduced to $4.95. While subscribership grew to 800 at that point, and the revamped system seemed promising for a short while longer, it was estimated that Telemovies would have needed 1,600 subscribers to break even. In summer 1958, after Telemovies had lost over $1.25 million, Griffing suspended operations.[54]

One problem facing Telemovies had been a lack of success in negotiating a method for paying Hollywood studios for the use of their films. Another problem was that subscribers increasingly were dissatisfied with Telemovies' offerings, particularly when paying for movies not actually watched. Most were aware that other proposed pay-TV systems allowed subscribers to pay directly for individual programs. It also has been observed that, throughout the nine months of Telemovies' existence, Tulsa broadcast stations more than quadrupled the number of movies they showed, providing a selection of free movies with which Telemovies' pay fare increasingly was unable to compete.[55]

Telemovies was ahead of its time as a concept, but its failure also points to essential differences between the U.S. entertainment industry of the 1950s and that of more recent years. Shapp and Griffing may have had beneficial Hollywood connections, but modern pay-cable networks operate in a very different climate. Being subsidiaries of large media conglomerates helps outfits like HBO and Showtime to negotiate movie exhibition windows that follow theatrical releases by a few months— often the result of upfront financing arrangements. In this way, they do not compete with theaters for first-run dollars. Nor do they need to worry that broadcast networks and stations will show the same recent movies, since it typically takes years for a Hollywood movie to reach audiences via any broadcast television window.

Telemovies' demise did not discourage others in the CATV industry from becoming interested in pay-TV, though. Many viewed pay-TV as a promising way to fill vacant channels. A lot of attention was given by the NCTA to all forms of pay-TV during the late 1950s and early 1960s— as indicated by the number of articles on the topic appearing in *NCTA Membership Bulletin,* as well as several speeches made by pay-TV executives at the organization's annual meetings. In fact, so great was CATV's optimism about pay-TV that during the late 1950s a number of systems had their franchises amended in preparation for the addition of pay-TV channels. The Oneonta, New York, franchise, for example, was amended on 14 August 1958 in order that Oneonta Video might "transmit through its facilities, signals, programs, and other events of its own origin of all kinds, either live or on film or otherwise." Other cities with such franchise amendments included Dallas; Little Rock; Carlsbad, New Mexico; Oklahoma City; Meridian, Mississippi; and Austin, Texas.[56]

Nonetheless, the Palm Springs and Bartlesville experiments were the only instances of actual CATV/pay-TV joint ventures during the 1950s. At this early stage of CATV history, sufficient connections among CATV and other media industries had not yet formed. Even the Bartlesville system, actually run by a movie theater owner, had had difficulty securing an adequate supply of new product. An independent CATV operator certainly could not have hoped to fare any better. To give a concrete example of the situation, in the mid-1950s, Martin Malarkey, known for his early attempts at local origination, had proposed to his town's movie theater owners that movies be chained following theatrical showings and then shown to cable subscribers on a pay-TV basis. The CATV operator and the theater owner then would share the profits. But, as Malarkey explained many years later, "I thought it was a neat idea and they said, 'No way, absolutely not, we're not going to share any of our revenues with you.' . . . The movie distributors had never heard of cable."[57]

Pay-Television: The 1960s

The idea of pay-TV did not disappear along with Telemovies (even though it would be another 15 years before the appearance of either another flat-rate system or one that operated in conjunction with community antenna service). In the meantime, some older companies finally got the opportunity they had been waiting for. In March 1959 the FCC announced that it would accept applications for limited and tightly controlled tests of pay-TV systems, and several experiments were launched within the next five years. While none were directly integrated with CATV, these pay-TV experiments of the early 1960s were critical to the evolution of CATV (and later cable). They revealed certain types of programs, such as sports and movies, for which the public might be willing to pay directly, and also led to the formulation of regulatory guidelines that would have a powerful impact on modern satellite-delivered cable networks.

In the late 1950s, in the wake of the much-publicized failure of the Bartlesville system, International Telemeter had announced a reconfigured pay-TV system that collected program payments in nickel increments using a metered coin box. Transactions, including information about program selection, were recorded on magnetic tape inside the box—which, Telemeter claimed, was a more effective means of audience measurement than that of either Trendex or Nielsen. While the system prototype introduced in the late 1950s used wire for transmission, Telemeter promoted its coin-box mechanism as being usable with either wires or broadcast signals.[58]

Demonstrations of the new system began in 1957 and led to a full-fledged consumer market test in 1960. Even though Telemeter (by 1960 a fully owned subsidiary of Paramount Pictures) was based in New York, the site it chose for testing a wired version of its system was Etobicoke, Ontario, a suburb of Toronto, under the auspices of Famous Players, a Canadian theater chain partly controlled by Paramount. It has been suggested that Etobicoke was the ideal location to test pay-TV. Audiences there had regular access to U.S. network programming, and thus their viewing preferences could be equated with those of American audiences. Yet the Canadian location protected Paramount from allegations of antitrust and the various other rallying cries of pay-TV's opponents in the United States (Hilmes 1990, 127).

Service began in Etobicoke on 26 February 1960 with 1,000 subscribers.[59] Programming during the trial's first year consisted primarily of movies and fictional series, and a study released in November 1960 showed that it drew a prime-time viewership higher than that of American commercial broadcast networks (2.4 hours between 7 and 11 P.M., as opposed to 2 hours for the networks).[60] In 1961 Telemeter also secured rights to Toronto Argonauts football games and the away games of the Toronto Maple Leafs hockey team. Since the movies and other programs in use up to this point had been primarily second-run or low-budget fare, securing the rights to popular sports events was considered a major coup for the pay system.[61] Nonetheless, the Etobicoke experiment only lasted through 1965. By that point, Telemeter's subscribership had decreased from a high of 5,800 to only 2,500, and the company had lost an estimated $2 million (Howard and Carroll 1980, 30; Baer and Pilnick 1974, 22).

It is worth noting that when it discontinued the Etobicoke experiment, Telemeter was actively pursuing connections with the CATV industry. As company president Louis A. Novins had observed in 1959, the facilities appropriate for pay-TV were in wide use in more than 500 community antenna systems in the United States and about 200 in Canada, serving "well over a half-million homes."[62] In 1965 Telemeter was planning a programming experiment in Montréal that would offer three pay channels on an 11-channel CATV system (this experiment was never carried out). The company also had opened a U.S. subsidiary called Home Theatres, Inc. in 1962, whose employees were working with large CATV operators to find ways of making their two businesses compatible.[63] And throughout the mid-1960s, Telemeter executives strongly—though unsuccessfully—urged the FCC to authorize pay-TV as a part of CATV in the United States.[64] It is highly likely that if such authorization had been granted at the time, Telemeter's plan to combine community antenna service with pay-TV would have been successful.

Eventually, though, a frustrated Telemeter adopted a different strategy in its pursuit of CATV connections. In 1967, a year after Paramount had been acquired by Gulf + Western Industries, Telemeter (by that point a separate subsidiary of the new conglomerate) was building CATV systems in two states and had applied for franchises in more than 200 cities.[65] Although there is no evidence to indicate that Telemeter ever offered pay-TV channels on these systems, *Broadcasting* did report that the company had entered into CATV equipment design and was planning a 25-channel system.[66] Throughout the late 1960s and early 1970s, International Telemeter would continue, with very limited success, to develop new types of CATV and pay-TV equipment.

Meanwhile Zenith's Phonevision, another long-standing pay-TV company, launched an experimental over-the-air system in Hartford, Connecticut. Amidst loud protests from broadcasters and theater owners, the system began service on 29 June 1962. Phonevision programming was broadcast from WHCT, a Hartford UHF station licensed to RKO specifically for the Phonevision trial. WHCT broadcast scrambled pay programming for two to three hours per day, and offered free programming the rest of the time. Subscribers paid $10 for installation of a decoder box and a $3 monthly rental fee in addition to the charges for individual programs. Phonevision's first week of programming consisted of three 15-minute shorts for children at 25 cents for the package; the feature films *Escape from Zahrain* (1962), *One-Eyed Jacks* (1961), *Splendor in the Grass* (1961), and *Pleasure of His Company* (1961) at $1.25 each.

The programming was repeated about four times during a 10-day period.[67] Additional programming was added over the years.

In 1964 it was reported that major boxing matches were drawing Phonevision's largest audiences. The 25 February 1964 Cassius Clay–Sonny Liston fight was watched by 86 percent of all subscribing households. The second most popular programming category was first-run movies. By its second year of operation, Phonevision had acquired first broadcast rights to films from all the major Hollywood studios. *Whatever Happened to Baby Jane?* (1962) drew 66 percent of Phonevision's subscribers the first time it aired. Certain entertainment specials comprised the next most popular viewing category. A program featuring the Kingston Trio, for example, drew 44 percent. Cultural programming such as ballets and classical music concerts proved to be the least popular.[68]

Apparently Phonevision's pay-TV audience preferred the same programming categories as "free" television audiences—though it is likely that they found the programming quality to be higher on pay-TV. The lack of viewership for the so-called cultural category of programming seems ironic given that Phonevision's subscribers and potential subscribers had cited *absence* of these types of programming as a major reason for dissatisfaction with the system.[69] This suggests that people might be more idealistic when discussing television programming in the abstract than they are when actually viewing. Phonevision's viewer preferences prefigure the failure of specialized cultural cable programming services in the early 1980s.

The Hartford experiment continued, without much fanfare, through 31 January 1969, but ultimately failed because it did not attract the 20,000 subscribers (at a minimum) that it needed.[70] When pay-TV finally won FCC approval in 1970, it was too late for Phonevision specifically. However, the approval gave a green light to several other pay-TV operations that had been waiting to launch—including several of the earliest pay-cable networks.

Another wired pay-TV venture, Subscription Television Inc. (STV), was tested during the mid-1960s. While STV's trial had the shortest duration of all the 1960s pay-TV tests, it was also the most highly acclaimed. STV was the heir (through a complicated series of stock transfers) to Skiatron Corporation's Subscriber-Vision, tested in the early 1950s.[71] Skiatron had continued to promote an over-the-air system throughout the 1950s, but in 1963 it announced plans to operate wire-based pay-TV systems. The major figure behind STV, Skiatron's new operating company, was Matthew M. Fox, who had been involved with

Skiatron since the mid-1950s, but a new group of executives and investors—including a mixture of publishers, electronics firms, brokers, and baseball clubs—had joined STV.[72] Most notably, Sylvester L. "Pat" Weaver was brought in as president of the company.[73] Weaver arrived at STV already a veteran of television entertainment, with a career ranging from advertising executive to chairman of NBC.

Wired STV networks were constructed in both San Francisco and Los Angeles. The company's long-range plans were first to wire other major cities and later to incorporate existing CATV systems into a nationwide wired pay-TV network. Subscribers paid $10 for installation and a base charge of $1 per week in addition to charges for individual programs. Billing was from a central location. Like several other pay-TV systems, STV had a built-in ratings system. STV launched in Los Angeles on 17 July 1964, with 2,500 subscribers.

The system's three channels offered a mixture of sports, movies, children's programs, and theatrical performances. In addition to a Los Angeles Dodgers doubleheader, the inaugural weekend's programming included a children's ballet from Holland (at $1.50), a Broadway review starring Carol Channing ($2.00), a gospel jazz performance by the Los Angeles Community Choir ($.50), and a number of foreign films (most $1.00). Nearly all of the movies were obscure second-run features, and most other programming tended to come from inexpensive and lesser known sources. It was baseball that provided the foundation for STV's programming schedule, and Fox's acquisition of the rights to Major League Baseball games for STV's exclusive use has been cited as the greatest programming coup achieved by any of the early pay-TV operations.[74]

Apparently, though, even a maneuver such as this could not guarantee the success of the pay-TV outfit. STV discontinued service in November 1964, only four months after it had begun, the victim of the well-organized body of opposition to pay-TV. Even before STV's launch, the Citizens' Committee for Free TV and the California Crusade for Free TV had begun lobbying state legislators to pass Proposition 15, a measure to ban pay-TV in that state. Thomas Whiteside suggests that efforts to counter the "free TV" campaign drew resources away from business and programming aspects of the fledgling STV operation. In November 1964 Proposition 15 was passed—concluding a two-pronged attack on STV, which already had been drained to the point of bankruptcy because of the resources expended in the campaign. STV's San Francisco and Los Angeles operations already had gone out of business by the time Proposition 15 was declared unconstitutional in federal courts a few months later.[75] The company did not disappear completely. Rather, it continued as a subsidiary of Skiatron Electronics & Television Corp. As with other pay-TV companies, though, the vestigial operation never became an active player in the expanded television scenario of the following decades.

The CATV Industry and Pay-Television

By the 1960s joint CATV/pay-TV ventures seemed somewhat more likely due to the changing structure of the community antenna industry. During the 1950s CATV had been controlled primarily by small-town entrepreneurs, while pay-TV was run by Hollywood movie studios and other established entertainment companies. But a decade later, a few large media corporations were involved with CATV, and they were interested in expanding both the number of communities served by the medium and the number of services it offered. Adoption of pay-TV was one of the services they wanted to explore, as well as greater numbers of broadcast channels and expanded local programming. A major goal—though one certainly hampered by the regulatory climate of the 1960s—was to begin offering CATV/cable service in communities already served by broadcast television.

The largest of the new MSOs was TelePrompTer Corporation, a company that had built its reputation by marketing cueing devices for speeches. Following the success of this invention, the company, under the guidance of its president, Irving Berlin Kahn, began pursuing television technologies—the first of which was theater television. When first invented in the 1940s, theater television had involved the broadcasting of programming to movie theaters using special frequencies. That programming then was projected onto screens—either instead of, or as a supplement to, traditional filmed movies. This form of television was pursued actively by the Hollywood film studios, particularly Paramount, as a way to draw audiences away from home television and back to theaters. As Christopher Anderson explains, the income derived from direct viewer payments, as opposed to commercial television's indirect advertising support, could subsidize lavish productions—such as sporting events, plays, or ballets—not available to home viewers.[76] By the late 1940s many movie exhibitors had purchased television projection equipment for their theaters, believing this to be the key to their future economic success. But a spiral of legal and business events starting in 1948 gradually brought an end to the studios' pursuit of theater television.[77]

In the early 1950s the specially equipped theaters built by the studios were taken over by new companies planning to offer *closed-circuit* theater television—a form that used either microwave relays or land lines, rather than broadcast frequencies, for transmission. Among these firms was Box Office Television, which specialized in live industrial programming, such as product promotions, and sports events, including Notre Dame football.[78] In 1955 Box Office Television was bought by the Sheraton Hotel chain and was renamed Sheraton Hotel Closed-Circuit TV Corp. The following year, the company was acquired anew—this time by TelePrompTer, which continued the industrial programming and also added boxing.[79]

In a sense, closed-circuit theater television prefigured the development of pay-cable networks, since it suggested a willingness on the part of the public to pay directly for special-event programming. Kahn clearly was aware of this, as evidenced by the aggressive CATV acquisition policy he instituted in his company starting in 1960. The first CATV system TelePrompTer acquired was in Silver City, New Mexico, a system for which it paid $130,000. Upon discovering that the cash flow of the Silver City system was over $30,000 per year, the company purchased systems in Rawlins, Wyoming, and Farmington, New Mexico.[80] Along with the moneymaking potential of community antenna service by itself, Kahn saw these small, remote CATV systems as the ideal testing grounds for pay-TV—unlikely to draw the scrutiny of either antipay groups or government regulators. As he explained in a 1987 interview, "If you want to go to Silver City, you have to really want to go there. There is a grass airport. We figured if we tried out our Pay-TV there and it was successful, who will know? We can hide it until we develop it. If it's a failure, who will know? It was a no-lose proposition."[81]

In 1960, shortly after acquiring its first CATV systems, TelePrompTer became the first company to use an intercity closed-circuit network to transmit a special event to CATV systems. The event, a boxing match between Floyd Patterson and Ingmar Johansson, was carried by 13 CATV systems (including several not actually owned by TelePrompTer) scattered throughout the country. In the same year, Kahn also introduced a prototype for a pay programming system called "Key TV" that could be used in combination with CATV.[82] He wasted little time in making his interest in pay-TV known to the CATV industry. Kahn was among the featured speakers at the 1960 NCTA convention in Miami, but rather than speaking in person, he appeared before the delegates on a large television screen, live from New York via TelePrompTer's theater TV equipment.[83]

Throughout the 1960s and 1970s, TelePrompTer remained extremely interested in adding non-broadcast-derived programming to CATV systems. This was a line of business that complemented its early and aggressive efforts to bring CATV into broadcast markets. In 1961 TelePrompTer purchased a system in Elmira, New York, a community that had two UHF stations of its own and was within Binghamton's grade B contour.[84] It continued to acquire systems in smaller broadcast markets, and in 1964 became one of three successful bidders for CATV franchises in Manhattan. By 1965 the company was serving 46,463 subscribers in systems located throughout the United States. And by the late 1960s, TelePrompTer was not only the largest MSO but also a major player in the cable industry's efforts to develop satellite networks.

Other CATV operators also were interested in pay-TV, of course, but approached this line of business with much more trepidation than Kahn. The risk of a measure banning pay-TV was ongoing, and few independent operators could have sustained the losses that would have followed such a ban. As a 1964 *Broadcasting* analysis found, the likely cost for a CATV system to add pay channels would have ranged from 50 percent to 150 percent of the system's initial construction costs.[85] Still the growing coexistence of CATV and pay-TV as of the mid-1960s must not be overlooked when considering the history of either form of television. Pay-TV did not disappear in the mid-1960s, only to resurface with the introduction of satellites to the cable industry a decade later. Rather, at the time of pay-TV's supposed demise, its compatibility with CATV was just beginning to be explored.

There is little doubt the modern cable industry is the heir to the intentions of International Telemeter, Phonevision, Skiatron, and other pay operations. Had CATV operators been less encumbered by an uncertain regulatory environment (surrounding both CATV and pay-TV), their adoption of pay-TV might have taken place much earlier than it did. As it was, early pay-TV experiments indicated which types of programming could successfully supplement commercial broadcast programming, and they brought about regulations that shaped the development of pay-cable. Yet, as elaborate and promising as the various pay-TV schemes were during the 1950s and 1960s, they never amounted to more than curiosities. Many television viewers knew about pay-TV from newspapers and magazines, but very few experienced the technologies firsthand. For the American audience of the 1950s and 1960s, television was virtually synonymous with the system of advertiser-supported broadcast television.

CATV and Developments in Broadcast Television

So when discussing programming developments in CATV, one must not lose sight of the fact that its fortunes were inextricably bound to those of broadcast television. During the 1950s and 1960s CATV's sole reason for existence was to deliver broadcast programming, and the more of it a CATV operator could offer, the better. But it is also worth noting that even at this early stage broadcast television comprised more than simply the programming supplied by the major networks. As will become apparent in later chapters, many of the programming formats that characterize modern cable can be traced back to programming strategies used by stations not affiliated with one of the major networks. A reconsideration of just what was available on broadcast television during cable's early years seems in order in this regard.

Movies became a popular, reliable, and easily attainable television programming source during the 1950s, owing primarily to the fact that Hollywood studios had begun selling their pre-1948 film libraries to television distributors. Although few old movies showed up in network prime time before the 1960s, they served as a key programming source for both network affiliates and independent stations during the 1950s. As Barnouw (1990) explains, switching from live drama to movies allowed stations to reduce staff and discontinue costly studio operations. By 1956 New York independent station WOR's schedule was 88 percent film (197–198).[86] WOR and other major-market independent stations also served as the television homes to local sports teams, providing much more extensive coverage than was available from the broadcast networks. As discussed above, the emphasis on movies and sports encouraged many CATV systems to import the signals of independent stations—even over great distances.

While most independent stations still catered to the interests of the general public, a few niche-oriented operations also were forming— most notably in the areas of religious and Spanish-language programming. Religious broadcasting in the United States dates back to early radio, and made the transition to television during the 1940s and 1950s, with the rise of televangelists like Billy Graham, Rex Humbard, and Oral Roberts. These men reinvented the church sermon for television audiences, blending fire-and-brimstone exhortation with the charismatic showmanship of variety show hosts. It has been suggested that when Humbard's 5,000-seat Cathedral of Tomorrow opened in 1958, it was designed at least as much to be a television set as it was to be a church (Ostling 1986).

These early televangelists were joined by Marion G. "Pat" Robertson in 1961, when he purchased his own UHF station. Unlike his predecessors, who either rented blocks of time from stations or relied on broadcasters wishing to meet public service obligations, Robertson controlled entire programming days, which allowed him to experiment with a variety of different television genres. In this way he was able to carve out a distinct programming niche—one that held interest for viewers outside his local market. Throughout the 1960s his station grew into a network of affiliated religious stations called the Christian Broadcasting Network (CBN). In 1977, as will be discussed later in the book, CBN launched the third satellite-carried cable network. A few other early satellite cable networks also trace their origins to broadcast televangelism.

Like religious programming, Spanish-language television has a long history in the United States, as indicated by *Broadcasting*'s 1964 "Special Report" on that market.[87] The report lists dozens of radio stations broadcasting at least several hours a week in Spanish, as well as over a dozen Spanish-language television stations, seven of which offered Spanish-language programming full-time.[88] Two of these stations, KMEX–Los Angeles and KWEX–San Antonio, were started in 1961 by the Spanish International Network (SIN). During the 1960s and 1970s SIN—controlled by a partnership that included Emilio Azcarraga Milmo, owner of the Latin American broadcast giant Televisa—rapidly came to dominate Spanish-language broadcasting in the United States. In the late 1970s SIN would launch one of the earliest satellite-carried cable networks.

Another alternative to broadcast television's "big three" networks that took off in the early 1960s was educational television. The FCC's 1952 *Sixth Report and Order* had called for 242 frequencies to be set aside for educational television (ETV), with more to be added later.[89] ETV had a slow start, with most early stations operating on negligible budgets. But this was enough to reinforce the notion that advertiser-supported network television was not the only option. By the 1960s television reform was a major policy issue—one that led to the formation of the Corporation for Public Broadcasting in 1967 and PBS in 1969.

CATV was by no means left out of the policy discussions surrounding educational television. Certainly these contributed to increased expectations for cable during the Blue Sky period of the late 1960s and early 1970s. Even before that, though, CATV operators were encouraged by both the government and their professional organization to become involved with ETV. Clearly recognizing the public relations benefits associated with fostering the growth of ETV, in 1961, the NCTA asked its members, "How are you helping ETV in your area? Do you carry an ETV program? Have you contacted school officials to determine how you can help meet their ETV needs?"[90] For its part, the FCC agreed to suspend its recently imposed freeze on the granting of microwave permits in the case of CATV systems wishing to import educational stations.[91]

Programming developments within commercial network television itself also prefigured cable programming of the satellite era. Especially notable in this regard is the rise of syndication. The stockpile of broadcast network reruns that began to accumulate during the 1950s and 1960s would provide a significant programming resource for modern cable networks. When cable began to develop large-scale programming operations of its own, it would draw heavily from—and, in fact, expand upon—the conventions established by broadcast television in the 1950s. This would be a disappointment to those wishing to see cable develop as a medium substantially different from broadcast television, but it is not surprising given the role of CATV during its first decade. During the 1950s CATV built its identity around its ability to expand the coverage of broadcast television. And during the 1960s, in spite of new investment and improved technology, protracted regulatory debates stalled any significant developments in CATV programming, allowing broadcast television's programming and scheduling conventions to become even more entrenched.

Conclusions

One major significance of these years to the history of CATV/cable programming, then, is the CATV industry's de facto requirement to continue repeating broadcast fare. The 1950s witnessed the growth of CATV from a few small, pioneering systems to an industry encompassing 640 local systems, serving a total of 650,000 subscribers (out of 47.3 million television households).[92] As the number of systems grew, so too did the amount of programming they offered. Still, at this stage expanded CATV service almost always meant additional broadcast channels, often obtained through the use of microwave relays. Although a few operators experimented with local origination programming, and there were a few experiments in which CATV operated in conjunction with pay-TV, the appeal of CATV during the 1950s lay overwhelmingly in its ability to relay broadcast signals. This is hardly surprising given the novelty of broadcast television itself at this early stage.

The impulse to supplement broadcast programming was much stronger in the 1960s, owing in large part to a shifting industrial structure. Although CATV had remained primarily in the hands of small-town entrepreneurs throughout the 1950s, in the 1960s the systems began to be acquired by MSOs such as TelePrompTer Corporation. These corporations had observed the success and profit potential of CATV in smaller communities, noting carefully the various ways in which the basic antenna service had been enhanced. After acquiring several smaller systems, they would look toward expanding into cities where one or more broadcast television stations already were operating. At first, they speculated, CATV could supplement limited channel selections in smaller broadcast markets. Later it might offer channels of non-broadcast-derived programming that could be marketed even in cities with many available broadcast signals.

But as much as those in the industry wanted to expand and try new services, they were also encumbered by restrictive new regulations and other pressures from the government. Operators were extremely wary about starting program origination systems while the FCC was debating new bodies of rules and issues of copyright remained unresolved. And the equally shaky status of pay-TV forestalled its much desired and anticipated confluence with CATV. Following the *Carter Mountain* decision, even simple signal importation was a risky venture; however, this remained the most typical source of supplemental programming. Certainly it was the most feasible proposition for CATV systems operating in the isolated rural areas that were least affected by the tide of regulation.

It has been argued that the 1948–52 licensing freeze on broadcast television virtually guaranteed the future of a three-network oligopoly in that industry.[93] Similarly, a poorly conceived and uncompromising set of regulations allowed cable to remain little more than a retransmission medium for broadcast programming. But ironically the debates, hearings, and regulation between 1960 and 1967 gave CATV a level of recognition it had not had in the previous decade. Representatives of many different constituencies began to reassess CATV's functions and to suggest ways in which its parasitic relationship with broadcasting might be diminished. Following the 1966 *Second Report and Order,* a wave of articles about CATV began to appear in the popular press. Their purpose typically was both to inform the general public about the existence of the wired medium, still considered something of a rural oddity to many, and then to present suggestions (sometimes lengthy treatises) on the medium's potential social benefits.[94] Certainly by this point, much of the American public realized that CATV (by then known as cable television) was no longer simply a *temporary* solution to insufficient broadcast television coverage. The next chapter will examine how new levels of recognition for CATV/cable contributed to a climate of expectation and optimism, known as "Blue Sky," in which the groundwork for modern cable was finalized.

New Directions for Cable, 1968–1975

In spite of dramatic technological innovation that would shape cable in the late 1970s, after the introduction of communications satellites to the industry, the years from 1968 to 1975 arguably were the period in which cable changed the most. During these years policies, programming precedents, and industrial structures were established that would guide the development of cable programming during the satellite era. In 1960 CATV had been perceived as a mere novelty by other entertainment industries, and was little known to television audiences not relying on it for basic service. Even the group of broadcasters who actively opposed CATV around that time had based their arguments almost solely on CATV's retransmission potential—for the most part, leaving issues of non-broadcast-derived programming to those who were debating pay-TV. Only eight years later, broadcasters, regulators, and the general public were increasingly aware of cable's capacity to deliver much more than broadcast signals. As the Sloan Commission pointed out in its 1971 document:

> In the end, cable must grow as conventional television has grown: on the basis of its own accomplishments. As it takes on an identity of its own, the current debate over distant signals and the passion it arouses, as well as the disputes concerning the rights over local broadcast signals, will come to appear insignificant stages in the growth of a total television system. (Sloan Commission on Cable Communications 1971, 62)

The industry's 1968 name change—from "CATV" to "cable television"—effectively symbolized the medium's evolution from an elaborate antenna service to a promised cornucopia of televised entertainment and information that could be delivered to the home via a single wire.

One reason for the changed perceptions was that, by the late 1960s, the cable industry no longer was controlled by the independently owned systems that had dominated it a decade earlier. It was expanding both horizontally and vertically, with most of the major MSOs also involved in broadcast television or other entertainment and information industries. Also by this time, channel capacity on most systems had increased to 12 or even 20, microwave relay networks covered large areas of the country, and satellites promised even more widespread distribution of cable's purportedly vast array of programming. In a few isolated instances, cable systems had even begun to draw revenue from the sale of advertising during local programming. This was of relatively minor significance at the time, but it foretold a future in which cable would become an advertiser-supported medium.

Throughout the late 1960s and early 1970s, cable's development remained subject to the vicissitudes of a rapidly shifting regulatory terrain, as in earlier years. But while the 1965 and 1966 regulatory efforts had been aimed primarily at protecting the existing broadcast industry, much of the regulation that followed tried to assure a future in which cable could supply locally oriented and special-interest programming, rather than merely extend the offerings of broadcast television. The publicity brought about by the FCC's mid-1960s hearings and regulations combined with the promise of satellites and other new technologies to generate a flood of visionary statements and treatises.

Indeed, many parties expressed hopefulness about cable's ability to satisfy unmet television programming needs. In addition to government agencies, private research firms and the cable industry itself labored diligently to produce plans by which satellites could feed multiple channels of television programming to terrestrial distribution networks throughout the United States. Existing coaxial cable networks frequently were cited as the ideal foundation for such networks. The same planners also were making elaborate claims about cable's potential for local programming, especially in communities not served by their own broadcast television stations. These statements and treatises had a profound effect on cable policy initiated during this period.

The Blue Sky documents were part of an even larger set of optimistic discourses—reflecting a wide range of political philosophies, interpretations, and agendas—that were aimed at reforming television programming generally. Beginning in the late 1960s there was a renewed interest in public television, and various policies were initiated to reform commercial broadcast television. While not all of these were directly related to cable programming, they did contribute to a climate in which expectations for any television programming were quite high. When applied to cable specifically, perhaps they were unrealistically high. A sense of urgency accompanied the plans for cable programming reform, leading to what most analysts now regard as haphazard and ineffective regulations.

This is the issue examined in the present chapter. What factors led to modern cable programming patterns, and might cable's course have been altered by more effective policy during the years from 1968 to 1974? For during this period, cable programming underwent more changes than it had in all of the preceding two decades. Within a very short time span, policymakers tried to force a complete reversal of cable's primary function: from a basic rural retransmission medium to the locally oriented and content-specialized medium broadcast television could never be. Local programming strategies were developed for cable. The concept of public access programming was introduced. The earliest pay-cable networks were started. And yet, with all of these new programming possibilities, the enduring legacy of the period from 1968 to 1975 was a continued—in fact expanded—reliance on broadcast-type programming. By 1975 and the industry's first use of a communications satellite, cable had gone through an extraordinarily rapid series of policy shifts and programming experiments, and finally had settled into a set of programming conventions that was strikingly reminiscent of broadcast television. What happened?

Blue Sky

As discussed in the previous chapter, the verdict in the *Fortnightly* copyright case gave the cable industry some degree of encouragement in exploring programming sources that did not derive from broadcast signals. As never before, cable operators developed new programming schemes—ranging from low-budget local news programs to elaborate movie and specialty channels (for which they hoped to charge additional fees). As will be discussed in more detail below, cable interests actively pursued promising new television technologies, particularly communications satellites.

These initiatives received considerable support from the public-at-large due to the prevailing climate of technological optimism and expectation. As mentioned above, discourses of television programming reform were emanating from every imaginable constituency, and they guided policy in widely varying ways. For example, the years 1968–1974 saw the rise of the Corporation for Public Broadcasting and PBS, as well as active debate over the government's policy on public broadcasting (with perspectives ranging from strong support on the part of the Johnson administration to Nixon's veto of a major PBS funding allocation).[1] Publicly funded television programming also was seen by various parties, notably the Ford Foundation, as an important use of satellite technology. There was extensive discussion about who might best control such an operation in the public interest.

Also, in the early 1970s the three major broadcast networks (following a Department of Justice antitrust suit) signed consent decrees designed to make their programming more competitive and diverse. The decrees contained two major provisions. First, the Prime Time Access Rule (PTAR) limited to three (four on Sundays) the number of prime-time hours during which networks could provide programming to their affiliates. The remaining hour (or two) had to be used for locally produced or syndicated programming. In the top 50 markets, the syndicated programming could not consist of off-network reruns. Second, the Financial Interest and Syndication Rules ("Fin-Syn") limited the number of hours per week during which networks could use programming they had produced themselves. These rules also prevented networks both from having a financial interest in program syndication and from syndicating their own programs.[2]

One intended effect of PTAR and Fin-Syn was to encourage more independent production companies to sell programming to the networks. The rules, complemented by a new interest in drawing educated, upscale audiences, encouraged the replacement of some of the lowest-common-denominator programs of the 1960s with socially relevant, "quality" sitcoms such as *All in the Family* and *The Mary Tyler Moore Show*. This so-called sitcom renaissance might indirectly have fueled the optimism about cable's programming potential, since it meant that television in general was being taken more seriously. Another effect of PTAR and Fin-Syn was to encourage the production and stockpiling of large amounts of syndicated programming (both first-run and off-network). The abundance of syndicated material would have a strong impact on cable programming in the years to come, since satellite-carried cable networks would draw heavily from syndication libraries. This is a very significant point and will be discussed in considerable detail in later chapters.

In the meantime, expectations for cable programming were being guided by a gradual shift in the FCC's cable policy, which paralleled public service and programming-diversity goals for broadcast television as reflected in PTAR and Fin-Syn. In the late 1960s the Commission began to focus on how to recognize and foster any underutilized or emerging technologies that might help repair its local television service mandate. This meant recognizing, as the Commission put it, that "the CATV industry generally is placing increased emphasis on program origination, both of a local public service nature and of the entertainment type, and on the provision of other services to the public" (U.S. FCC 1968b). Because of its large channel capacity, cable had become the promised mode of delivery for these sorts of programming, and so the FCC was under increasing pressure to implement new regulations to promote the medium's growth.

New optimism about cable's programming potential was circulating both within regulatory circles and among the general public, and centered around the notion that cable could—and definitely should—provide the American public with multiple channels of non-broadcast-derived programming. Various proposals forwarded during this time period envisioned local news channels, programming produced by community members, niche-interest programming, political debates, interactive services, and myriad other program types that were seldom, if ever, available from broadcast networks and their affiliates. The proposals appeared in the form of popular press articles, government reports, and privately commissioned studies. They reflected a dissatisfaction with the FCC's cable policy that was widespread and spanned a broad range of political philosophies. As Robert Britt Horwitz explains: "Liberals and broadcast reformers saw the problem of commercial broadcasting as a problem of citizen access, thus championed cable TV as an abundant wellspring for such access. Free market economists saw the problem of commercial broadcasting as an artificially produced paucity of competition, thus advocated the end of regulatory restrictions on cable TV as a way to let the broadcast market function 'naturally'" (Horwitz 1989, 252).

The first major round of popular press articles—those appearing immediately after the 1966 rules had been implemented—did little more than explain CATV technology and the medium's regulatory status to a naive public.[3] Soon, however, more definitive statements regarding cable's potential future began to be seen. Among the first voices was that of FCC commissioner Nicholas Johnson. In an October 1967 speech at an NCTA regional meeting in Philadelphia, Johnson asserted a belief that cable could help establish localism in television programming. Johnson noted that the 36 percent of systems then originating programming (weather, movies, and news) were "a start," and recommended that cable regulation be pursued with enough leniency to foster the development of more local programming.[4]

Johnson further articulated his position a month later in a *Saturday Review* article titled "CATV: Promise and Peril," where he pointed out that

> cable's potential . . . lies in two technical advantages. First, its channel capacity permits the simultaneous carrying of a wide variety of programming aimed at a wide variety of audiences. Second, a cable system could, if so designed, reach precisely selected geographic portions of a city—or the nation—which may correspond to particular social, economic, or other special interest groupings. Cable could become a viable medium for interconnection of what would, in effect, be a number of large closed-circuit systems. Whereas a local broadcaster may not be able to justify programming aimed just at ballet enthusiasts, or the local Negro community, or *aficionados* of sports cars, a regional or even a national cable network might be developed which could enhance its appeal significantly through such specialized programming. (1967, 88)

Johnson's words capture the optimistic outlook of cable's "Blue Sky" era. Like many others, he believed the medium's large channel capacity gave it the potential to provide a newsstandlike cornucopia of special-interest channels at the national level. At the same time, cable's economics and technology enabled it to specialize at the local level to an extent impossible for broadcast television.

Still, Johnson's optimism, wherever it was expressed, always was tempered by a concern that without a well-considered regulatory plan this remarkable potential might never be realized. He contrasted the understaffed and underfunded FCC, which held responsibility for television's public service functions, with various large entertainment and communications corporations, including AT&T, that eventually could control a networked cable industry. Past experience told him that the public service mission easily could be abandoned in favor of higher profits for entrenched entertainment and information corporations. The cautiousness that mitigated Johnson's enthusiasm demonstrates an awareness of how deeply entrenched the existing television programming infrastructure was by the late 1960s—not only in terms of industrial practices and precedents, but also in terms of public expectations for television programming. Subsequent developments in cable would show that his concern was well founded.

In his memorable 1972 book, *The Wired Nation* (which had appeared in article form in *The Nation* two years earlier), policy analyst Ralph Lee Smith expressed a similar blend of caution and enthusiasm, arguing that "under any circumstances . . . the cable will be built, and the aim must be, through positive policy and intelligent action, to take every advantage of its tremendous potentials for social good" (98). He envisioned a common carrier model of cable systems that would allow independent programmers, including community groups and nonprofit organizations, to set the agenda for cable programming. Smith's proposed system, strikingly similar to the "toll broadcasting" of early radio, would allow an individual or a business to pay directly for the right to transmit a message during an allotted portion of the broadcast day. This, he believed, could bring about not only expanded program options, but also such services as home libraries, facsimile data, delivery of mail, crime detection and prevention, and travel information (Smith 1972, 86–88).[5] It is clear, though, that he also believed a well-planned and strictly enforced regulatory plan was necessary to steer cable away from its long-standing antenna function (which, Smith asserted, had been cultivated by the FCC's illogical and restrictive policies on CATV).

Smith, like Johnson, was aware that pulling cable out of its symbiotic relationship with broadcast television would require a monumental effort on the part of all concerned. Yet he felt the time was right for such a shift. And he certainly was not alone in this. By this point, a variety of government task forces already had begun working on plans for cable's future. Lengthy studies had been commissioned by the U.S. government as well as municipal governments (including New York and Philadelphia) to assess the existing television and telecommunications infrastructure and suggest ways to improve it.

One of the most influential studies at the federal level was initiated in 1967, when President Johnson launched a Task Force on Telecommunications Policy under the direction of Eugene V. Rostow, former undersecretary of state for political affairs. One chapter of the completed study, titled "Future Opportunities for Television," looked at various alternatives to the current domination of American television broadcasting by the commercial networks. These included a strengthened UHF system, low-power UHF, pay-TV, a fourth network, direct broadcasting from satellites to homes, noncommercial educational TV, and cable TV.[6]

Out of all these, it considered cable to be the most practical means of re-forming television, and explained thus:

> Cable television can provide an abundance of channels at a rela-tively low cost per channel; it is potentially well adapted to selec-tive distribution to particular audiences, even if they are scattered throughout a city or area; it provides an effective vehicle for rais-ing money to support television from the viewers themselves (through subscription fees), thereby increasing the resources avail-able for the support of additional programming; and it is already a thriving business able to prosper without governmental subsidy or protection.[7]

It is well worth noting that Rostow's group strongly advocated local origi-nation (l.o.) programming for cable systems, but only as an accompani-ment to the existing selection of broadcast channels. The group reasoned that it would take a while before cable service would be affordable to all sectors of the existing television audience.

While the federal government task force did not go so far as to en-dorse a closely regulated telephone-type common carrier like the one proposed by Smith, they did recommend a high degree of regulatory vigilance for cable's future. Much more of a hands-off approach can be seen in the Sloan Commission report. Claiming to be speaking on be-half of the public interest, the Sloan Commission recommended dereg-ulation of the cable industry in as many areas as possible, including pay services;[8] in other words, cable could best be developed by those al-ready working in that industry—but only if they had the capital needed to subsidize new programming ventures. The Sloan Commission held that a common carrier model, such as that forwarded by Smith, would deny cable operators the programming revenues they needed.

The Sloan Commission report did not completely dismiss a need for regulatory oversight. Rather, it advocated the sorts of regulations that would force the cable industry to impose its own controls. For example, the report stressed the need for revised copyright legislation, speculat-ing that a comprehensive plan for payment of copyright royalties would eliminate any need for distant signal restrictions. The Sloan group also came out strongly in favor of localism in cablecasting, objecting to multiple-system ownership and recommending that a limit be set on the number of subscribers to be served by a single owner. Still, the overall tenor of the report was that the combination of viewer demand and ca-ble's multichannel technology was the best assurance of future programming diversity. In statements that foretold the guiding logic of cable's programming future, the Sloan Commission (1971) reasoned that short-term profits from inexpensive broadcast-type programming were needed to ensure development of more expanded program options in the future:

> [F]or the most part, first-run entertainment will be beyond the reach of [the cable operator's] purse as long as his installation, and the cable system as a whole, are young or adolescent. He must fall back upon second-run and subsequent material: "I Love Lucy" the third or fourth or fifth time around—the fare with which independent stations have made most viewers familiar. (48)

In retrospect, of course, this statement reflects a great deal of prescience. As we now know, modern cable networks have used off-network reruns to recover start-up costs before starting to produce or acquire original programming. Still, the Sloan group probably did not realize how difficult it would be to dislodge the reruns from the cable schedule—even long after most cable networks had acquired the resources to provide more original material.

Another manifestation of the Blue Sky climate is represented by a group of studies carried out by the Rand Corporation, a California research firm. In early 1969 the Ford Foundation awarded a $165,000 grant to Rand for completion of a series of reports on the expansion of cable programming. The Ford Foundation had a two-decade history of supporting projects to further diversity in television programming, including grants to National Educational Television, the Corporation for Public Broadcasting, and various local and regional educational television initiatives.[9] When completed, the Rand studies generally advocated measures to protect broadcasters, but also pointed out that existing policies protected the largest broadcasters at the expense of both smaller broadcasters and cable television. Therefore, like the Sloan Commission, they called for the removal of virtually all restrictions on CATV regarding distant signal importation, program origination, advertising, and interconnection. And, also echoing the Sloan group, these reports called for copyright payment by CATV systems for all distant signal programs.[10]

The large policy studies just discussed show that the desire to reform cable programming extended to the highest levels of both government and private enterprise. But by the early 1970s, the mood of Blue Sky was apparent in many other sectors of American society, as well. Even groups without the resources or need to embark upon full-scale policy studies of their own nonetheless echoed the hopeful sentiments of the studies described above. For example, in 1973, *Writer's Digest* pointed out that "cable is expected to generate about $4.4 billion worth of new jobs throughout its 5,000 projected new systems, requiring six times as many writers as are employed by broadcasting industry today" (Kleir 1973, 31) The new job openings said to be on the rise included journalism, screenwriting, and research for the new educational and public access channels (31–32). Schools also jumped on the cable bandwagon, as teachers and administrators considered the possibilities of increased educational programming and interactive "electronic classrooms." The National Education Association showed a strong interest in the development of cable, as demonstrated by two lengthy reports that appeared in *NEA Journal–Today's Education* in the early 1970s.[11]

It is difficult to characterize the Blue Sky reports according to the goals underlying them or the recommendations made in them; there simply were too many of these documents, representing too many interests and political agendas. And yet there was something about the ideals and inspirations they expressed individually that reflected a pervasive climate of technology-centered optimism. As Thomas Streeter (1987) suggests, a "quasi-religious faith" in cable's capabilities made it seem as though the technology not only existed independently of ideological differences, but also could help people overcome those differences (224–225). One must wonder in retrospect if any practicable plan could have matched the sort of cable utopia conjured up in the popular imagination.

The Sloan Commission report, the document that most closely predicted today's cable landscape, cautioned:

> It is tempting to venture into the blue sky of technological imagination, and to write knowledgeably about widespread low-cost two-way point-to-point television systems; about home communications centers which can deliver printed copies of any volume in any library on any continent; about coaxial cable systems which will cook dinner, wash the windows and tend the babies. . . . But the hard facts of technology, wedded to the even harder facts of economics, provide no warrant for the belief that any of them will come to fruition upon a time-scale that can confidently be established in advance. (1971, 9)

Certainly in retrospect we can see that the economic forces, policy initiatives, and social impulses that needed to come together to change the direction of cable never materialized—at least not to the extent that was envisioned during the Blue Sky era.

Blue Sky had started when a critical mass of the population became aware of cable's capacity to deliver more than simply retransmitted broadcast signals. But basic technical specifications quickly were absorbed into a much larger belief in progress through technology. Eventually, it seemed, the technological optimism took on a life of its own, becoming a vaguely defined platform to which virtually any party could attach its particular interests. The apparent paradox of the Blue Sky climate is that while the sense of both hopefulness and urgency was voiced by the widest possible spectrum of constituencies, no clear policy consensus ever was reached.

Policy Changes

Clearly, the public perception of cable was changing very rapidly in response to the idealistic discourses that surrounded the medium during the Blue Sky years. Policymakers, for their part, were eager to see a scenario emerge in which cable would provide the local and minority-interest programming so long neglected by broadcast television. The first formal evidence of this changing attitude appeared in December 1968, when the FCC adopted a *Notice of Proposed Rulemaking and Notice of Inquiry* that both recognized the cable industry's recent expansion and encouraged the development of new services. This document was grounded in the Commission's belief that "it [is] generally appropriate to condition CATV's use of broadcast signals upon a requirement that it further the allocations policy of achieving a multiplicity of local outlets" (U.S. FCC 1968b). The proposal expressed a strong belief that cable needed to break free of its dependence on broadcast signals and work toward providing distinctive types of programming to complement them. Of course, this was an abrupt turn away from the regulatory goals evidenced in the *Second Report and Order*—passed less than three years earlier.

Following up on the recommendations, in 1969 the FCC issued a *Report and Order* requiring that all systems with 3,500 or more subscribers begin originating programs by 1 April 1971.[12] Clearly, the FCC was beginning to perceive cable as the means by which to achieve the localism and minority television service that essentially had been precluded by its inefficient 1952 broadcast license allocation policy. While any signal importation continued to be scrutinized relentlessly, program origination suddenly was perceived as an arena in which cable operators might compete more fairly with broadcasters. The Commission even anticipated possible protests from broadcasters regarding unfair competition by incorporating the following statement into the rules:

> [I]f the public is to be provided with additional program choices and different types of services and chooses to take advantage of them, it appears inevitable that there may be less viewing of the previously existing services. However, we do not think that the public should be deprived of an opportunity for greater diversity merely because a broadening of selections may spread the audience and reduce the size of the audience for any particular selection. Such competition for audience attention is not unfair, since broadcasters and CATV originators . . . stand on the same footing in acquiring the program material with which they compete. (U.S. FCC 1969)

Clearly, the Blue Sky discourses had had an impact on the FCC's stance toward cable and its possible threat to broadcasting. At this point it was embarking upon what previously had been considered contradictory goals: both to maintain protection of broadcast interests *and* to foster the growth of cable in programming areas not served by broadcast television. But it is important to keep in mind that within only a few years the Commission had been presented with a completely new set of challenges. As some scholars have suggested, the climate of Blue Sky had made it virtually impossible for regulators to ignore the public demand for cable reform (Horwitz 1989, 252; Streeter 1987).

The wording of the 1969 *Report and Order* left it unclear as to how much programming cable operators should be doing or which types of programming they should be offering. Much as the concurrently developing PTAR and Fin-Syn guidelines were attempts to improve broadcast television without prescribing specific types of programs, the 1969 *Report and Order* on cable tried to create an environment in which the cable industry would develop its own programming strategies and conventions. No doubt the goals of this new regulation were insufficiently articulated, but in retrospect this is not really surprising, since regulatory precedents for *encouraging* the development of cable programming were virtually nonexistent at the time. As the 1969 rules were being implemented, it was also clear that their provisions would need much more clarification.

In February 1972, after lengthy debate and hearings, the FCC passed its *Cable Television Report and Order*. Unlike previous sets of rules, this body of policy reflects political and economic goals of the Nixon administration, particularly those of the executive office's Task Force on

Telecommunications Policy. In 1970 Nixon appointed Clay T. Whitehead, a management specialist and electrical engineer with three degrees from MIT, to chair the task force. The following year, the task force became the Office of Telecommunications Policy (OTP), which played a major role in shaping cable and, as will be discussed below, satellite policy during the early 1970s. The OTP's recommendations were much more in line with President Nixon's conservative political agenda than were those of the FCC, especially in the way they loosened restrictions on big business.

Whitehead's free-market economic perspective, in turn, had a remarkably strong influence on the Nixon administration—probably more than had been expected. As Don R. LeDuc (1973) explains, the OTP "was created more as a gesture of presidential interest than as a full-scale effort to generate policy, but the OTP itself seemed to have a broader vision of its role" (198). Whitehead, obviously a proponent of big business, wanted to see a cable industry that was strong, independent, and free of constraints from regulators. Speaking at the 1970 meeting of the NCTA, Whitehead asserted that the federal government no longer wanted the cable industry to be known simply as a community antenna service. He also gave strong indications that the industry would be granted more freedom in choosing its program sources if it were to show more interest in local programming.[13]

The lengthy 1972 Cable Television Report and Order reflected precisely this sentiment. The rules were aimed toward improving localism in cable programming, but they also allowed cable operators to carry more of the broadcast signals they felt would subsidize local programming operations. A minimum channel capacity of 20 was specified for systems in the top 200 markets, and quotas of local signals, distant signals, and locally originated programming were designated for most of those channels.[14] The rules specified must-carry provisions for all local signals in a system's coverage area. Leapfrogging (importing additional broadcast signals from outside the local market) was permitted, but, with the exception of the smallest systems, was limited to stations within the vicinity of (or at least the same state as) the cable system. Syndicated program exclusivity provisions were outlined for the top 200 markets. And all systems with 3,500 or more subscribers were required to provide free public, educational, and government (PEG) access channels and to make leased access available on all unused channels.

The 1972 Report and Order is approximately 400 pages long. However, except for a lengthy section on technical specifications, most of its provisions encompass two major issues: signal importation and public access. As with the existing l.o. rules, the FCC, by writing stringent cable access provisions into the rules, was attempting once again to ensure localism and minority-interest programming as components of television service. By relaxing the restrictions on signal importation in broadcast markets, the Commission was trying to give cable the penetration and economic base it would need to expand its services. While the new regulations did not give cable operators quite the free rein they would have liked, the guidelines did provide a framework within which cable could expand into the highly desirable major broadcast markets. So in one sense these rules reflected the discourses of the Blue Sky years as well as the Commission's mandate to act in the public interest. But in another sense, they reflected the government's increasingly lenient stance toward big business.

Awareness of the latter point—that the 1972 rules allowed cable operators to maintain, indeed augment, their historical reliance on broadcast programming—is critical to understanding the development of modern cable programming. The relaxed signal importation restrictions ended up reinforcing, not altering, cable's primary use as a source of additional broadcast programming. While the rules mandated a minimum of 20 channels for larger systems, most systems filled the channels with their quota of broadcast signals. The access channels remained largely unused. Furthermore, the signal importation allowances written into the rules represented only the start of a trend toward allowing cable to increase its reliance on broadcast programming. In 1974 the FCC permitted cable systems to import an unlimited number of distant signals at night to replace broadcast stations that went off the air at the end of the day. In 1976 the antileapfrogging provision was lifted completely. This increasing leniency regarding signal importation served to increase the carriage of a select group of major-market independent stations—including New York's WOR and Chicago's WGN—that had become popular with CATV systems in the early 1960s. These stations, along with Atlanta's WTCG (later TBS), would prove popular enough outside their home markets to become satellite cable "superstations" in the late 1970s. As some of the earliest satellite-carried cable networks, they were among the trendsetters in modern cable programming. Yet their program schedules remained virtually unchanged after they became available nationwide. The enduring popularity and widespread carriage of these superstations would become critical in reinforcing cable's ongoing resemblance to broadcast television.

Also in 1974 the FCC repealed its mandatory l.o. rules. Naturally, this gave cable systems even more incentive and opportunity to use broadcast signals. Many operators had claimed inability to meet the l.o. requirements set forth in the 1972 *Report and Order*. Ironically, this limitation did not seem to correspond directly to a particular system's size or subscriber number. It seemed, rather, to relate to ownership— the sense of responsibility individual cable operators felt toward their communities. In 1973 the NCTA completed a study revealing that of 585 systems then originating programming, 40 percent were systems with fewer than 3,500 subscribers—that is, systems not even required to originate programming.[15] It hardly seems coincidental that these small systems also were the most likely still to have local ownership. Of course, the larger MSOs would have had more lobbying clout than the independently owned systems. Thus, the repeal of the origination requirement probably had more to do with MSOs' desire to achieve greater economies of scale than with the financial difficulties of individual operators.

After revoking the origination requirement, the FCC continued to require that operators maintain production equipment for use by members of the community for an additional five years. However, in the 1979 *Midwest Video II* case, all public access requirements at the federal level also were abolished. Due to local franchising agreements, cable systems in some communities have had the incentive to maintain successful l.o. and public access programs, but overall neither the FCC's initial requirements nor the subsequent performance of individual cable operators has ever come close to meeting the need for localism in cablecasting.

Riding a tide of optimism about cable's potential, the FCC had tried to force a nationwide scenario in which cable would provide the local, grassroots, and minority-interest programming that broadcast television generally has lacked. At the time the rules were implemented, a number of cable systems were originating programming—as heralded by the cable trade press. However, few of these systems were doing so as anything other than a community service. Fewer still were making access channels available to the general public. So it seems that, with regard to origination and access, the Commission had asked for too much too soon. Unlike signal importation, l.o. and access programming were not established components of cable service. Implementing these types of programming as a way to undo the programming patterns cable had inherited from broadcast television would have required a much greater degree of regulatory guidance than what cable operators were receiving as of the mid-1970s. And even if the regulatory climate had been stricter, it is far from certain that the television-viewing public would have traded even a small amount of time watching broadcast network programs—even overexposed reruns—for watching lower-budget local programs.

Local Origination

The demand for local programming on cable systems has always been low. Nonetheless local programs have been available on some cable systems since the 1960s. Several cable operators already had begun local origination programming by the time the FCC's 1969 *Report and Order* was instituted. A number of others began shortly thereafter. As of 1969, 206 cable systems were originating programming (U.S. FCC 1969), and the cable trade press was filled with origination success stories. These represented a wide—and often eclectic—variety of local program formats and production styles. Although the FCC eventually would become more rigorous in requiring locally *produced* programming, at first the term "origination" referred to virtually any programming available on a cable system that did not derive directly from broadcast signals. This meant that several inexpensive and technologically simple solutions were becoming available to meet the new programming requirement. As discussed in the previous chapter, cable operators of the late 1960s had access to time and weather channels, as well as text-only news services such as AP, UPI, Reuters, and the local news bulletins used by several suburban systems.

A number of systems did offer programming produced locally, either by the cable operators themselves or by members of the community using equipment provided by the operators. Common program formats included local news, coverage of local sports, talk shows, children's programs, and instructional programs. A typical early 1970s program origination manual advised cable operators to "aim at a collection of small audiences with very focused, inexpensive programming directed at each separate audience" (Woodard 1974, 70). It recommended using separate channels for commercial-free movies, adult education for credit, a "message wheel," news services, time and weather, and public access.[16] Rudimentary narrowcast formats like these reflected the cable industry's belief that their medium's future lay in its ability to serve local needs and specialized interests—at fairly little expense.

Of course, any locally *produced* cable programming involved significant financial commitments for cable operators. The manual mentioned above lists the following equipment as the minimum needed for an 8,000- to 15,000-subscriber system:

One complete portable Sony 1/2-inch black-and-white videotape recorder unit

One backup camera with zoom lens

One Sony 1/2-inch record/playback unit with editing facility

One tripod

One portable monitor (Panasonic or equivalent)

One set Mini-pro lights (Colortran)

One audio cartridge record and playback unit with bulk eraser

Three single-tube color cameras (for use in the studio and mobile unit)

Two 1-inch color videotape recorders (VTRs) with editing facility (for use in the studio and mobile unit; IVC 870 the only one recommended at this writing)

One 1-inch color videotape playback unit (IVC 825 the only one recommended at this writing)

Three studio–mobile unit color monitors (Sony Trinitron or equivalent)

One movable audio/video switching console (for use in studio and mobile unit)

Four lavalier microphones (Electrovoice recommended)

Two desk microphones (Electrovoice recommended)

One processing amplifier

One mobile unit (the smallest that can hold the equipment and one man at the switcher)

Studio—20 x 20 feet with a 20 foot ceiling, soundproofing, and separate air conditioning

Studio lights

One 16-mm film chain with one-tube camera and 35-mm slide projector

Plus miscellaneous supportive and test equipment

(Woodard 1974, 97–98)

Similar specifications were given for smaller and larger systems.

Although the necessary equipment was a significant expense, some cablecasters saved money on actual productions by using amateur talent both behind and in front of the camera. In Honesdale, Pennsylvania, for instance, the local mortician was cameraman, a high school art teacher hosted interview shows, a petroleum salesman provided commentary for sports events, and a lawyer interviewed political candidates.[17] Advertising sales also helped sustain origination efforts on many systems. In most instances, one or two local merchants sponsored a particular program in exchange for recognition on that program—a sponsorship style reminiscent of the one early broadcast television had inherited from radio. The following is a trade publication's description of a program produced by Santa Rosa CableVision of Santa Rosa, California:

> [Studio manager John] Cardenas' own *Coffee Break* show is a parade of interesting guests for an hour and a half each morning. Musicians, physicians, housewives, and professors—if they live in Santa Rosa and do something interesting in their work or hobbies, or if they are "big name" from elsewhere[—]are potential *Coffee Break* guests. A local bakery delivers a box of doughnuts to the set and participants drink coffee and eat doughnuts as the mood moves them, thanking the bakery in the process.[18]

Local programs such as this still exist in communities where local franchises mandate program origination or public access facilities. However, early on there were signs that this promise of Blue Sky was inherently flawed. Not long after the 1969 rule had been passed, it became clear that in most cases local origination had to be seen as a community service exclusively—not as a source of revenue for cable operators. Much as the cable trade press hailed l.o. efforts, virtually none of the programs were earning substantial profits for the cable systems that carried them. Programs were considered extraordinarily successful if they even recouped production costs. It seems that even the advertiser-supported programs were intended more as gestures of community service than anything else.

Many—if not most—cable operators complained that implementing local programming posed too great a financial burden, even with the sale of advertising. Competition from established local media such as radio and newspapers, whose overhead was much lower, only worsened the situation. Following four years of program origination in Pittsfield, Massachusetts, and Winter Haven, Florida, Don Andersson of Television Communications Corp. explained:

> The cost of providing 90 minutes of programming daily, five days a week, in each of these two cities . . . runs $4,000 monthly. To recover that sum, each system must sell 14 spot advertisements at an

average of $20 a spot. This adds up to $5,600 monthly, but trying to sell 100 percent of the advertising potential is unrealistic . . . particularly where the CATV is in competition with local radio stations that charge from $1 to $5 per spot.[19]

Furthermore, l.o. programming tended to prove disappointing in its public appeal. Production values of local programs could never match those of the well-funded broadcast networks and national syndicators. As the Sloan Commission had predicted, broadcast reruns, old movies, and other syndicated fare proved more popular, profitable, and convenient for cable operators—a suggestion of things to come after the advent of satellite networks.

Half of the 300 exhibitors at the 1970 NCTA convention were program packagers or syndicators. A few of these offered the sorts of non-broadcast-derived programming being produced for local audiences. In this case the production values were probably better, though local flavor was certainly sacrificed. For example, National Telesystems Corp.—a joint venture between Dick Clark Enterprises (a program syndicator) and International Video Corp. (a video equipment manufacturer)—offered a 20-hour-per-week package consisting of such programs as *Everywoman's Village* (subjects ranging from home decor to the stock market), *The World of Skipper Frank* (a children's program), *Foundations* (a nondenominational religious program), and *Perception* (a series of hour-long lectures); other titles included *Rock Palace, What's Cooking?* and *Pittsburgh Fight of the Week*.[20] Recorded music and various "program lead-ins" (local news bulletins, introductions to movies, etc.) were also included in the package. There were other, similar ventures: in its *Cablecasting Guidebook* (1973), the NCTA listed a total of 23 companies, including National Telesystems, that were distributing programming directly to cable systems.[21]

The use of syndicated off-network reruns and old movies for local origination proved even more successful. Made-for-cable programming was of lower quality than broadcast network programming, even when produced for nationwide distribution. In contrast, reruns and old movies were inexpensive and already known to be popular with audiences, and offering these types of programming on l.o. channels gave cable operators a degree of scheduling flexibility that was not possible with broadcast signals alone. For example, operators could use this material during fringe time as a way to draw audiences who either could not watch television during prime time or wished to continue watching television late at night. Cox CableVision, for example, claimed success with cablecasting late-night movies on its Lewistown, Pennsylvania, system. As Cox executive Thomas C. Dowden explained:

> On all the stations that come into Lewistown, there is no late movie, only talk shows. Lewistown is a three-shift town, a lot of people are up late and a lot of people would simply rather see moving, talking movies than people sitting and just talking.
>
> So we bought a package of inexpensive movies—believe it or not—Italian-made westerns with English dubbed in. They are pretty bad, but we could afford them and 25 different local sponsors bought them. So far, the sponsors are getting results. Now— our next step is to up-grade the movies, expand our original programming, and hopefully keep the sponsors happy by getting further advertising results for them.[22]

Targeting fringe-time audiences in this way would become a significant factor in the launch of national satellite-carried networks during the late 1970s.

It is essential to remember that, as of the late 1960s and early 1970s, the territory served by cable was still made up primarily of towns and smaller cities. Even the most enterprising operators generally lacked the critical mass of subscribers necessary to develop high-quality local programming. For the most part, communities large enough to have broadcast television stations had no use for cable—but there were some notable exceptions. The cable systems in San Diego, Los Angeles, and San Francisco all were known for their origination facilities.[23] And the most widely acclaimed origination facilities were in Manhattan—a result of that borough's early development of CATV service. Because Manhattan *was* able to garner a critical mass of cable subscribers, it stands as an example of the sorts of local programming that could be started under favorable conditions. Ironically, it had been Manhattan's extreme population density that created a demand for cable there at a very early date. Clearly these large cable systems were much more likely than smaller systems to have adequate resources and talent for meeting the FCC's program origination goals. Ironically, then, sophisticated local cable programming was enjoyed by the same communities that already had good broadcast television service.

CATV in Manhattan

Unlike most large metropolitan areas in the 1960s, New York City had fairly strong demand for community antenna service because, even though the market was served by a number of broadcast stations, the tall buildings made clear reception difficult. The "ghosts" caused by signal refraction proved especially problematic as color television became dominant. For this reason, nonbroadcast television services such as theater television and other forms of closed-circuit television had gained a foothold in New York by the early 1960s.

In spring 1964 Sterling Information Services began to lay cable throughout Lower Manhattan for a closed-circuit television network designed to provide professional and informational programming to hotels and businesses.[24] Later that year Sterling and TelePrompTer Corp., by then a major force in the emerging industry, filed competing bids for CATV franchises.[25] In November 1965 they, along with a third company, CATV Enterprises, were granted two-year franchises to serve portions of Manhattan.[26] Since the franchises did not permit distant signal importation, at first the only programming planned for any of these companies was clear delivery of the local broadcast signals.

Then in July 1967, New York mayor John V. Lindsay appointed a seven-man committee, headed by former CBS News president Fred Friendly, to evaluate the city's three CATV systems and recommend ways in which they might better serve the public.[27] Their conclusions reflected the Blue Sky sentiments that were sweeping the nation. In December 1968, before the report had even been completed, New York's existing cable franchises were amended to allow program origination. The lower Manhattan amendment restricted origination to "local public-service programs of a social, artistic and cultural nature," and prohibited the showing of "purely entertainment motion pictures." It also prohibited both the use of commercials on the cable-only channels and the charging of any additional fees for the service. Reminiscent of the sentiments expressed against pay-TV during the late 1950s and early 1960s, the new rules represented a compromise: between CATV operators, who wished to offer extra services in hopes of drawing additional subscribers, on the one hand, and broadcast station and movie theater owners, who had argued that CATV program origination would pose unfair competition, on the other.[28]

In the first half of 1969 Sterling Manhattan Cable was offering such programs as *Manhattan Issues, The Community Bulletin Board,* and *Town and Village News,* along with occasional sports and culture specials.[29] The *New York Times* reported in May of that year that Sterling's typical program day consisted primarily of talk shows, news updates, movies, and old radio shows (which ran while a stationary announcement covered the screen). Manhattan Cable also incurred a small amount of controversy with regard to the franchise's program origination amendment when it began showing classic movies such as *Citizen Kane* and *The Magnificent Ambersons,* as well as various "art house" films. Sterling's president, Charles Dolan, explained that the films featured on his cable system would be "films which have the cultural and artistic qualities which the board's action requires." He further justified the practice by running the films without commercials and by hiring film critic Judith Crist to provide opening and closing remarks.[30] Across town, Tele-PrompTer's origination scheme featured such programs as neighborhood news, children's shows, adult education courses, Spanish-language shows, and religious shows (Harrington 1973, 9).

The New York franchises came up for renewal again in July 1970, following completion of the long-awaited Mayor's Advisory Task Force report. This time there were only two companies in the running, Sterling and TelePrompTer, and the contracts would be for 20 years. As a result of both recommendations included in the report by the task force and awareness of the FCC's ongoing push toward localism in cablecasting, the new franchises required the cable companies to set aside channels for use by the general public on a first-come, first-served basis and to provide free time on the public channels to all nonprofit and noncommercial groups. Thus, on 1 July 1971 both TelePrompTer and Sterling Manhattan began the nation's first public access services. TelePrompTer did not charge for use of its studios and equipment, but made only a limited amount of equipment available. Sterling charged for equipment use—starting at $25 for one black-and-white camera.[31]

Manhattan no doubt was perceived as a microcosm of the futuristic "wired nation" scenarios so widely discussed during the early 1970s. At a time when the future of cable was a hotly contested issue throughout the United States, the franchising debates in New York were understood as a critical precedent-setting scenario. Policymakers repeatedly cited the cable systems in Manhattan as a program origination and public access success story. And they used the Manhattan situation to justify requirements that other cable systems offer public access facilities. Nonetheless, it should be obvious that Manhattan was not a typical cable community—in terms of either talent or resources. And, as one writer expressed it, "New York . . . is an isolated experience [because] New Yorkers are, almost by necessity, more 'media-sophisticated' than the citizens of other areas. And there are simply more people."[32] And even New York did not experience the public rush to use access facilities that had been expected. Most program production was done by nonprofit organizations or by community outreach groups such as Open Channel and Restoration Corporation (Price and Wicklein 1972, 32–33). The Center for the Analysis of Public Issues found that during New York's first year with public access facilities "10 or 12 groups produced 60 per cent of the programs and provided 60 per cent of the money" (Harrington 1973, 38). Thus, we can see that for the vast majority of U.S. communities, much more was needed to turn cable into a community service medium than simply making channels available to the public.

Pay-Cable

Another type of supplementary cable programming in Manhattan, as well as other cities, also contributed a great deal to the growth of modern cable, specifically the emergence of the pay-cable industry. Pay-cable was the latest incarnation of pay-TV—which, after decades of regulatory contention, once again looked as if it might improve the nation's television service. Unlike l.o. channels, pay-cable channels promised even small-town operators the possibility of charging subscribers directly for non-broadcast-derived programming, thus easing their financial burden.

On 12 December 1968 the FCC adopted its *Fourth Report and Order* on pay television. This rulemaking, which did not go unchallenged by lingering anti-pay-TV forces,[33] finally gave both over-the-air and pay systems formal permission to operate—though a number of restrictions applied. Wired forms of pay-TV were prohibited from using films between two and ten years old. They were prohibited from showing sports events that had been shown on broadcast television at any time in the preceding two years. They were also prohibited from showing "series-type" programming that featured an "interconnected plot or substantially the same set of characters." And feature films and sports were not permitted to constitute more than 90 percent of the systems' total programming hours (U.S. FCC 1968a).[34] The restrictions were complex. Nevertheless, they did not prevent either the development of new pay-cable technologies or the formation of pay-cable businesses.

By this point, it seemed clear to most of those involved that the future of pay-TV lay in the addition of pay channels to existing cable systems. Three over-the-air systems had been licensed by the FCC as of 1974: Zenith's Phonevision, planned for Los Angeles and Chicago; Blonder-Tongue Laboratories' BTVision, authorized for Boston and Newark; and Teleglobe Pay-TV Systems, Inc., planned for San Francisco, Milwaukee, and Washington, D.C. (Baer and Pilnick 1974, 41).[35] None of these systems ever launched, however, and no other over-the-air system would begin operations until the late 1970s (as will be discussed in Chapter 4).

Meanwhile, a number of *wire-based* systems had begun operating in conjunction with cable systems. Since cable increasingly was entering markets already served by broadcast television, operators were eager to expand the services they offered. Pay services presented the opportunity both to recover costs without seeking advertising support and to provide programming with the high production values and national prominence viewers had come to expect from the broadcast networks. For the most part, the earliest pay-cable systems operated in isolation from one another, and there was no standard method of billing, program selection, or program distribution.

One of the largest of the early pay-cable companies was the Los Angeles–based Optical Systems Inc., which used a system of punched plastic cards ("tickets") and an optical reader, allowing subscribers to pay only for the programs they wanted to watch. These tickets could be purchased individually, in packages, or on a subscription basis. Optical Systems used no commercials, and the programming consisted exclusively of movies—though there were plans to expand. Optical Systems either leased cable operators the use of its system on a profit percentage basis (maintenance included) or sold them the system outright as a turnkey operation. The technology was designed to be compatible with most CATV equipment. In 1972 Mission Cable in San Diego became the first cable company to use the Optical Systems arrangement—under the name "Channel 100." The following year, three other cable systems adopted Optical Systems.[36]

Another planned pay-cable operation first announced in 1972 was TheatreVisioN Inc., a New York–based joint venture of Laser Link Corp. and Chromalloy Corp. Former Hollywood movie executive Dore Schary was the company president. TheatreVisioN, which also used plastic tickets, charged a flat fee of $15 per month. A monthly package of seven movies ran on alternating days and times. This system was tested briefly on a Storer Broadcasting cable system in Sarasota, Florida.[37]

In 1973 the Los Angeles–based Home Theater Network (HTN) tested a pay-TV system in Redondo Beach, California. HTN's programming plans included sports, home shopping, live concerts, and even college courses—though initially it limited its program selection to two movie channels. For ordering, HTN used an electronic device called a "PERK" connected to a subscriber's telephone. Orders were transmitted to a central computer that could either bill customers directly or accept credit cards. HTN president Dick Lubic noted that the PERK also was capable of gathering demographic data from HTN subscribers—anticipating later efforts to apply broadcast rating systems to cable.[38]

In addition to these early pay-per-view systems, several pay-cable systems of the early 1970s charged flat monthly fees for their programming. For example, Gridtronics, a subsidiary of Warner Communications (a major MSO), tested its videotape-based movie service in several small towns during this period. Other flat-rate pay-cable systems were tested by TelePrompTer and Viacom in suburban New York; by TelePrompTer in conjunction with Hughes Aircraft ("Z Channel") in Los Angeles; by Cinca Communications in Long Beach, California; by American Multi-Cinema in Columbus, Ohio; and by Digital Communications in Pensacola, Florida, and Decatur, Georgia.[39]

All of these systems were managed and programmed by individual cable operators. However, on 8 November 1972 Home Box Office Corporation, a subsidiary of Sterling Manhattan Cable, began using microwave networks to transmit pay-cable programming to systems throughout the Northeast. Sterling's movie origination efforts had proved so successful in the New York metropolitan area that the company decided to expand. Microwave promised an efficient and cost-effective means of distribution, at least in places where microwave networks already existed. In fact, advertising executives attending the 1970 NCTA convention had encouraged cable operators to consider the value of microwave-served national cable networks that could cater to narrow audience tastes.[40] By the early 1970s several companies were proposing to link cable systems throughout the country by microwave. HBO apparently was the only one to do this successfully. Since HBO went on to become a satellite-carried network, its development will be discussed in more detail in subsequent chapters, along with the TelePrompTer system, which evolved into Showtime, and Gridtronics, which evolved into The Movie Channel. At this point, it is necessary to discuss the arrival of satellite technology to the cable industry, and how this made the transition into the modern cable era possible.

Satellite Technology and the Cable Industry

By the mid-1970s both the broadcast and cable television industries were well aware of the potential of satellites for program delivery. Many of the Blue Sky reports—particularly the Rostow Report—had been touting the possibilities of using satellites in combination with broadcast and cable television. The FCC also had suggested a role for satellite transmission:

> The so-called "wired city" concept embraces the possibility that television broadcasting might eventually be converted, in whole or in part, to cable transmission (coupled with the use of microwave *or other intercity relay facilities*), thereby freeing some broadcast spectrum for other uses and making it technically feasible to have a greater number of national and regional television networks and local outlets. (U.S. FCC 1968b; emphasis added)

The commercialization of the domestic satellite industry was in the works at exactly the same time the pay-cable systems discussed above were being launched. These two factors, combined with the extensive new set of cable regulations discussed above, led to the first satellite-served cable networks and the beginning of modern cable.

Excitement over the possibilities of communications satellites actually predated the cable industry's first use of this technology by nearly two decades. In 1957 the Soviet Union had launched *Sputnik*, the first artificial satellite, beginning an era heavily influenced by discourses about space exploration. Among the various uses considered for the technology was the long-distance relaying of electronic messages, and by the end of the decade speculation was rampant that satellites eventually would enable instantaneous and potentially worldwide televisual communication. The first communications satellite to be tested was Bell Laboratories' *Echo*, launched by NASA in 1960. *Echo* was a "passive" satellite — essentially a low-orbiting metallic balloon that served as a mirror off which to bounce electromagnetic signals. *Echo*'s transmissions were weak, but had enough of an impact to convince policymakers of the technology's promise. In 1962 *Telstar*, the first satellite with an active transponder (i.e., retransmitter and responder), was launched. *Telstar* carried the first intercontinental television broadcast. In 1963 *Syncom 2*, the first geosynchronous satellite, was launched, and the following year *Syncom 3* transmitted portions of the Tokyo Olympics.[41]

In 1962 Congress passed the Communications Satellite Act, which, along with various other policy initiatives, established the Communications Satellite Corporation (COMSAT). COMSAT was a public corporation intended to develop a commercial, international satellite communications system. It was owned jointly by the major communications corporations and a group of independent investors. In establishing COMSAT as a government-regulated, yet nonetheless commercial, corporation, legislators were demonstrating an eagerness to develop the new technology in the fastest and most cost-effective manner possible (Magnant 1977, 59). They also were advocating a key role for private industry in developing the new technology. The use of commercialization to speed up the development of new technologies would become a powerful force in shaping cable programming.

Many television interests were drawn to the idea of using satellites to bypass AT&T and its overwhelming dominance of terrestrial forms of long-distance transmission, but they also expressed concern that COMSAT might develop a similar monopoly in satellite communications. Thus, in 1964 Hughes Aircraft Corporation approached ABC with the idea of providing a satellite for the network's exclusive use. ABC expressed strong interest in the idea, and the following year it presented an application to the FCC for satellite authorization. This set in motion a series of debates as to how the new medium might best serve the public interest (Magnant 1977, 91–92).

The Commission, realizing that a comprehensive satellite policy was needed, took ABC's application under consideration, but did not act upon it immediately.

Instead, beginning in 1966 a number of meetings were held to determine who would finance and oversee a satellite communications system and how its use might be regulated.[42] As discussed earlier, the future of communications satellites was given strong consideration by President Johnson's Task Force (the Rostow group), and was reflected in various policy studies and visionary statements of the time. Most predicted that satellites would complement the existing terrestrial communications network. However, the studies generally wavered on how effective policy might be implemented to guide the transition into this phase of telecommunications development. Among the major issues was the question of whether satellites should be designated for specialized uses (such as television programming) or operated as common carriers for all communications uses.[43] Another concern was how minority and educational television programming might be subsidized under each of the various systems that were proposed.

Most earlier studies were set aside with the arrival of the Nixon administration. At that point, the FCC began new inquiries under the guidance of its new chairman, Dean Burch. Burch was known to be both an advocate of the public interest and a champion of laissez-faire capitalism. He apparently worked well under the new administration. A January 1970 memorandum from the White House to Burch had indicated a strong interest on the part of the president in opening the domestic satellite industry to open-entry competition (Magnant 1977, 156–160). And in the coming years the FCC was strongly influenced by the White House in matters of satellite policy.

One major step the new Nixon administration took toward opening the satellite industry to big business was appointing Clay Whitehead as head of the OTP. When an FCC plan of "limited entry" for satellite use conflicted with the "Open Skies" plan favored by Whitehead, the Commission found itself capitulating to the OTP's recommendations.[44] On 16 June 1972, following a 4–3 vote, the Commission issued its *Second Report and Order* permitting open entry in the domestic communications satellite industry to any financially and technically qualified applicant.[45] Only four months earlier, the FCC had approved the final version of its 1972 *Cable Television Report and Order*. These two rulemakings would be the two most important policy decisions shaping the growth of cable during the 1970s.

Conclusions

The FCC had intended the two major programming provisions in the 1972 rules to complement each other—by requiring very specific types of local programming, and by allowing operators to carry enough of a variety of marketable broadcast signals to subsidize the local programming. Unfortunately, one of these provisions gradually would be revoked, taking the goals that had guided its initial formulation down with it. The other represented the first in a series of deregulatory measures that would make it very easy for cable to continue providing a selection of programs that deviate very little from what has been available on broadcast television for decades.

The 1972 rules and the subsequent amendments to them were one major factor in the creation of what became the modern cable industry. Another was the 1972 deregulation of the domestic satellite industry under the Nixon administration's "Open Skies" policy. A third major factor was the FCC's approval of pay-TV and the ensuing development of pay-cable networks. These three factors came together in 1975, when the movie and sports programming service Home Box Office became the first satellite-carried cable network. They also would shape the development of many subsequent networks in what was becoming a highly commercialized industry.

Two years before the 1972 rules were passed, former CBS News president Fred Friendly had written an article warning that if extreme caution were not taken in guiding cable's future, "the current [broadcast] monopoly could give way to a new Tower of Babel, in which a half-hundred voices scream in a cacophonous attempt to attract the largest audience" (Friendly 1970, 59). His prognosis—one no doubt formulated through years of experience in broadcast television—could not have been more accurate. Federal policymakers had tried to mandate local and special-interest programming. And many cable operators actually attempted to comply. However, these operations frequently were hurried and makeshift. They easily were replaced by broadcast programming as soon as federal policy permitted.

As of the mid-1970s cable operators, particularly MSOs without ties to the communities they served, had very little incentive to offer anything but the cheapest, most readily available, and most popular types of programming. The advent of communications satellites to the cable industry, while sometimes considered revolutionary, would do nothing to remedy this situation. On the contrary, because they increased the economies of scale for the distribution of inexpensive programming, they helped ensure cable's continued resemblance to broadcast television. By 1975 pay-cable sports and movie networks were ready to launch as satellite-carried networks. Major-market independent stations were ready to launch as cable "superstations." And there was a growing stockpile of syndicated and other ready-made program material waiting to fill the schedules of any cable network that desired it.

Satellites could not possibly have aided the development of local programming, since the economics of satellite use necessitate the largest possible networks of cable systems. And even niche-oriented programming, with potential audiences spread across the nation, cannot promise the large numbers of viewers that familiar movies and broadcast reruns can. More recently, established entertainment corporations have spun off niche-interest cable networks, but most early satellite cable networks, already paying for transponder rental and uplinking equipment, opted to minimize program production and acquisition costs rather than invest in new program production. Program types already proven successful on broadcast television and in movie theaters stood out as the safest bets for those launching satellite networks. In other words, the cable programming legacy of the early 1970s—which actually was the legacy of the 1950s, as well—would become the model for cable programming in the satellite era.

When examining economic and regulatory causes for the programming patterns that have emerged in modern cable, it is also important to consider cultural factors. Could it be that the Blue Sky writers and policy analysts gave more weight to the American public's idealism than to its actual uses and expectations for television programming? Nearly all Blue Sky documents somehow suggested that cable's great strength lay in its ability to serve ever smaller, ever more specialized constituencies. Yet fundamentally lacking in the studies was any exploration of the cultural reasons for the popularity and endurance of the three major broadcast networks and their programming. The Blue Sky writers and policy analysts, by and large, chose to believe that audiences would favor cable's variety and specialization over anything broadcast television had to offer. Yet audiences by this point had had two decades in which to become accustomed to the high production values and familiar formats of broadcast programming. Moreover, the networks offered American audiences a common and reliable source of information about what affected the nation as a whole. They provided, as they always have, a sense of unity and a common cultural agenda. As will become apparent in the next chapter, several established television operations—with widely varying origins—were able to take advantage of this as they successfully launched satellite cable networks.

The Rise of Satellite Cable, 1975–1980

The 1975 satellite debut of Home Box Office might be described as a revolution in cable programming since this was the first instance of a non-broadcast-based cable network becoming available to audiences nationwide. Indeed, this pioneering use of satellite technology for a pay-cable network—an event that marked the beginning of modern cable television—was a breakthrough in cable communications. The cable industry's goal of offering packages of programming to supplement re-transmitted broadcast channels, a goal firmly established in the early 1970s, was aided tremendously by the advent of an efficient means of widespread distribution. In effect, satellites created an entirely new market for cable service among television viewers already well served by broadcast stations—a market that would grow exponentially as more satellite networks launched and more cable operators gave their sub-scribers access to this programming. However, to describe the intro-duction of satellite technology as a programming revolution is to neglect both the evolution in cable that preceded it, as detailed in Chapters 2 and 3, and the legacy of that evolution in modern cable programming. In fact, by the mid-1970s a programming infrastructure already was in place that would be expanded tremendously, though not fundamentally altered, by the introduction of satellites.

Satellite cable's first half decade was by no means a period of pro-gramming innovation for the medium. Approximately half the satellite networks launched before 1980 can be described as "narrowcast," in that they targeted subsections of the larger television audience or specialized in particular topics. Yet nearly all of them offered program genres—often actual programming—already proven successful either on broad-cast television or elsewhere. They relied heavily on sports, movies (first-run as well as syndicated), and broadcast reruns. In some cases, as detailed later in this chapter, early satellite networks were nothing more than independent broadcast stations whose signals had been uplinked to satellite. However, even the more specialized networks tended to resemble broadcast television. The Christian Broadcasting Network's cable network, for example, filled much of its schedule with broadcast reruns. And the Spanish-language network Galavision drew heavily from programming originally produced for Latin American broadcast television.

Cable's brief but conflicted regulatory history has a great deal to do with this reliance on broadcast-type programming, since it had cultivated an environment in which the cable industry had little incentive to use its resources for developing new types of programming. No sooner had CATV become a viable industry in the 1950s and early 1960s than it was forced by government regulators to limit its expansion into new areas of service—notably the development of new programming categories. CATV already was heavily dependent on broadcast television, and the FCC regulations of the mid-1960s only cemented this relationship.

A shift in the official position on cable's development during the late 1960s and early 1970s did not alter this trajectory nearly as much as expected. While Blue Sky optimism was the discursive climate in which many enduring cable policies were formulated, those policies ultimately did not encourage nearly the degree of innovation that had been anticipated. In efforts to foster both localism and diversity in cable programming, the FCC mandated several different types of locally originated programming. In the 1969 *Report and Order,* regulators set goals for the development of original programming, yet offered very little guidance for implementing those goals. They essentially were requiring the cable industry to build its own programming infrastructure—a huge demand, especially given that up to that point cable operators had been discouraged from exploring most types of original programming. The follow-up to this was the 1972 *Report and Order,* which extended local programming goals through its access provisions, but offered even stronger incentives for operators to increase the amount of broadcast programming they used. As the present chapter discusses, provisions mandating original and local cable programming were eroded over the course of the 1970s until, by 1980, virtually none were left.

Furthermore, the federal government—particularly the White House's Office of Telecommunications Policy (OTP)—had been eager to see the domestic communications satellite industry develop in the fastest way possible. Virtually ignoring plans laid out by the Ford Foundation, the Rostow task force, and other researchers, the FCC (under the OTP's influence) deregulated satellite communications in 1972. The new open-entry form of competition favored companies able both to launch networks quickly and to draw large audiences. Consequently, there was a proliferation of satellite networks launched by established programming operations. By the mid-1970s the rapid and unrestricted expansion of the cable industry was favored both by available technology and by government bodies that looked very positively upon free enterprise. These factors were, of course, compounded by Americans' long-established network television viewing habits and expectations.

It also needs to be pointed out that, by the mid-1970s the term *cable industry* referred more to a group of powerful corporations than to the independent small-town entrepreneurs who had organized formally in the 1950s. While it is true that many cable systems—particularly in smaller communities—still were locally owned and operated during the 1970s, they were no longer the influential decision makers for the industry. Teleprompter Corporation, which had begun accumulating multiple local CATV systems in the early 1960s, had been joined by such powerful players as American Television & Communications (owned by Time Inc.), Viacom, United Video, Cox Cable, and Warner Cable. Not only did these companies control multiple local cable systems, they also, increasingly, were involved in cable programming. Cable clearly was becoming part of the trend toward both horizontal and vertical integration that was going on throughout the entertainment industry as a whole.

This chapter outlines how those corporations that possessed the finances and programming infrastructures necessary to launch satellite networks in the late 1970s were able to establish positions of incumbency and power for themselves in the highly competitive cable programming environment of the 1980s and 1990s. It also looks at how, by the mid-1970s, the meager efforts to make cable a medium distinct from broadcasting gradually had given way to an atmosphere in which the cable industry had every reason to continue being a provider of broadcast-type programming. Finally, this chapter begins to explore strategies modern cable networks have used to distinguish their uses of broadcast-type programming from those of actual broadcast stations and networks.

Changes in Cable Policy

The 1972 *Cable Television Report and Order* was the decade's first major body of cable policy; its creators had set out to foster the growth of cable, while also protecting the broadcast television industry. As in the 1960s, their stated goal was to ensure local television service in as many communities as feasible and to make cable a true *supplement* to existing television programming choices. Yet in the long run cable programming's development would be influenced the most by concessions the *Report and Order* gave to the cable industry—by amendments to those rules, by the repeal of some of them, and by the resolution of regulatory issues that the *Report and Order* had not even covered.

In 1974, under pressure from the cable industry, the FCC withdrew the requirement that systems with more than 3,500 subscribers originate programming, but the Commission continued to require that cable systems maintain equipment and studios for PEG access program production. Still, even this access requirement subsequently was lifted—a result of the 1979 *FCC* v. *Midwest Video Corp.* (*Midwest Video II*) case. In *Midwest Video II*, the Supreme Court ruled that in making the maintenance of PEG access facilities mandatory, the FCC had exceeded the authority granted to it in the 1934 Communications Act. The majority opinion, as noted by Justice Byron White, was that the 1972 rules had denied cable operators "all discretion regarding who may exploit their access channels and what may be transmitted over such channels." At this point, the issue of whether or not cable systems would provide access facilities was left to individual franchising processes.

Another step toward deregulation involved lifting the "antisiphoning" rules the FCC had imposed on pay-TV in 1969. These rules had been written at a time when cable was little more than a community antenna service, with its major threat still being perceived as the one involving distant signal importation. Pay-television at that point largely was controlled by Hollywood studios—which were viewed as powerful entertainment corporations with the ability to withhold their product from "free" television should they have a financial incentive to do so. By the early 1970s the situation had changed, and direct-payment forms of television no longer seemed a major threat to broadcast television. The major pay-TV businesses of the 1960s—STV, Phonevision, and Telemeter—either had gone out of business or had changed ownership. In any event, none were active as of 1972. For the most part, start-up pay-cable networks of the early 1970s were controlled either by cable MSOs or by independent investors. Furthermore, the Hollywood studios themselves were in an economic slump at this point, and it was believed by some that they needed pay-cable distribution capabilities almost as much as pay-cable needed their product. Apparent support for this point lies in the fact that Jack Valenti, president of the Motion Picture Association of America, was a vociferous proponent of pay-cable during these years.[1]

In November 1973 the FCC opened hearings on whether or not to liberalize the antisiphoning rules. Certain long-standing pay-TV opponents, most notably broadcast networks and movie theater owners, maintained their opposition (in fact, most felt that the existing rules were *too* lenient), and made compelling cases against relaxing the rules. The Commission ultimately chose not to lift the rules, though in March 1975 it added certain qualifications and exemptions in an attempt to make the rules less restrictive. The compromise proved no more satisfactory to the pay-cable industry than to its opponents, though. Pay-cable interests wasted no time in initiating a court challenge to the continued existence of the antisiphoning rules, calling them a violation of their First Amendment rights and an unfair restraint of trade. Pay-cable won their case. In *Home Box Office* v. *FCC* (1977), the U.S. Court of Appeals for the District of Columbia held that the FCC had, in fact, exceeded its authority over cable television in issuing program restrictions for pay-cable, and stated that there was no evidence to support the need for regulation of pay-cable programming. The court of appeals also found that the FCC had failed to state clearly the harm its regulations sought to remedy and its reasons for supposing that harm existed. Later in 1977, the Supreme Court declined to review the *Home Box Office* decision, leaving the lower court's decision intact.

The ruling permitted pay-cable networks to acquire recent movies and sports programming—the main sustenance of pay-cable for decades to come. Most significantly, it allowed cable to replace broadcast television as Hollywood's first television exhibition window, not only boosting the popularity of networks like HBO, but also encouraging those networks to enter into financing and exhibition agreements with Hollywood studios (as will be discussed below). Thus, the ruling was a boon to existing pay-cable networks, and also encouraged the development of others in the future. Furthermore, in this ruling, the court had observed that because cable does not use the electromagnetic spectrum for transmission of programming, it is more akin to newspapers than to broadcasting—a suggestion that cable might have some First Amendment rights not enjoyed by broadcast television (Horwitz 1989, 258).

As discussed in Chapter 3, another unresolved issue affecting the cable industry as of the 1970s involved the use of copyrighted program material. The *Fortnightly* and *Teleprompter* cases had highlighted a pressing need to update the Copyright Act of 1909 and thereby create statutory guidance for issues involving copyright and electronic media. Several copyright bills were, in fact, introduced in Congress during the early 1970s, and lengthy debate and hearings were held before a measure finally was passed in 1976. Not surprisingly, cable operators were active lobbyists throughout the copyright hearings. While most of them considered some sort of royalty fee to be fair compensation for the programming they used, the operators also insisted that too steep a tariff would threaten the success of their industry. Cable's lobbying efforts were countered by three major groups: the National Association of Broadcasters, the Motion Picture Association of America, and various professional sports organizations.

The version of the Copyright Act that finally passed established a mandatory compulsory license for all cable systems that transmit distant, nonnetwork television signals. Under the compulsory license arrangement, a Copyright Royalty Tribunal (composed of five commissioners appointed by the president for seven-year terms) was to calculate each individual cable system's copyright liability based on a statement of account covering a six-month period. The statement would consider distant signals carried, total number of subscribers, and gross receipts for basic service. The tribunal would use this information to determine a system's payment category. Systems with the smallest incomes would pay a negligible flat fee; moderate-income systems would pay a percentage of gross receipts; and systems with the highest incomes would pay according to the number and types of distant signals carried. The royalties collected by the tribunal then would be distributed among any copyright owners who claimed to have had their material distributed by cable systems or other forms of secondary transmission.[2]

For the most part, the cable industry found the new copyright guidelines to be reasonable. Once they were in place, however, operators immediately began petitioning the FCC to relax its rules on signal importation and program exclusivity, on the grounds that the 1972 provisions and the copyright requirements *together* amounted to an excessive regulatory burden. Influential House Communications Subcommittee chairman Richard E. Wiley backed the cable industry's position by referring to the 1972 importation and exclusivity provisions as a "copy-right substitute."[3] The FCC assented and moved quickly to lift the 1972 antileapfrogging provisions, stating that those provisions had led to awkward patterns of signal importation that sometimes even proved costly, as was the case when more than one microwave route was needed to meet the requirements. As will be discussed below, this helped pave the way for the cable "superstation," an early and precedent-setting type of cable network.

At the same time, the FCC also agreed to allow cable operators unlimited distant signal importation after local stations in their markets had gone off the air, another major benefit to the growth of the cable superstation. The provision was extended in 1980, when the FCC removed all distant signal quotas and repealed the program exclusivity rules (U.S. FCC 1976, 1980). Clearly, this liberalization signaled a radical change in federal regulators' conception of "the public interest." In the span of a decade, they had gone from policies aimed at fostering local media, whether broadcast or cable, to policies that sought the speediest possible development of new technology. In explaining the Commission's 4–3 decision in the distant signal matter, Chairman Charles Ferris stated that "the FCC has removed the regulatory debris of a previous decade; we have thus expanded the choices that consumers will have in the future. . . . Cable has not and will not destroy broadcasting, as was once feared" (Brown 1980a). This was the beginning of the Reagan era, a period that favored both the rapid growth of cable as an entertainment medium and the synergistic integration of cable with other entertainment industries.

By 1980 virtually the only programming restriction left for cable was a rule affecting the showing of sports events, one of the most popular types of cable programming. Although hearings on this issue had begun in 1973, at approximately the same time as the antisiphoning hearings, the outcome was much less favorable to cable programming efforts. The sports hearings involved two related issues. The first was whether or not cable carriage of sports events cut into potential ticket sales. This was a long-standing concern of both professional sports franchises and college athletic programs. As early as the mid-1960s, representatives of Major League Baseball, the National Football League, and the National Collegiate Athletic Association had formally voiced concern that CATV might destroy their control over how and where their games would be televised.[4]

The second issue considered in the hearings related to the sports contracts that prohibit broadcast stations from televising sports events within their local markets (known as a "blackout" rule). The ability of a cable system within a given market to pick up a distant signal carrying a local sports event was considered unfair to broadcasters as well as to sports franchises. After lengthy debate, in April 1975 the FCC passed a rule prohibiting any cable system within a 35-mile radius of any broadcast station blacked out for a particular sports event from importing that event on a distant signal. While not considered satisfactory by either cable or broadcast interests, the blackout rule created for cable remained in place.[5] This regulatory measure was an anomaly in an otherwise deregulatory period for cable.

Satellite Technology

The cable industry's adoption of satellite transmission and the ways in which the new technology was implemented were as much a matter of policy as of technology. This is evidenced by the fact that the first satellite-carried networks were begun by powerful media corporations such as Time Inc. and Viacom, rather than by the Corporation for Public Broadcasting or alternative media coalitions as many Blue Sky visionaries had intended. As discussed in Chapter 3, communications satellites had been in use since the mid-1960s, but it was the "Open Skies" policy instituted during the Nixon administration that gave cable MSOs and other private interests permission to use this powerful technology as they thought appropriate.

This policy decision would profoundly affect the types of programming available to cable subscribers in the future. "Open Skies" no doubt was a disappointment to those who envisioned cable as an educational or narrowcast medium, since in the new scenario there would be no subsidies for worthwhile but underfunded programming operations. Of course, the increasingly corporate-controlled cable industry's response to the new policy was extremely favorable. "Open Skies," combined with the various deregulatory measures of the mid- to late 1970s, ensured that cable programming would be dominated by wealthy conglomerates, most with established operations in broadcast television or other media. During the early 1970s various cable interests did advance satellite programming plans under which educational, public service, and minority-interest programming would be subsidized; however, in retrospect it is apparent that there were neither programming precedents nor economic incentives to favor the implementation of such plans.

The cable industry, particularly the larger MSOs, had been interested in using satellites for at least a decade by the time "Open Skies" was instituted. As early as the 1960 NCTA convention, Teleprompter's Irving Kahn had proclaimed that cable was "the most practical, economical and effective medium of distribution after the TV signals have been beamed to earth from the satellite."[6] Study of the new medium's potential appears to have been carried on quietly by Teleprompter (and some other MSOs) throughout the 1960s, culminating in part in a panel discussion titled "CATV via Satellite" that took place at the NCTA's 1969 convention.

The cable industry's early interest in satellites is further evidenced by the many trade press articles on the subject during the late 1960s and early 1970s. But while the industry as a whole was extremely interested in this topic, Teleprompter seemed the least daunted both by the relatively untested nature of the technology and by its expense. In 1965, according to rumors within the CATV industry, Teleprompter had been actively researching the use of satellites for transmitting programming.[7] And by March 1973 the large MSO, ready to explore the possibility of forming a nationwide satellite-served cable network, hired former COMSAT employee Robert E. Button as a full-time consultant.[8] Almost immediately after hiring Button, Teleprompter filed an application with the FCC to operate receive-only earth stations (i.e., receiving dishes). The programming transmitted to these dishes would be produced by Teleprompter and unspecified "others."[9] The company outlined compelling credentials for such an undertaking, as described in this passage taken from the application:

> Teleprompter's experience in the planning and production of programming for broadcast television, closed circuit for military, government and commercial users, and CATV is requisite to establishment of a CATV networking system for itself and for others desiring to participate. Teleprompter has established a major program origination facility which presently serves its cable television system in the City of New York. Similar origination facilities are currently being established in Los Angeles. Much of the programming originated in these centers and by Teleprompter's other program production facilities is of national rather than purely local interest. . . . Furthermore, Teleprompter's experience in national networking of special-events programming is particularly relevant to the instant applications.[10]

The application reads like a roster of the various cable-related businesses and technologies that Teleprompter was involved with at the time.

Later in 1973 Teleprompter and more than 40 other cable operators—including American Television & Communications (owned by Time Inc.), Viacom, United Video, Cox Cable, Warner Cable, Daniels Properties Inc., Sammons Communication, and Continental Cablevision—formed an organization called Cable Satellite Access Entity (CSAE) for the purpose of financing research in satellite technology. CSAE, though officially a separate entity from NCTA, was made up of many of the organization's members, including both large MSOs and independently owned systems. The well-financed group had no trouble raising $140,000 to commission the research firm of Booz, Allen & Hamilton to complete a satellite feasibility study.[11]

This study, completed in August 1974, identified consumer demand for various types of specialized programming not available from broadcast television and recommended the use of cable networks to provide that programming in the most cost-effective way possible. One significant finding of the study was that most cable nonsubscribers were willing to pay a fee (even a fee somewhat greater than the current cable average) for programming not available from broadcast television (Final Report 1974, 23–24). Since no pay-cable network had yet made a profit, the CSAE members undoubtedly considered this finding encouraging. However, the study also accurately predicted that, in the short term, the economics of satellites would make extensive use of that distribution medium impractical. Instead, the study recommended a three-part approach to implementing cable networks, outlined as follows:

"Bicycling" [i.e., physically transporting] is best when the number of program hours and distribution points are both relatively low, the probable situation in the early stages of CATV network development. Satellite distribution with taped repeats is the best economic choice for moderate numbers of program hours and distribution points and offers "real time" capability when needed. Multi-channel satellite transmission of the full schedule becomes the most economic choice when the number of program hours and distribution points becomes large, as can be anticipated with maturation of the CATV network. (Final Report 1974, 45)

The study cautioned CSAE members against an all-or-nothing approach to the new technology. It recommended instead that satellites be introduced gradually so as to allow new programming infrastructures to be built and investments to be recovered before the heavy costs of uplinking and transponder rental were incurred. Apparently, though, some cable operators and others interested in satellite use ignored this advice. While the exact impact of the feasibility study on most of the CSAE group cannot be determined, four of its most powerful members (Time Inc., Warner Cable, Viacom, and United Video) had launched national satellite networks prior to 1980.

Several other members lent their support to a satellite-dominated cable industry by purchasing the earth stations (receiving dishes) needed to complete satellite transmissions—as ended up being the case with Teleprompter. The earliest MSO to show an interest in developing a satellite-served network became the first MSO to supply receiving dishes for most of its systems. As Teleprompter vice president Hubert ("Hub") Schlafly told a cable trade magazine, the $100,000 price tag per earth station was not unreasonable for his company. Because the dishes were low maintenance and expected to last at least 10 years, the long-term cost would be under $1,000 per month—less than some terrestrial distribution arrangements.[12] Time Inc. also subsidized the cost of receiving dishes for cable systems agreeing to offer its Home Box Office pay-cable network.

Although the CSAE study had recommended very specific categories of specialty and non-broadcast-derived programming, the planning and cooperation within the industry necessary to accomplish this simply did not occur. For those wanting to start satellite cable networks, it was more important to have popular and inexpensive programming available and ready for immediate use than it was to introduce distinctive new services at a pace that was feasible economically—as will become apparent in the rest of this chapter. While some early cable networks were able to introduce programming that was new to American audiences, this tended to be subsidized by schedules otherwise filled with sports and movies, typically repeated at intervals throughout the programming day.

Pay-Cable

Two types of cable networks emerged in the late 1970s: basic and pay (premium). Basic cable is a level of service comprising retransmitted broadcast channels, PEG access and other locally originated programming, and a number of cable-specific networks that developed following the introduction of satellites to the industry. Basic cable will be discussed in detail below. Pay-cable channels are available to subscribers on an unbundled or "à la carte" basis for a monthly fee. Pay-cable had its beginnings in the late 1960s and early 1970s, when the pay-TV industry's goals merged with those of the CATV industry.

The earliest pay-cable networks were of two types: pay-per-view systems like Optical Systems (Channel 100) and TheaterVisioN, and flat-rate systems like Gridtronics and Home Box Office. Even though there was a fair amount of optimism about the potential of pay-per-view systems, all of them quickly went out of business following the cable industry's adoption of satellite technology (other systems would begin during the 1980s). It seems likely that many cable systems at the time would have lacked the appropriate two-way technology, as well as the additional staff needed to operate those systems. Flat-rate systems proved to be better suited to the emerging satellite-served programming environment, since billing was less complicated and the only technology required to limit access was a filter at the subscriber's home (scrambling of pay-cable signals would not begin until the mid-1980s). The three earliest satellite pay-cable networks—HBO, The Movie Channel, and Showtime—all had existed as flat-rate pay-cable networks prior to being uplinked.

Gridtronics/The Movie Channel

The Movie Channel's origins date back to the Gridtronics videotape-based movie network that was launched by Warner Communications in 1973. The Gridtronics concept actually had been developed by Alfred Stern and Gordon Fuqua of Television Communications Corporation (TVC), an MSO, in the late 1960s. The system was designed to include an arts and current events channel, an instructional channel, a channel for medical professionals, and a movie channel (Smith 1972, 27–28; Lachenbruch 1973). Stern and Fuqua presented their concept to cable operators at the 1969 NCTA convention, and spent the next several years signing up cable systems and trying to secure permission to use Hollywood movies. However, the network did not actually launch until a year after TVC had been purchased by Warner. As Frank Cooper, the president of Gridtronics, explained, it was the company's acquisition by Warner that finally made it possible for Gridtronics to obtain the program material it needed:

> It became obvious when Warner bought out TVC, it had, in effect, become a cable operator and would in fact, provide film for "pay" purposes. That was indeed something to motivate the other movie studios. The majors then fell into line. They decided they better

share the pie rather than allow Warner to get this tremendous hold on the cable industry all by themselves. They weren't about to let that happen.[13]

Shortly after the Gridtronics movie network launched, its name was changed to Warner Star Channel. In 1979 it was uplinked to satellite and was renamed The Movie Channel.

Home Box Office

HBO's roots can be traced back to the uncut movies and sports that Sterling Manhattan Cable began offering its Lower Manhattan subscribers during the late 1960s as a standard part of monthly cable service. Sterling's programming was fairly sophisticated for its time, and undoubtedly drew more subscribers than community antenna service alone could have done. Nonetheless, by 1969 the company was having financial troubles and was looking for additional sources of revenue, including a mechanism by which Manhattan subscribers could pay additional fees for some of the non-broadcast-derived programming they received. At the time, Sterling was part owned by Time Inc., the magazine publisher, which recently had entered into cable system ownership. Thus, it was to Time Inc.'s board of directors that Sterling president Charles Dolan presented the idea for what he called "The Green Channel." Dolan envisioned a pay-cable sports and movie programming network that would serve Manhattan, as well as any other cable systems wishing to pay for the service.

Dolan's plan won approval by Time's board in November 1971, and shortly thereafter the name of the proposed pay-cable network was changed to Home Box Office. Ironically, due to a franchise prohibition on pay-TV, HBO actually was not able to launch on the Lower Manhattan cable system for which it had been designed.[14] Instead, in November 1972 the cable system in Wilkes-Barre, Pennsylvania, became the first to carry HBO programming—a selection that reportedly included six feature films, New York Knicks basketball, New York Rangers hockey, live boxing matches from Madison Square Garden, "miscellaneous" sports events (such as Roller Derby), and some children's movies.[15] This programming was transmitted to Wilkes-Barre from the company's New York City headquarters via microwave.[16]

HBO was the first pay-cable network to use microwave successfully—due in large part to extensive microwave networks that already existed in the Northeast. Within its first year, carriage grew to include 14 affiliate cable systems in Pennsylvania and upstate New York, for a total of

8,000 subscribers. By 1975 there were more than 100 microwave-served affiliates.[17] At that point, HBO's executives were extremely interested in expanding their service to other parts of the country. Still, building new microwave networks in areas not already served would have been both costly and time-consuming. Satellites presented an obvious solution to this problem, even though the technology had not yet been tested by the cable industry. From the beginning, HBO's founders had been well aware of the potential of satellites for program distribution. As Dolan had expressed in a January 1972 memo to Time's board of directors:

> In the long run, we may think of ourselves as the Macy's of television, shopping everywhere for programs that some public, large or small, will buy. If we are successful in meeting these "retail" program needs of the region we are attempting to serve in 1972–73, we will later use whatever efficient transmission systems become available, from microwave to satellite, to sell television programs worldwide to any public that signals its specific demands to us. ("HBO" 1992)

HBO's move to satellite actually was initiated by a new executive team. In early 1973 both HBO and Manhattan Cable were bought out entirely by Time Inc. Dolan left the company to pursue other cable ventures, and Gerald Levin, an entertainment attorney who had been with Sterling since 1971, became HBO's president.

The new owners were eager to expand HBO's service using the new distribution technology. Nonetheless, the actual transition to satellite needed not only extensive research but also a demonstration of the technology's potential to a skeptical industry. Simply making the programming available via satellite was not enough; cable operators had to be convinced that the expensive receiving dishes would be a worthwhile investment. HBO was only a year old when it assumed a key role in this promotional effort.[18] During the 1973 NCTA convention in Anaheim, HBO, Teleprompter, and Scientific Atlanta (a cable equipment manufacturer) held a demonstration of satellite technology. The televised event was a boxing match from Madison Square Garden. Boxing probably had been selected for the demonstration because of both the general popularity of televised sports and HBO's previous experience with this particular sport.

HBO's first satellite telecast to subscribers, in September 1975, also was a boxing match: Muhammad Ali versus Joe Frazier live from the Philippines (the "classic" bout that came to be called "The Thrilla in

Manila"). Already at this early stage, HBO was carving out "trademark" programming niches such as boxing—a sport with a long history on cable (dating back to Teleprompter's closed-circuit telecasts of the early 1960s) but not widely covered by broadcast television. HBO also quickly became known for its exclusive movies and original comedy specials (in 1977, *The Bette Midler Show* won the first Cable ACE award). HBO also had been developing scheduling and promotional strategies that would further differentiate its fare from that of broadcast television. For example, in 1974, the year before its satellite debut, HBO had used a promotional campaign called "Gasless Saturdays and Sundays" (in response to the energy crisis), a strategy that prefigured the marathons and theme days introduced by many cable networks during the 1980s and 1990s ("HBO" 1992). In 1977 HBO introduced the concept of systemwide free previews, also popular with modern cable networks, in a campaign called "Tonight's On Us" ("HBO" 1992).

HBO also introduced the now widespread cable programming practice of showing series that have been rejected or abandoned by U.S. and foreign broadcast networks. In October 1975 it purchased the rights to a package of BBC programs that included the 26-episode hour-long drama, *The Pallisers;* the six-hour *David Copperfield;* and the three-hour *Heidi.*[19] Less than a year later, HBO similarly ran two episodes of the canceled CBS drama, *Beacon Hill*—reportedly to a favorable audience reception.[20]

Of course, HBO was in a fortunate position with regard to its resources for program production and acquisition. Although it did not actually earn a profit until 1978, its programming was subsidized by a wealthy parent company. This privileged status was especially apparent in June 1976, when HBO announced that Time Inc. would help Columbia Pictures finance a number of major feature films in exchange for the first television rights to those films.[21] This was a strategy HBO would continue to pursue through partnerships with studios, financing of independent films, and multinational coproductions.

Premiere

HBO's movie-financing strategy did not go unnoticed by the Hollywood studios. In fact, HBO's exclusivity deals demonstrated to the studios what a profitable aftermarket pay-cable could be for the films they produced and distributed. In late 1979 a group of Hollywood studios (Columbia, Paramount, Universal/MCA, and 20th Century Fox) agreed to form a pay-cable network called Premiere to compete with HBO (and any other pay-cable networks that might emerge). The studios were joined by the Getty Oil Corporation, which already was active in cable programming through its ownership of the basic cable sports network, ESPN, and thus able to provide a satellite transponder. Premiere would be available for three or four hours every evening of the week, and some 150 different films would be shown each year—half provided by the studio partners, and the rest acquired elsewhere on a nonexclusive basis. Since the Hollywood studios were not vertically integrated within the cable industry, as HBO and other pay-cable networks were, Premiere would require a unique marketing strategy in order to compete for channel space on cable systems. The studios opted to retain a nine-month television exclusivity window for each of the films they produced. This would give Premiere first pay-cable rights to over half of Hollywood's annual film output.[22]

Premiere was scheduled to launch in January 1981. However, in August 1980 the U.S. Justice Department filed an antitrust suit charging that Premiere's exclusivity window would fix movie prices at artificially high levels and would restrain competition among pay-cable networks. On 31 December New York federal district court judge Gerald L. Goettel barred the Premiere partnership from going ahead with the network's launch. Goettel found that, even without the exclusivity window, Premiere would not only restrain trade within the cable industry, but would also raise the prices of films made available to broadcast television. Unable to have the ruling overturned, Premiere's five investors abandoned their plans, sustaining a multimillion-dollar loss.[23]

Even though Premiere never actually launched, it is worth mentioning for several reasons. First, it shows that satellite cable was not developing in isolation from other entertainment industries. The Premiere plans are evidence of Hollywood's alarm over HBO's rapid rise to prominence within the American entertainment industry. Second, comparing Premiere's situation with that of HBO makes it clear that cable networks were able to exploit a lingering public perception of their industry as small, experimental, and therefore fairly benign compared to the Hollywood movie giants at the time. This perception is, of course, glaringly invalidated by the rapidly increasing power held by Time Inc.—not to mention the increasing absorption of both cable networks and cable systems by synergistic entertainment conglomerates throughout the decades that followed. By 1980 Time already was more vertically integrated than any of the Hollywood studios had been since the 1948 consent decree, and it was becoming clear that other cable interests would fall into the same pattern. Finally, the Premiere episode signifies one facet of a major redefinition that Hollywood was undergoing in the late 1970s as a variety of new media outlets became available for its product.[24]

Showtime and other pay-TV networks

In spite of Premiere's demise, serious competition had emerged for HBO following its satellite debut. Most notable was Viacom's Showtime network. Showtime had launched in July 1976 as a regional network in the New York City and Long Island area, packaging taped and microwave-carried programming. It began by targeting systems not willing or able to acquire satellite receiving dishes. Unlike HBO, Showtime's programming required little or no new equipment. But when Showtime finally uplinked its network to satellite in March 1978, it quickly became a rival to HBO, signing on 250,000 HBO subscribers from Teleprompter systems alone in early 1979.[25] The two pay networks were not substantially different, as both featured movies and entertainment specials weekday evenings and from 2 P.M. to 2 A.M. on weekends. The only significant difference between them was that HBO produced many of its specials and some of its movies in-house, while Showtime contracted out for all of its programming.

In 1980 The Movie Channel, HBO, and Showtime were joined by Bravo and its sister network, Escapade. Bravo was a culture channel, while Escapade featured R-rated movies and other "adult" entertainment. HBO also spun off Cinemax, an all-movie network, in 1980. Other pay-cable networks, including The Disney Channel, were launched during the 1980s.

Pay-cable versus over-the-air systems

For a brief period during the late 1970s and early 1980s, the various pay-cable networks were challenged by over-the-air pay-TV—an industry that had lain dormant since Phonevision's Hartford operation shut down in 1969. Following the FCC's approval of pay-TV in the early 1970s, several companies had filed applications for over-the-air systems, though none actually began operation until 1977. The first two over-the-air pay stations were WWHT in Newark, New Jersey, and KBSC in Corona, California (a Los Angeles suburb). WWHT (Wometco Home Theatre), known as "WHT, the Movie Network," was licensed to Wometco-Blonder-Tongue (a company formed by Blonder-Tongue Laboratories of Old Bridge, New Jersey, and Wometco Enterprises, Inc.

of Miami Beach). WHT had an installation fee of $49.95 and charged $17 monthly. KBSC (National Subscription Television) was owned jointly by Oak Industries of San Diego and Chartwell Communications of Los Angeles. This system had an installation fee of $39.95 and charged $19.95 per month. By 1980 other systems had been launched, and six additional pay-TV stations were on the air (Howard and Carroll 1980, 35–38 and 84–85).[26]

For a few years it was uncertain whether pay-cable or over-the-air pay-TV would become dominant. Each seemed to have certain advantages over the other. Cable already was available in many communities and offered multiple channels of programming. Nonetheless, for the many large metropolitan areas that still lacked cable systems it would have been much cheaper to buy or build a UHF station than to construct an entire cable system (Howard and Carroll 1980, 157–158). Since some of the most desirable markets for pay-TV also happened to be markets in which cable was not yet established, over-the-air pay-TV was believed to have a short-term advantage. So strong was the optimism surrounding over-the-air pay-TV around 1980 that its proponents estimated that before 1990 there would be at least one STV station in each of the top 40–50 broadcast markets. The airwaves, not cable, were believed to be the future of pay-TV at this stage.[27] In fact, as of 1980, broadcast pay TV subscribers numbered more than 400,000 (Howard and Carroll 1980, 54).

Still, this number was dwarfed by HBO's 4.1 million subscribers (as of January 1980) and Showtime's 1 million.[28] Satellite-served pay-cable quickly had become a powerful force in American television entertainment. One of the reasons over-the-air pay-TV ultimately went out of business was its inability to deliver more than a single channel of programming. By contrast, cable systems provide multiple channels of programming. Since the early 1980s, most cable systems have had at least 20 available channels, but premium networks use only a few of these. The other channels are used for basic cable, a level of service over-the-air pay-TV could never provide.

Basic Cable

Of the three components of basic cable service—broadcast channels, access and other local programming, and satellite-carried program networks—retransmitted broadcast stations historically have been the most popular with cable subscribers. Even in communities where broadcast stations can be received using a home antenna, cable delivers clearer, more reliable signals. The term "basic cable," however, normally refers to satellite-carried networks that are not available over the air. These cable-only networks typically are sold to subscribers as a package ("bundled"). With a few very notable exceptions, they are sustained both by advertising and by a "per-subscriber" (or "per-sub") fee—a monthly fee that cable operators pay networks based on total numbers of subscribers. Basic cable networks substitute other sources of revenue, usually a combination of per-sub fees and advertiser support, for the large monthly fees each individual pay-cable service charges its subscribers.

Several satellite-carried basic cable networks were introduced during the late 1970s. As will become evident in the sections that follow, these represented an eclectic mix of program categories. Like the pay-cable networks started in that decade, most basic networks had origins predating the introduction of satellite technology, and thus had their programming infrastructures in place. Uplinking to satellite was enough of a financial gamble already; they did not need to risk precious resources on programming experimentation at this stage. Those networks that had not existed in any form prior to satellite transmission took even fewer risks in terms of programming innovation. Ironically, hardly any of the basic cable networks started in the late 1970s failed—either in the short term or in the long term. The same cannot be said of networks started during the 1980s and 1990s. This is due in part to the fact that the early networks established a position in the industry when there were few competitors. It is also due to their conservative programming practices; they did little to disrupt the audience's expectations of television.

By the late 1970s it was becoming quite clear that the most popular and profitable cable networks would be those that reflected what was popular on broadcast television. The most blatant example of this (outside the category of broadcast signals received by community antenna or microwave relay) is the rapid rise of the cable "superstation," essentially a popular broadcast station whose signal is distributed nationwide by satellite. As discussed in earlier chapters, the importation—usually via microwave relays—of major-market independent stations foreshadowed the rise of superstations. For those stations already widely carried by microwave, moving to more efficient satellite distribution was a logical next step. Within only a few years of HBO's pioneering satellite debut, three satellite-carried independent stations, operating as basic cable networks, also became available to cable subscribers.

Superstations

The rise of the superstation can be attributed to a variety of factors. Major-market independent stations had been popular cable channels ever since technology first enabled systems to carry more than a few of the nearest available signals. FCC regulations severely restricted the ability of larger CATV/cable systems to import distant signals during the 1960s, though even at that time the "proto"-superstations received a great deal of carriage by smaller, more rural systems. Carriage of these independent stations increased tremendously following the institution of the 1972 rules, which outlined a framework allowing virtually any cable system to import some distant signals. The stations then received a boost in both carriage and recognition in 1974, when the FCC allowed unlimited signal importation at night if must-carry stations had gone off the air. By 1980 virtually no regulations existed to limit cable systems' importation of these popular stations.

The first satellite-carried superstation was the Atlanta station that would become the WTBS (later TBS) superstation. In 1968 Ted Turner, the owner of a billboard company, purchased a bankrupt Atlanta UHF station, WJRJ, which he immediately renamed WTCG (for Turner Communications Group). For programming, Turner used old movies and syndicated television series, many of which he wisely purchased outright with a view toward unrestricted future showings. He first made a name for WTCG by counterprogramming the network affiliates, especially during evening newscasts. Turner also made WTCG a home for local sports, offering far more sports programming than any broadcast network or affiliate. By the early 1970s WTCG was covering a broad selection of Atlanta teams—first professional wrestling and then Braves baseball, Hawks basketball, and Flames hockey. In 1976 Turner actually purchased the Braves, thereby securing long-term access to what would become the station's single most important source of programming.

Turner quickly put Atlanta's only other independent station out of business, and as early as 1972, WTCG was earning a profit and boasted a 15 percent share of the Atlanta audience (Bibb 1993, 84). In addition, the station's signal had begun to be carried by microwave to cable systems in the Atlanta region. Since there were so few professional sports teams in the South, Turner believed that he could successfully expand WTCG's coverage to include cable systems throughout Georgia and surrounding states. Microwave would have been both cumbersome and costly for such an undertaking, however, and when Turner heard about

HBO's satellite debut, he quickly began investigating ways to use the same technology to extend WTCG's signal. Through a series of adroit negotiations, Turner set up (as a business separate from Turner Communications) a company called Southern Satellite Systems, Inc. to uplink WTCG's signal to an RCA communications satellite. In 1976 WTCG became the second satellite-delivered cable network and the first satellite superstation. The superstation was renamed WTBS in the late 1970s.[29]

Within the next few years, the signals of two other major-market independent stations began to be carried on satellite as well, and several more independent stations would attain this status in the 1980s. The stations that followed WTBS to satellite carriage represent a different type of superstation, though. WTBS is considered to be an *active* superstation because it has pursued superstation status as part of day-to-day operations; programming targets a nationwide market more than a local market, and national advertising is sought by its owner. WTBS currently is the only active superstation. By contrast, the *passive* superstations that followed WTBS to satellite (including New York's WOR, WPIX, and WNEW; Chicago's WGN; Boston's WSBK; and Los Angeles's KTLA) initially did little or nothing to market themselves as superstations.[30] Instead, satellite common carrier companies (most often the same companies that had been delivering the signals by microwave) retransmitted these stations' signals without any formal consent, sometimes even against the stations' wishes. In spite of their potential to be viewed thousands of miles away, passive superstations continued to direct the greater portion of their programming and advertising toward local or regional markets.

As with any cable network, cable operators pay per-sub fees for the use of passive superstations' signals. Ironically, though, for many years the fees were paid to the common carriers, not to the stations, and passive superstations received no compensation for the carriage of their signals. In fact, in 1979 the FCC formally permitted common carriers to sell superstations' signals to cable systems, a permission unsuccessfully challenged by Metromedia Inc., the owner of one of the stations affected.[31] It was not until 1992, with passage of a major body of cable-related legislation, that a mechanism was established by which passive superstations could be compensated for the use of their signals.

After Turner, then, the second satellite superstation entrepreneur was Roy L. Bliss, president of United Video, which was both a cable MSO and a microwave and satellite common carrier company. In November 1978 United Video uplinked WGN-Chicago, which already was extremely popular throughout the Midwest as a microwave-carried station. Bliss rented a transponder for $600,000. He subsequently claimed that by selling the network to 500 systems for a 10-cent subscriber fee (up to $3,000 per system), he was able to break even after only a year.[32] In April of the following year Eastern Microwave, Inc., the upstate New York common carrier responsible for the microwave relaying of several independent stations to cable systems in the Northeast, uplinked New York's WOR to satellite.[33] Thus, by 1979 the superstation already had become an established and popular fixture in cable channel lineups.

Superstations (especially passive superstations) have made extremely economical cable programming sources. With their programming infrastructures already in place, turning independent stations into cable superstations is primarily a matter of acquiring and maintaining uplinking facilities, leasing a transponder, and marketing the superstation as a basic cable network. Still, there does appear to be a limit to the number of superstations that can exist at any one time. Since the late 1980s, the total number of national superstations has remained at six. There are several reasons for this. First, cable systems have limited channel capacity, or "shelf space," and a superstation represents only one of hundreds of possible networks an operator might offer subscribers. Second, while any independent broadcast station technically is capable of becoming a superstation, only a select few possess the reputations and programming resources to compete with other nationally available networks. Essential programming resources include extensive movie libraries or coverage of professional sports. Third, superstation carriage is considered to be a use of a nonnetwork broadcast signal and therefore makes cable operators liable for fees under the provisions of the 1976 Copyright Act.

In spite of their popularity, the existence of superstations did not preclude or limit the growth of more specialized cable networks. In fact, several of the earliest basic satellite networks can be considered narrowcast. This was not the result of a comprehensive policy guiding cable programming development, as Blue Sky visionaries had hoped. Rather, it was a matter of which programming interests had adequate financing and existing programming infrastructures. In some cases, satellite cable networks were launched by well-established special-interest programming operations. In other cases, they were started by well-backed individuals or partnerships wanting to specialize in specific program genres.

For all of these entrepreneurs, the late 1970s was a laboratory period for determining which types of programming could succeed on cable and how schedules might be refined so as to ensure profits in the future.

Religious programming

Some of the earliest specialty programming to emerge on cable was religious programming—a genre with a lengthy history in broadcasting, as discussed in Chapter 2. Several of the more successful religious broadcasters began satellite cable networks with nationwide distribution during the 1970s and 1980s. Religious networks demonstrate the important role nontraditional funding sources have played in helping launch cable networks; most have had a substantial revenue stream from viewer donations, allowing them unusual flexibility in producing or acquiring original programming for their market niche. Nonetheless, even with this additional revenue, networks that adhere strictly to religious themes have not succeeded in receiving widespread carriage or in drawing large audiences. The case of cable's first religious programming network, CBN-Cable (the third satellite cable network to be launched overall), supports this point.

CBN-Cable was started as an extension of televangelist Pat Robertson's Christian Broadcasting Network (CBN) in 1977. As discussed in Chapter 2, CBN's existence actually dates back to 1961, when Robertson purchased a bankrupt UHF station in Portsmouth, Virginia. A few years later, Robertson acquired another UHF station (this one in Atlanta) and began to describe his operation as a television network.[34] Due in large part to contributions from Robertson's television congregation, CBN grew rapidly during its first decade. By 1967 Robertson was able to build a multimillion-dollar headquarters for his operations (Donovan 1988, 86–87).

The key component of CBN's early schedule was *The 700 Club,* a show that features celebrity interviews, current events, fund-raising, and religious exhortation. This religious program debuted in 1965, and has remained Robertson's trademark program ever since.[35] Other religious programs were used as well. However, by the late 1960s, CBN also had begun to use some old movies and off-network reruns to fill out its schedule. By the early 1970s CBN's audience size had increased considerably, with local advertising sales growing accordingly. And it appeared that much of this success was attributable to the inexpensive reruns and old movies CBN was using to fill out its program schedule.

Apparently, audiences and advertisers were drawn to a schedule that represented a mixture of religious and nonreligious programming.

Discovering this led Robertson to an important programming innovation: presuming that other independent stations could combine religious and nonreligious programming as successfully as CBN had, he began to package and sell four-hour blocks of CBN-produced religious fare. Robertson began to think of the stations that bought his tapes as network affiliates.[36] Bicycling the tapes was considerably less expensive than leasing AT&T land lines (the method the major broadcast networks were using to deliver programs to their affiliates), yet an effective means of distribution nonetheless. And since reruns and old movies are fairly interchangeable components of an independent station's schedule, the four hours of original CBN programming could give these stations a distinctive CBN identity.

By the 1970s CBN's broadcast television operation had become a familiar television "brand" and was earning a profit both from the sale of its syndicated programming and in the form of advertising revenue on its own stations—in addition to donations from the faithful *700 Club* viewers. The popular program schedule that had developed around Robertson's TV pulpit already had taken on a life of its own by the time Robertson launched the cable network. Over the course of its evolution into The Family Channel during the 1980s, CBN-Cable shifted its identity even further from strictly Christian-oriented programming and toward a much broader appeal.

PTL, a cable network launched in 1978 by televangelists Jim and Tammy Faye Bakker, offers a different example of how a religious programming enterprise could develop as a satellite network. The Bakkers had gained experience in religious broadcasting during the 1960s and early 1970s. In fact, they had begun their careers working for CBN from 1965 to 1972. After also working at Trinity Broadcasting Network for a year, they moved to Charlotte, North Carolina, in 1974 and started PTL, a network of affiliated religious stations. Similar to CBN's *The 700 Club, The PTL Club* became PTL's flagship program.[37] In 1978 the Bakkers launched a PTL satellite network. By that point, PTL programming already was available on 181 broadcast television stations.

Unlike CBN-Cable, PTL offered 24 hours of religious programming. This consisted primarily of talk shows and fundraisers, but also included religious soap operas, children's shows, and comedy/variety shows. The Bakkers continued using this format in the 1980s until, in the latter part of the decade, scandals and bankruptcy brought an end to the their control of PTL (by then called PTL Inspirational Network). New owners chose to keep the network within the religious programming niche, renaming it The New Inspirational Satellite Network (a name that subsequently was shortened to The Inspirational Network).[38]

Both CBN-Cable and PTL entered the field of satellite cable programming at a very early stage. They were added to channel selections at a time when operators still were looking for ways to fill empty channels. Within only a few years, this situation would change dramatically; the proliferation of start-up cable networks in the 1980s, coupled with the limited channel capacity of most cable systems, made shelf space a scarce commodity in that decade. So early entry into cable gave the religious networks discussed above a distinct advantage in years to come. Nonetheless, CBN-Cable and PTL used this advantage in two very different ways. PTL chose to remain within its religious niche, while CBN-Cable chose to boost its carriage and viewership by programming most of its schedule for general audiences—content virtually identical to that of superstations and other mainstream cable networks. In 1986 PTL boasted only a third of CBN's viewership, a discrepancy that grew during the years that followed, as CBN-Cable jettisoned even more of its religious programs and other signifiers of a fundamentalist Christian identity, as will be discussed in Chapter 6 (Ostling 1986, 62).

Another early religious cable network was Trinity Broadcasting Network (TBN), which had begun in 1973 as a group of affiliated broadcast stations and started distributing programming via satellite to affiliates and cable systems in the late 1970s. TBN's programming, while all within the religious niche, remained multidenominational, covering a broad spectrum of program genres. TBN's situation is unusual in that it chose to operate as both a satellite cable network and a broadcast network. During the 1980s and early 1990s TBN's cable viewership was about half that of CBN-Cable/The Family Channel, but its combined cable and broadcast viewership was, for many years, larger than that of any cable network.

As cable networks, religious programmers have been helped tremendously by the fact that their targeted audiences consist of people who feel underserved by mainstream television. Indeed, these audiences comprise enough cable nonsubscribers that a network like TBN can maintain a substantial broadcast audience in addition to its cable viewership. A similar situation has occurred with Spanish-language cable networks.

Spanish-language programming

As discussed in Chapter 2, SIN (the Spanish International Network) started several Spanish-language broadcast stations in the United States during the 1960s. By the mid-1970s additional stations had been added to SIN's broadcast network. In 1976 SIN began to distribute programming to its affiliates via satellite. Then during the 1980s some cable systems picked up this feed and marketed it as a cable network.[39] In 1979 SIN also launched Galavision, the first cable-only Spanish-language network. Initially, Galavision was a premium network, but low subscriber numbers brought about an early relocation to the basic tier.

During the late 1970s and early 1980s about 90 percent of programming used by SIN and Galavision was recycled fare, initially produced in Latin America. A large portion of it consisted of "telenovelas" (highly popular Latin American soap operas). Other popular programming included sports (especially soccer, baseball, and boxing), movies, talk shows, children's shows, game shows, and variety shows—a varied selection similar to the schedules of most English-language networks, stations, and cable networks.[40] In this respect, SIN and Galavision—while unquestionably minority targeted—nonetheless fit within the paradigm of start-up cable networks that relied on secondhand broadcast programming.

Spanish-language programming has retained a solid hold both in broadcasting and in cable since those early years. The existing networks have increased their use of original programming, but still rely heavily on popular programs from Latin American broadcast markets. Also, the 1980s and 1990s witnessed the launch of several additional networks—including the broadcast/cable network Telemundo (1987); the cable networks Canal de Noticias NBC (1993), Canal Sur (1991), CineLatino (1994), GEMS (1993), MTV Latino (1993), and Viva (1993); and either Spanish-language versions or second audio feeds for The Cartoon Network, TNT, Cable News Network, HBO, Request Television, and EWTN: The Catholic Cable Network.

QUBE and Nickelodeon

The children's network, Nickelodeon, was one of the earliest satellite cable networks. And like many of the other early satellite networks described above, it had a prehistory as a nonsatellite operation. Nickelodeon started in December 1977 as Pinwheel, one of the more popular channels offered on Warner Communications' QUBE interactive cable system, which was tested in Columbus, Ohio. The only show featured on Pinwheel was *Pinwheel House,* oriented toward preschool children. *Pinwheel House* was similar in format to *Sesame Street,* featuring puppets, educational material, and animated films (including several obtained from the National Film Board of Canada). The program ran from 7:00 A.M. to 7:00 P.M. every day of the week (Denisoff 1988, 10). In the long term, this children's network would be the only lasting part of the QUBE system.

QUBE initially offered a wide range of programming. There were three categories of QUBE channels: "P" channels, which provided premium programming; "C" channels, which offered various categories of locally originated programming; and "T" channels, which included broadcast stations and public access. The selection of P channels included Free Program Preview, First Run Movies, Movie Greats, Performance, Better Living, Sports, Special Events, QUBE Games, College at Home, and Adult Films. As a means of parental control, the premium channels required a key for access. C channels included Pinwheel, along with Columbus Alive, Columbus Information, News Update, Sports News & Scores, Stocks & Business News, Religious Programs, Time & Weather, Selected Audience Programs, and Live and Learn. There were 30 channel choices in all. The QUBE selector box also was equipped with five response buttons, which could be used for everything from interactive game shows to town meetings to home shopping.

In the late 1970s both the trade and popular presses were filled with articles about the futuristic cable scenario QUBE had initiated. Many believed that systems like QUBE could help the cable industry achieve the goals intended by Blue Sky visionaries. They could foster democratic participation by allowing viewers to watch public meetings and to vote using their selector boxes. They could further educational goals by allowing at-home students—children and adults alike—to participate in classes they otherwise might not be able to attend. And they could provide participatory forms of entertainment to replace passive television viewing. Because of its interactivity and extensive channel selection, QUBE was believed to represent the cable system of the future.

In fact, QUBE itself ended up doing more to highlight the enduring success of *established* television genres than it did to revolutionize the medium of cable.[41] Not surprisingly, of the interactive programs offered on QUBE, game shows with cash prizes were the most popular. But even these only drew an average of 2 percent of QUBE subscribers.

Three quarters of QUBE subscribers never used the interactive networks at all. Although the Columbus system continued into the mid-1980s, and Warner Amex also expanded the network into a few other cities (Cincinnati, Pittsburgh, Dallas, Houston, and St. Louis), QUBE's novelty value had faded by 1984 and interactive programming was cut back drastically. QUBE's primary use during its few remaining years was for distributing pay-per-view movies and special events.[42]

Although QUBE itself did not survive, its Pinwheel children's service did. The success of *Pinwheel House* in Columbus had led Warner Cable to use the show on some of its other systems, where it also fared well (Denisoff 1988, 10). In April 1979 Pinwheel was uplinked to satellite, its name was changed to Nickelodeon, and its programming day was expanded to 13 hours on weekdays and 14 on weekends. These were hours not used by Warner's Star Channel/The Movie Channel, so one transponder could be shared by the two networks.[43] Warner boasted of Nickelodeon's programming originality. At the time of its satellite debut Warner Cable chairman Gustave M. Hauser proclaimed, "To my knowledge Nickelodeon is the first all-cable channel the industry has ever had. It doesn't consist of materials from other places that have been packaged like motion pictures, etc."[44]

Original material notwithstanding, Nickelodeon has targeted the interests of a well-established television audience. Even though children's programming historically has been a site of struggle between the interests of advertisers and those of parents, educators, and social reformers, its presence on television cannot be denied. It is worth noting that during its earliest years Nickelodeon—unlike other basic cable networks of the time—remained both commercial-free and free to cable systems. Of course, it did not actually make a profit until the mid-1980s, after it had begun to sell advertising and had launched its evening subservice, Nick at Nite, which relies exclusively on reruns.[45]

From the start, almost all of Nickelodeon's programming (excluding the semiautonomous Nick at Nite portion) has been original material, both first-run acquired programming and in-house productions. It also has introduced a number of new program formats since it was founded. Nickelodeon quickly became one of cable's top-rated networks—a success its executives attribute to having filled a previously unmet need in television programming. Nickelodeon's publicity materials have often boasted that moving away both from the strictly educational programming seen on PBS and from the often violent and commodity-linked programming on commercial broadcast networks has been the key to success. The cable network has managed to strike a balance between what children want to watch and what parents feel is appropriate.

Sports programming

Children's programming had a long television history that predated the launch of Nickelodeon—offering an established audience that gave the new cable network a foot in the door. The same can be said of sports, the type of programming offered by the Entertainment and Sports Programming Network (ESPN), which launched in September 1979. Although at first it was unable to secure rights to most major professional sports events, ESPN did have a fairly strong beginning because it showed sports not available elsewhere: various NCAA events and Canadian Football League games, for example. Although college football was featured on a tape-delayed basis in order to protect an exclusive ABC contract, ESPN was able to show many more games than the broadcast networks did. ESPN also scored a small coup by showing minor league baseball during a major league strike.[46] As the network grew in popularity, it attracted more advertisers and was able to replace most of the minor sports it had been using as filler with big-ticket events.

From the beginning, ESPN had little difficulty finding financing. Getty Oil owned 85 percent of its stock, and commercial sponsors included Anheuser-Busch, Sony, Hertz, Gillette, Goodyear, Toyota, and Chevrolet (Waters and Wilson 1979). As with the superstations, a 24-hour schedule was a major factor in giving ESPN its start. Its founder, William Rasmussen, explained, "Many people work the 4-to-midnight shift, and lots of them are sports enthusiasts."[47] Clearly ESPN was able to convince major advertisers that there is no shortage of television sports fans, even in the earliest hours of the morning. Its early and rapid success provides evidence for the claim that a cable network can specialize successfully in one traditionally popular television genre. It is the dynamic interplay between viewership and advertising revenue that determines whether or not a cable network can succeed in a free market situation such as the one brought about by "Open Skies."

Another sports network, Madison Square Garden Sports Network (which had been operating as a regional terrestrial service since 1969), uplinked to satellite in 1977. MSG was a subsidy of UA-Columbia Cablevision, at the time one of the largest MSOs. During its first three years of operation, MSG added several subservices to its feed. These included Calliope, a children's network; Black Entertainment Television (BET), beginning in January 1980; and the Cable Satellite Public Affairs Network (C-SPAN), discussed below. Initially, these were discrete services, distributed individually to cable systems. In 1980, however, portions of MSG and Calliope were blended to form USA, a general-interest network with a strong emphasis on sports programming. Kay Koplovitz, who had first developed Calliope for Learning Corporation of America, became head of the cable network.[48]

Black Entertainment Television

BET continued to share USA's transponder for two more years, programming 2–3 hours per week, while operating on a tight budget.[49] Although its founder, Robert Johnson, had secured investments from some MSOs, BET also made its programming available to cable systems free of charge and was struggling to sell advertising. Thus, it relied on extremely inexpensive programming, consisting mainly of sitcoms featuring African Americans and blaxploitation films from the 1960s and 1970s. Johnson also had obtained the rights to show some films produced for segregated theaters during the Hollywood studio era. The founding of BET involved a combination of a narrowcasting vision and the ability to make do on extremely limited funds (Shales 1979). As BET began to recover its start-up costs during the late 1980s, it was able to begin providing original programming. In open-entry competition, this pattern was typical for cable networks that successfully targeted specialized audiences.

C-SPAN

The founding of C-SPAN, another network that had started on MSG's transponder, represents a very different sort of narrowcasting—indeed an anomaly in cable programming. C-SPAN was the brainchild of Brian Lamb, one-time member of the Nixon administration's OTP. By the mid-1970s Lamb had departed the White House staff and was working as Washington bureau chief for *Cablevision* magazine. While there, he came up with the idea for a cable network that would continually monitor the federal legislature. Some interest in Lamb's plan came from Speaker of the House Thomas P. "Tip" O'Neill (D-Mass.), who wanted to begin allowing cameras into House sessions. Lamb received additional support from Lionel Van Deerlin (D-Calif.), chair of the House Communications Subcommittee. In late October 1977, shortly after an interview with Lamb, Van Deerlin made a very persuasive speech to the House that led to acceptance of Lamb's idea.

Initially, Lamb received little support from cable operators, who generally saw no profit motive in diverting from broadcast-derived programming patterns. However, UA-Columbia Cablevision president Robert Rosencrans, whom Lamb had met while doing a story for *Cablevision*, seemed more enthusiastic about the idea. After formally receiving permission to use television cameras in the House of Representatives, Lamb approached Rosencrans about using MSG's less-popular daytime hours to launch C-SPAN. Rosencrans not only agreed to share the transponder; he also chaired C-SPAN's board of directors during the two years prior to its launch. Rosencrans was able to convince executives of other MSOs to lend their support, and with $25,000 provided by the cable industry, Lamb established C-SPAN as a nonprofit corporation for gavel-to-gavel coverage of House sessions.[50] The innovative network launched in March 1979.

A major condition in Speaker O'Neill's agreement to allow C-SPAN cameras into the House of Representatives had been that the legislators—not the cable network—would have final say in how those cameras would portray what took place there.[51] Part of this agreement was that C-SPAN's programming would include continuous coverage of all House sessions. This still left C-SPAN with the challenge of programming lengthy periods in the mornings before the House convened, as well as times when it was not in session. By the end of C-SPAN's first year, Lamb had begun using committee hearings as morning programming. Other times were used to cover speeches at National Press Club luncheons—a small additional source of revenue for C-SPAN, since Lamb charged the club $200 to cover each event. Beyond this, C-SPAN's programming day was open to ideas suggested by its staff. Over the course of its first few years, the network added various call-in shows, discussion forums, and Lamb's own *Booknotes,* hour-long interviews with prominent authors.[52]

Of course, C-SPAN has represented a radical break from existing television coverage of the U.S. Congress and other news. In interviews Lamb has been unapologetic about the long, often tedious coverage that does not resort to soundbites or sensationalism. In television programming, two things afford such a luxury: a medium with the channel capacity to include C-SPAN *along with* many other sources of programming, and an exemption from the need to amass ratings points and sell commercial time. Ever since the first contributions Lamb received from MSOs in the late 1970s, C-SPAN has been sustained by contributions from the cable industry—most notably small monthly subscriber fees charged by cable operators.

In the world of cable narrowcasting, an arrangement such as the one that enables C-SPAN to operate is rare. C-SPAN draws a small but loyal audience from among those who find television's other public affairs coverage inadequate. Networks such as this had been intended for cable ever since people first became aware of the medium's potential to supplement broadcast television with a wide variety of programming, designed for individualized viewing constituencies. Ultimately, though, C-SPAN would remain in a class by itself. Agreeing to finance C-SPAN (and later C-SPAN 2) represented the only gesture the cable industry would make voluntarily toward fulfilling the public service goals of the various Blue Sky studies and articles. The 1980s would witness the launches of several specialty networks. However, as will be discussed in the next two chapters, the programming of those networks, like that of the narrowcast networks launched during the late 1970s, would come to represent a compromise between cable's "promise" to serve niche interests and television's overall economic need to draw the largest possible audiences.

Conclusions

In 1972 Ralph Lee Smith, in *The Wired Nation,* wrote:

> There is still enough flexibility in cable TV to create national electronics highways in accordance with any pattern the nation may select, but if planning is delayed, and if federal and state policies are not created to turn plans into reality, short-term commercial considerations will dictate the form of the network. A wired nation so created will almost certainly fail to incorporate services that would be strongly in the public and national interest—just as the present broadcasting system has failed from lack of national planning and policy. Unfortunately, no branch of the federal government has evolved such planning, nor is any in the process of doing so. The time when effective national decisions can be made and implemented is running out. (83–84)

In fact, the 1970s witnessed the realization of precisely this scenario. Despite the warnings of Smith and others during cable's Blue Sky period, the only enduring federal policies affecting cable were those that allowed big business to use satellite technology to pursue its short-term profit goals.

Beginning in 1975, several well-backed corporations with established programming infrastructures launched cable networks. Pay-cable networks—including HBO, Showtime, and The Movie Channel—offered schedules of sports, movies, and entertainment specials. Superstations WTBS, WGN, and WOR were simply major-market independent stations whose signals had been uplinked to satellite. The religious networks CBN-Cable, PTL, and TBN had begun as networks of religious broadcast stations. Similarly, the Spanish-language network SIN/Galavision was launched by a company that owned several Spanish-language broadcast stations. Other early cable networks offered full-time schedules of established broadcast genres. These included the sports networks ESPN and MSG/USA and the children's networks Nickelodeon and Calliope (which was absorbed by USA).

With the telling exception of C-SPAN, the goal of almost all of the cable networks launched in the late 1970s was to draw large numbers of viewers in the fastest and cheapest way possible. They had been helped tremendously in this by the rapid removal of any regulations that might have curbed such growth. The cable industry's first use of satellites followed a decade and a half of regulatory uncertainty and miscues. The 1960s had been a period of heavy regulation for the emerging cable industry—in many ways a result of fear about cable's perceived encroachment on the established broadcast television industry. Severe regulations had been imposed with very little attention given to how cable might be encouraged to develop substantially different content from that of broadcast television. Yet efforts to liberalize cable regulation in the early 1970s, following several studies that touted cable's enormous potential for programming innovation, in many ways were fraught with just as much confusion and misjudgment as those in the previous decade had been. Zealous policymakers passed extremely stringent requirements for improving cable service—many of which, cable operators claimed, simply could not be implemented. The FCC, as well as various federal courts, generally saw the industry's claims as valid. As a consequence, throughout the 1970s, whenever a particular regulation seemed an unreasonable burden on cable systems, it was revoked. In very few instances were the rules modified rather than simply lifted, and little consideration seems to have been given to the reasons for having made the rules in the first place.

Along with a regulatory environment that was becoming less restrictive, limitations on the use of satellite technology were virtually eliminated in the early 1970s. There was little delay in seeing outcomes of this policy, since the cable industry rapidly embraced the new technology. HBO's early satellite debut signaled a gloomy prognosis for any terrestrially based networks. They simply could not attain the economies of scale to produce or obtain the high-budget programming needed to compete with satellite-carried networks. This, in conjunction with the *Midwest Video II* decision, struck a crippling blow to efforts to initiate local cable programming on a widespread basis. Also, because no controls were instituted to ensure subsidies for narrowcast networks, the future for these types of programming on cable would be determined by the interests of those who could finance them, by the number of viewers they could draw, and by program production or acquisition costs. In the decade to follow, many of the more innovative narrowcast networks, particularly the so-called culture networks, would fail due to lack of audience and advertising revenue. Others would have to adjust their schedules so as to have a broader appeal. In most instances, established broadcast television genres proved to be the safest bet for accomplishing this. While some of the networks that emerged in the early 1980s could be considered of high social value, hardly any of them introduced new types of programming to television audiences. Chapter 5 looks at the categories of cable programming that dominated the period from 1980 to 1995. Chapter 6 discusses the unique and innovative scheduling and promotional strategies cable networks developed as ways to distinguish their fare from that of broadcast television.

Broadcast Television's Resource-Starved Imitator, 1980–1995 PART I

As the previous chapters demonstrate, the U.S. cable industry evolved considerably in its first three decades—from a rural retransmission medium to a multichannel supplement to broadcast television. This reflects the coming together of a distinct industry as well as the increasing consolidation of operations within that industry; as cable operators increasingly shared profit-generating ideas, cable increasingly carved out its own niche within the larger entertainment industry. It also reflects a regulatory climate in which a fledgling industry grappled with continually shifting constraints on its growth. Even though the 1980s and the 1990s were a time of relative leniency in terms of programming choice and technological development, we cannot overlook the precedents that lingered from a time of greater restriction. This chapter and the next move in a different direction methodologically, attempting to analyze satellite cable's program sources and selections more than to provide a chronological history of these decades. However, the foregoing historical material is essential to understanding cable's inability to innovate along the lines laid out by the Blue Sky visionaries: satellite cable did not begin with a blank slate—either in terms of programming resources or in terms of audience expectations.

The industry's growth during the late 1970s is particularly striking. Although the increase in the number of cable systems between 1975 and 1980—from 3,506 to 4,225—was not significantly greater than what had taken place between 1970 and 1975, *subscriber numbers* grew at a remarkable rate. Basic cable subscribership alone went from 9.2 million in 1975 to 17.7 million in 1980; the rise in the number of pay subscribers was even more dramatic. The growth in subscribership relative to total number of systems was due primarily to construction of cable systems in larger communities—in other words, markets already well served by

Table 1

YEAR	NUMBER OF LOCAL CABLE SYSTEMS
1975	3,506
1980	4,225
1985	6,600
1990	9,575
1995	11,218

Source: *Television and Cable Factbook.*
Also available from NCTA website: *http://ncta.cyberserv.com/qs/user_pages/CableIndustryAtAGlance.cfm*

Table 2

YEAR	BASIC CABLE SUBSCRIBERS (IN MILLIONS, ROUNDED TO NEAREST .1 MILLION)
1975	9.2
1980	17.7
1985	39.9
1990	54.9
1995	62.9

Source: *Cable Television Developments.*
Current data now available at: *http://ncta.cyberserv.com/qs/user_pages/CableIndustryAtAGlance.cfm.*

broadcast television. Since cable, by this point, had more to offer urban dwellers than simply retransmitted broadcast signals and (occasionally) local origination programming, its days of being simply "a rural curiosity" were over. This growth trend would only continue over the next two decades.

By early 1980 cable operators across the nation were able to offer their customers three superstations (WTBS-Atlanta, WGN-Chicago, WOR–New York); Pat Robertson's CBN-Cable; Jim and Tammy Faye Bakker's PTL; the Spanish-language network Univision/Galavision; the sports network ESPN; Nickelodeon for children; C-SPAN, the public affairs network; and premium networks including The Movie Channel, HBO, and Showtime. During 1980–81 more than a dozen additional networks were launched, including BET, USA, Cinemax, Bravo, The Learning Channel, CNN, MTV, and several others. Nonetheless, this rapidly growing selection of channels did not represent the range of specialty networks so many Blue Sky visionaries had proposed. Rather, it represented a range of market-dictated compromises—based on funding sources, popularity with audiences and advertisers, and available programming.

At one extreme was C-SPAN, with a unique funding arrangement that made it largely independent of the programming constraints imposed by, and on behalf of, advertisers. C-SPAN came closest to fulfilling the visions of Blue Sky, but (as discussed in the previous chapter) it was hardly a typical basic cable network. At the other extreme were the superstations, which, by their very definition, were inextricably linked to the conventions of broadcast television. Most of the successful early cable networks fell somewhere between these two extremes. Perhaps they had found a viable market niche that was underserved (BET, Nickelodeon) or that represented a highly popular broadcast genre (ESPN, CNN). Or, perhaps, they had an ability to draw from nontraditional funding sources and offer a more eclectic scheduling mix (CBN-C, PTL).

Regardless of whether or not these early networks appeared to serve specific audience constituencies, most of them relied heavily on program genres—often actual programs—already proven successful on broadcast television. Typically, these consisted of movies or off-network reruns. Traditional broadcast genres including news, sports, and children's programs also found a home on cable—especially when the programs could be produced on relatively low budgets. This only became more apparent during the 1980s. There appear to be two major explanations for cable's ongoing resemblance to broadcast television at this stage: one economic and the other cultural. At the economic level, uplinking to satellite was a major expense for cable networks, and the additional costs associated with the development of new programming might have put them out of business. At the very least, the networks enjoyed much better economies of scale with broadcast-type programming, which was known to have widespread appeal. Thus, unless a network had an unusual source of funding, such as C-SPAN's public service contributions from cable MSOs, it had little reason to use programming that was not inexpensive, familiar, and already popular with audiences.

As discussed in Chapter 4, the situation might have been different if cable regulation had proceeded along a less troubled path in the decades prior to the introduction of satellites. In fact, though, cable had gone very quickly from being a retransmission medium virtually banned from developing its own programming to being the promised multichannel solution to the inadequacies of broadcast television. During the early

1970s government regulators had enacted various rules designed to foster the development of original cable programming at both the community and the national levels. But the rules did not end up having this effect. Cable operators had complained that the provisions promoting original programming posed an intolerable technical and financial burden, and therefore the rules were lifted, one by one. Meanwhile, throughout the 1970s the cable industry was given more and more freedom to expand its use of broadcast-derived programming—the types of programming that would come to shape cable's identity during the 1980s and 1990s. By 1980 virtually no federal guidelines existed for cable programming content. And the only barriers to entry in the satellite market were economic constraints. Therefore, the parties with the strongest incentives to form satellite-carried cable networks were those with the deepest pockets, rather than those with the most innovative or public service–oriented programming plans.

A more complex set of cultural mechanisms was also at work in delaying cable's move away from broadcast-type programming. These are related to the notion that television established itself, very early in its history, as a locus of common stories and shared understanding. Over the course of more than three decades, Americans developed a familiarity with, and reliance on, three major suppliers of television programming. The simple fact of having only three widely available programming sources is of course conducive to the formation of a common cultural agenda. Add to this the oligopolistic character of NBC, CBS, and ABC—which, as Barry Litman (1990) explains, has led to various common industrial behaviors—and the likelihood of overlapping program categories and content seems obvious (115–144). To give one example, nearly every American is deeply familiar with the basic narrative structure of the domestic situation comedy. Yet it would be virtually impossible to attribute the sitcom's "invention" or "discovery" to any one of the three networks, since all have contributed to the evolution of this popular genre. To give another example, historically there has been only minimal divergence among the nightly newscasts of the three networks: each day's 18–20 minutes of actual news somehow end up covering mostly the same material, even though the actual range of possible news stories is limitless. As Herbert J. Gans (1980) observed, the main variations in network newscasts have tended to be in the area of editorials—content intended more to give each network its own marketing cachet than to disrupt the status quo. This situation did not change in the years following Gans's observation.

So, although many American citizens had been upholding the benefits of cable as a niche-interest medium ever since the years of Blue Sky, it seems likely that most of these people also would have felt disoriented by any major deviation from their long-established viewing habits. Perhaps they would have sensed this as being left out of the "cultural conversation," for indeed, many of the topics we discuss daily with friends, relatives, and coworkers are derived from recent television viewing. This is not to say that all audience members watch television for the same reasons, or that we all take away the same understandings. Rather, as Horace Newcomb and Paul M. Hirsch (1987) explain it, "the television text functions as a cultural forum in which important cultural topics may be considered" (460). There is plenty of evidence that the emerging cable industry itself—at least some of its players—was willing to provide serious alternatives to broadcast programming, as will be discussed in Chapter 6. However, the inevitable reality of unfamiliar faces and lower-budget production styles in such programming would have come as an unpleasant surprise to anyone familiar with the well-funded programming of the broadcast networks.

The goal of this chapter, then, is to establish the degree to which satellite cable relied on the conventions and programming of broadcast television during the 1980s and early 1990s. This is a largely descriptive project, intended to set the stage for Chapter 6, which identifies and discusses areas in which cable was able to innovate and expand beyond the boundaries set by its predecessor medium during these years. These two chapters together reveal what is probably the most telling aspect of modern cable's programming history: that the recycling or imitating of broadcast-type programming not only sustained most cable networks during their start-up years, but in many cases also proved popular enough to warrant continued use—*along with* more original cable programming—long after those cable networks had begun to make profits.

The Television Landscape since 1980

Before beginning an analysis of cable programming developments since 1980, it is important to look at the larger American entertainment environment in which modern cable developed. The effects of regulatory leniency and free-market competition definitely have not been limited to the cable industry; mergers and buyouts permeated all of corporate America during the 1980s and 1990s. Since the early 1980s, entertainment industries have ceased to be centered around discrete media, as they were in previous decades. Instead, huge media conglomerates have come to encompass such diverse industries as movies, broadcast radio and television, cable, home video, music recording, book publishing, and even theme parks—resulting in the use of centralized management structures and media cross-promotion. The buzzword of the late-twentieth-century media industries was "synergy," as large media conglomerates strove to combine an ever more diverse array of media-related products and services under their corporate umbrellas.

Cable became both horizontally and vertically integrated in this environment, as both local cable systems and national cable networks were acquired by massive corporations such as Viacom and Time-Warner.[1] The financial resources of these corporate parents offered the potential for funding original cable programming (as was the case with HBO). These synergistic media corporations also supplied the cable networks they controlled with major movie and television syndication libraries, contributing significantly to cable's existing reliance on recycled programming material. In turn, cable offered syndicated program suppliers one more distribution/exhibition window for their products, creating an incentive to build even larger libraries.

Of course, cable was only part of a larger television environment, in which a variety of new television outlets sought inexpensive programming material for the short term. Most notably, in 1982, the FCC revised its broadcast television licensing policy, allowing the total number of independent stations to grow to 260 by 1986, triple the number that had existed in the previous decade (Downing 1990, 30). A major consequence of this was the formation, in 1986, of Rupert Murdoch's FOX television network, which would prove to be serious competition both for established broadcast networks and for emerging cable networks. By only its third year of operation, FOX was reaching 90 percent of U.S. households (Grover and Duffy 1990, 114). FOX affiliates, other independent stations, and cable networks together created a huge demand for syndicated programming. In turn, this demand encouraged network producers to experiment with more pilots per season and more episodes per series, thus generating an ever-larger stockpile of recyclable program material to supply the new programming outlets.

During the 1980s Americans' television viewing began to be shaped by technologies such as remote control devices and VCRs. These allowed audiences an unprecedented degree of control regarding the hours when television could be viewed and the amounts of time spent with individual programs (and commercials). As will be discussed throughout the rest of this book, technologies such as these, complemented by cable's multiple-channel viewing environment, prompted the development of new programming and scheduling strategies. Moreover, the growing presence of home VCRs brought about the home video phenomenon— yet another distribution window for movies and, increasingly, television programs. Like the new broadcast outlets mentioned above, home video both competes for cable's viewership and contributes to increased demand for material for all distribution outlets, including cable.

Cable's role in this new media scenario seems clear: to complement existing and emerging technologies, not to supplant them. A major restructuring of cable's regulatory framework, as well as sets of clearly defined goals, would have been needed to alter a programming trajectory begun when the sole purpose of cable (as CATV) was to retransmit broadcast signals. However, policymakers failed to accomplish this. Instead, parties with the necessary financing and programming infrastructures were given every incentive to start satellite networks as quickly and cheaply as possible. This meant that most networks drew extensively from recycled programming fare, such as old movies and off-network reruns. Even original programming tended to remain well within established television genres, such as sports and children's programming. Thus, a powerful programming precedent was set during satellite cable's earliest years: cable would become an extension of broadcast television, rather than taking a different course from it as the Blue Sky visionaries had intended.

The Persistence of Broadcast Programming: The Superstation and Its Followers

The overarching characteristic of modern basic cable is its continued resemblance to and dependence on broadcast television. During the 1980s and early 1990s old movies, off-network reruns, and sports constituted the bulk of cable programming. If any single feature of modern cable could be identified as evidence of this ongoing relationship, it is the enduring popularity of the cable superstation. As discussed earlier, a superstation is an independent major-market broadcast station whose signal has been uplinked to satellite by a common carrier for nationwide (or, sometimes, continent-wide) distribution. By the early 1980s four cable superstations were available nationally: WTBS-Atlanta, WGN-Chicago, WOR–New York, and WPIX–New York (*Cable Television Developments*). The role of these modern superstations is essentially the same as that of

Table 3
Cable Carriage of Major-Market Independent Stations/Superstations

YEAR	WGN-CHICAGO		WSBK-BOSTON		WPIX–NEW YORK	
	Systems	Subscribers	Systems	Subscribers	Systems	Subscribers
1970	41	86,800	10	N/A	50	200,000
1982	1,035	3,456,000	110	1,700,000	279	2,603,841
1995	N/A	N/A	350	4,100,000	416	4,600,000

Source: *Broadcasting Yearbook, Broadcasting & Cable Yearbook*

the major-market independent stations that first were carried via microwave to small CATV systems during the late 1950s and early 1960s. Whether distributed by microwave or by satellite, the main selling point of these independent stations always has been sports coverage (followed by syndicated movies and off-network series). A 1983 *Broadcasting* article noted that the market value of major-market independent stations was approaching that of network affiliates—largely because of their desirable programming lineups.[2] It is no wonder, then, that these stations would make popular cable channels as well.

Like the early CATV entrepreneurs who built elaborate microwave networks to import the signals of major-market independent stations, Ted Turner came to realize the value of this type of channel to cable operators. By the mid-1970s microwave carriage of WTCG, his Atlanta independent station, had begun to spread throughout Georgia and into neighboring states. Wanting to play an active role in spreading the station's coverage even farther, Turner acquired a financial interest in satellite distribution. Initially, his intention in adopting the new technology was merely to facilitate his station's reception in the South (Vaughan 1978, 38). But he found that a benefit to this mode of distribution was that the large area covered by a satellite footprint enabled reception in more distant locations—as far away as Alaska. For this reason, WTCG/WTBS, the station that would in 1976 become superstation TBS, rapidly gained popularity nationwide. Several superstations followed Turner's station to satellite carriage during the late 1970s without diminishing the demand for this type of cable network.

As of the mid-1980s some analysts believed that superstations, in spite of their continued popularity, still represented a transitional phase of cable programming development and soon would give way to more specialized program outlets. It was believed that truly national basic cable networks such as ESPN, American Movie Classics, and Nick at Nite could provide continuous coverage of the various program genres that had made the superstations so successful.[3] These predictions were inaccurate, though. Many cable-only networks became successful during the 1980s, particularly those that catered to a range of viewing interests. But superstations continued to thrive alongside them and, in fact, increased in number. In the late 1980s Eastern Microwave uplinked WSBK-Boston and United Video uplinked KTLA–Los Angeles (both of which already boasted extensive terrestrial carriage).

Even a 1990 reimposition of the syndicated exclusivity (syndex) rules, requiring cable systems to black out superstation programs that duplicate programs shown on local broadcast stations, did little to diminish superstations' popularity. Major common carriers even began to consider it a reasonable expense to offer blackout-replacement programming for most of the superstations they carried. Ted Turner, for example, wasted no time in offering cable operators a guarantee of national exclusivity for the programs shown on his superstation.[4] And United Video advised cable operators, "Just send every blackout notice you receive to our SyndEXPERTs, and we'll make sure you're in full compliance with any of your system's programming from any source."[5]

Passive superstations have continued to serve as ready-made cable networks—to the benefit of those who uplink their signals.[6] One might expect that Turner's success with WTBS, the only *active* superstation, would have prompted other popular independent stations to pursue cable viewership more aggressively, rather than continuing to be uplinked by unaffiliated common carriers. By managing their own satellite carriage, the independent stations would have been able to pursue lucrative national advertising deals. Nonetheless, representatives of most superstations have expressed a desire to keep the local market as their top priority. As WGN vice president and general manager Dennis FitzSimmons explained in 1989, cable viewership is "a nice bonus to have, but the only thing we sell on that basis is the Chicago Cubs baseball telecasts. We need to be competitive in Chicago first. We're approaching close to a $600 million marketplace here."[7] This sentiment was echoed a few years later by WSBK's program director, Meg LaVigne, and director of research, Lee Kinberg, who attributed the Boston superstation's success to the idea that "what Boston likes is what a lot of other people like, as well."[8]

The superstation boom of the late 1980s tells us quite a bit about the nature of cable viewing—notably Americans' insatiable appetite for broadcast-type fare. In the 1980s cable operators had many incentives to discontinue their carriage of superstation signals. In addition to the satellite fees and copyright royalties they were required to pay, and the imminent reimposition of the syndex rules, operators were faced with increasingly tight channel capacity. Replacing superstations with cable-only basic services should have seemed like the solution to several problems. Yet this obviously did not occur.

It is debatable whether or not Ted Turner himself was among those predicting the demise of the superstation. But there was speculation around 1988 that the debut of his TNT network in the fall of that year was an attempt to offer a cable-only version of TBS. Turner did, in fact, suggest that operators might substitute the new service for a distant signal (though presumably not that of TBS itself).[9] One might argue more persuasively, though, that with TNT Turner was drawing from the fortunes of his superstation to create a basic cable network that more closely approximated the programming lineups of cable's premium services. Of course, Turner planned to use the classic films in his recently acquired MGM library. He also planned original productions including biography (Michelangelo, Billy the Kid, Donald Trump) and original sequels to such classics as *An American in Paris* and *The Time Machine*.[10] Time has shown that it is precisely these sorts of original productions, along with sports and reruns, that have made TNT popular. In short, it seems that the perceptive Turner was planning more for a future in which cable systems would be able to accommodate many more channels than for a future in which the superstation format would actually lose its popularity.

Cutting Programming Expenditures

Although the endurance of superstations is the most obvious evidence of broadcast programming's lasting presence on cable, cable-only networks also have exhibited a strong reliance on broadcast-type genres and program sources. Initially treated as a short-term way to economize and build financial assets, syndicated movies and television reruns have remained popular and profitable scheduling components for many cable networks. More recently when the women's network Lifetime added *Cagney & Lacey* to its schedule, the Nielsen rating for that time slot (previously occupied by a portion of a movie) increased by 43 percent. Even more remarkably, The Family Channel (formerly CBN-Cable) replaced *Country Music Spotlight* and a religious program called *In Touch* with a two-hour block of *Columbo* reruns and experienced a 332 percent increase in ratings for the time slot. Anticipating similar ratings success, in 1996 TBS paid a record $1.2 million per episode for *ER* reruns.[11] Joseph Turow (1997) points out that movies and off-network reruns have played a major role in defining the programming "brands" for which cable networks are recognized. Original programs are more directly associated with the cable networks that show them and garner any critical recognition those networks might receive, but it is the secondhand material that draws viewers in the first place (104). As USA's programming vice president Neil Hoffman remarked, "When viewers see *Quantum Leap,* they know the show instantly and it brings them to our channel. Once they're there, we introduce them to the original programming we produce" (Katz 1993, 28–31).

Even a percentage of cable's "new" programming is actually recycled. For example, during the 1980s, foreign programming emerged as a major supplier to the U.S. cable market. In particular, several networks have used programming originally produced for British television. BBC movies and series have a reputation for "quality" in the United States, primarily because of their association with PBS, and easily fit the schedules of arts networks like Bravo. In spring 1982 USA acquired the rights to *Coronation Street,* a long-running drama produced by Granada Television (a British production company). A few months later, it acquired the rights to *Brideshead Revisited,* another popular Granada production. Premium networks like HBO, whose viewers pay a substantial monthly fee for programming not available on U.S. broadcast television, have also had success with British programs.

Other English-speaking countries have also supplied programming to U.S. cable networks. For example, when The Discovery Channel debuted in June 1985, it saved money by scheduling mostly documentary reruns originally produced by foreign companies for foreign markets. These included the BBC, the Canadian Broadcasting Corporation, the Australian Broadcasting Corporation, Granada Television, TV Ontario, and the National Film Board of Canada. At the time, Discovery claimed that 75 percent of its programming had never been seen on American television.

The use of foreign programming has not been limited to what is available in English, either. In February 1987, concurrent with ABC's airing of the made-for-TV movie *Amerika* about life in the United States following a Soviet takeover, Discovery aired 66 hours of Soviet television programs, taken directly off satellite. In May 1988 it aired portions of the Soviet news show *Vremya* to coincide with the Reagan-Gorbachev summit. And one way C-SPAN was able to expand its government affairs programming during the 1980s was by adding coverage of foreign governments, including the Canadian and British parliaments and various government entities in France.[12]

These are just a few of the many examples of cable's use of foreign programming. In addition, several cable networks have entered into coproduction arrangements with foreign production companies. For example, the acclaimed documentary miniseries, *The Trials of Life*, which appeared on TBS in 1991, was coproduced by Turner Broadcasting, the BBC, and the Australian Broadcasting Corporation. And during the late 1980s and early 1990s The Family Channel began to coproduce some of its series programming with Canadian companies. The desirability of multinational coproductions for U.S. cable networks should not be surprising given the economics of producing for television. Television programs rarely earn profits when first shown; in some cases it takes years of repeat showings—as is likely to be the case with a lesser-known cable network. Any producer—and certainly one producing for cable specifically— would have good reason to consider potential revenues from foreign syndication in addition to domestic first-run and syndication revenues.

The 1980s also saw cable networks using increasing amounts of originally produced programming, though these were not always the types of original programming the Blue Sky idealists had recommended in the late 1960s and early 1970s. Operator-produced local origination programming and PEG access continued to be a presence on many local cable systems, but they did not make cable into the niche-oriented or locally centered medium that regulatory visionaries had intended. Many communities with production facilities are larger cities that also are well served by broadcast television. Most communities, however—large and small—have had little more local programming than they did in the 1950s. Thus, cable in no way remedied the FCC's flawed broadcast license allocation policy. Furthermore, with generally low production values and little publicity, those access programs that have been produced have not tended to draw large numbers of viewers. A strange irony of access programming is that a portion of its viewers apparently watch it primarily to laugh at its bizarre subject matter and low production values.[13]

During the early 1980s, some cable networks tested single-sponsor programming—a funding arrangement similar to those used by some local cable systems in the early 1970s as a way to meet the FCC's program origination requirement. For instance, starting in 1981, Bristol-Myers produced a series of "health-oriented magazine format" programs called *Alive and Well* for USA. This production arrangement benefited both the sponsor and the fledgling cable network, since *Alive and Well*'s production costs were under $20,000 per episode and each episode included 10 minutes of advertising time, five for Bristol-Myers and five for USA. Although narrowcasting was not the specific goal in this case, USA president Kay Koplovitz pointed out that health-oriented programs such as this could complement and build upon USA's image as a sports programming outlet.[14] USA also used programs sponsored individually by Proctor & Gamble, Clorox, Hallmark, and Mazda. Other cable networks also experimented with the single-sponsor format during the early 1980s, including programs sponsored by Pfizer on Lifetime, by General Foods on BET, and by Exxon and Quaker Oats on the short-lived arts network CBS Cable.

This practice would continue. As Carolyn Bronstein points out, Lifetime depended on major sponsorship and coproduction agreements with pharmaceutical and household products corporations throughout the 1990s. Proctor & Gamble, as the official sponsor of the long-running show *What Every Baby Knows* (1984 –), holds primary control of content decisions affecting the program (Bronstein 1994–95, 220). And when Lifetime decided to air new episodes of the former NBC series *The Days and Nights of Molly Dodd* in the late 1980s, it entered into a sponsorship agreement with Bristol-Myers that would allow the sponsor's products to be featured in the show.[15]

It seems apparent that, although they may have shied away from buying time on cable networks for traditional, broadcast-type commercials, advertisers have shown some interest in using cable to test new formats and scheduling strategies. Because cable sponsorship was so inexpensive during the early 1980s, corporations were able to experiment with non-traditional commercial lengths and formats. Quaker Oats, for example, ran a 106-second commercial cut from an old industrial film during CBS Cable's first evening of programming.[16]

Although cable advertising time eventually grew too expensive for the single-sponsor format to enter widespread use, cable continued to be a bargain compared to broadcast network television. It also holds the potential for more directly targeting specific audiences, making single-sponsor programming desirable under certain circumstances. One example is the travel documentaries used by Discovery, The Learning Channel, and The Travel Channel. Another example is the "Making of . . ." genre: half-hour specials used to promote soon-to-be-released theatrical movies. These commonly appear on premium networks that also hold the first television rights to the movies. MTV and E! Entertainment Television also use these programs to supplement their schedules.[17]

Another source of original cable programming worth mentioning is independently produced film and video, a source that has benefited little-known artists as well as fledgling cable networks. The need to fill 24-hour programming days, as well as the desire to distinguish themselves from competitors, has prompted several cable networks to seek out independently produced program material. This was particularly true of the various cultural networks that were launched in the early 1980s. In fact, one of these, Bravo (along with its spin-off pay service, the Independent Film Channel), has continued to enjoy a reputation for exposing cable viewers to lesser-known independent productions. Also, since shorter films can be used to fill gaps between feature-length productions, these gained some popularity on commercial-free movie networks.

Alternative sponsorship and production arrangements such as those described above have supplied cable networks with program types not seen on broadcast television, but these are used much too infrequently to be considered characteristic cable programming strategies. The vast majority of original cable programming has consisted of expanded versions of established broadcast genres—initially produced on very tight budgets, but otherwise similar in both sponsorship and narrative conventions to their broadcast counterparts. This is a far more reliable way to meet the primary demand of open-entry competition: drawing the largest audiences at the lowest cost. While narrowcasting did not come to dominate cable programming in the way that had been expected, some cable networks have been able to specialize successfully by using popular broadcast program genres—most notably movies, news, and sports.

The Popularity and Persistence of Broadcast Genres

By the early 1980s sports enthusiasts had access to selected sports shown on pay-cable networks like HBO, on superstations, and on more than a dozen regional sports networks.[18] Most notably, though, two 24-hour national sports networks, ESPN and USA, also were operating. Even this early in satellite cable history, ESPN and USA had managed to acquire the rights to a number of major professional and college events. In producing their sports programming, the cable networks imitated the production conventions of network sports programming—though at this stage, cable's weaker economic status was evident in the production quality. *TV Guide* writer Roger Director pointed out that although early cable sports announcers differed little from their broadcast network counterparts in terms of skill level and experience, they often lacked the high-budget technical support enjoyed by their broadcast network counterparts. According to Director (1982), "[The] production budget for one *Thursday Night Baseball* telecast (not including rights fees) runs to $15,000. This is roughly the same amount ESPN spends to cover a college football game. But it's just one-tenth of what a network will spend on the same event."

The production challenges eventually pushed ESPN and USA in two different directions. USA quickly moved from being primarily a sports network to being more of a general entertainment network, with the addition of a range of children's programs, health programs, business information, movies, and drama/action shows. Sports continued to play a small role in its programming strategy, but by the mid-1980s, few people would have described USA as a sports network specifically. In contrast, ESPN grew into the major supplier of televised sports. Recall that the network had begun with a few key sports events, primarily those that the broadcast networks had overlooked or not shown in their entirety. The rest of the schedule was filled with more obscure sports such as fencing, water polo, and Slo-Pitch softball (Waters and Wilson 1979, 124). Through the 1980s, though, ESPN began a practice of striking exclusivity agreements with major sports leagues. For example, in August 1985 ESPN acquired exclusive cable rights to National Hockey League games. In late 1987 it secured the rights to an eight-game National Football League package. And in early 1989 it acquired the four-year rights to show Major League Baseball games four nights a week.[19] By the early 1990s the 24-hour-a-day sports network had developed a trademark schedule that combined major sports with more eclectic or regional events (ranging from high school play-off events to mountain biking)— often using the former to draw new audiences for the latter. In 1992 ESPN had enough name recognition, income, and carriage to spin off a second network, ESPN2, to accommodate and encourage the growing demand for its sports programming (in the late 1990s, it would also spin off ESPNews, ESPN Classic, and ESPN International).[20]

News, like sports, has been one of broadcast television's most popular and entrenched genres. A wide cross-section of viewers have need for up-to-date news programming at varying times throughout the day. Thus, the extensive coverage provided by a dedicated cable network can compensate for the lower production values it must endure during its risky start-up period. And like sports, current events offer a virtually limitless supply of novel program material, even without superlative production values. This was the basis on which Ted Turner launched Cable News Network (CNN), a 24-hour news network, in 1981. Several writers have discussed how Turner and his staff were able to compensate for a limited production budget by enlisting bare sets and exposed technical equipment as signifiers of an open newsroom, thereby connoting a sense of up-to-the-minute news.[21] In addition to regular newscasts, CNN began using the talk show format—relatively inexpensive in-house productions that complement newscasts and add variety to the schedule. Thus, by concentrating on extensive and varied news coverage more than on lavish presentation, CNN quickly became both a highly rated cable network and viable competition for broadcast network news.

Other networks that have specialized successfully in news and information, using short, frequently repeated program segments, include CNN Headline News (launched in 1982), Financial News Network (early 1980s), Weather Channel (1982), CNBC (1989), CNN/fn (1995), and MSNBC (1996).[22] Similar to CNN's news updates, Weather Channel's weather bulletins and the various financial networks' business information can be updated continually throughout the day, making these networks' content more valuable to viewers than that of broadcast newscasts. Although local broadcast stations have increased the number of newscasts per day since the 1980s (no doubt in efforts to stay competitive with cable networks), at the time of CNN's debut most local stations had newscasts only once or twice daily. Full-service cable news networks also replaced videotext-based news services like UPI's North American Newstime and Reuters's NEWS-VIEW, which had been operating in some form since the 1960s.

With the advent of the continuous news networks, cable service became a more marketable package overall. Still, the news bulletins are not the type of cable programming that encourages sustained viewing. The "complete" cable package continued to be anchored by acquired programming. And of the various categories of acquired programming, theatrical film has always provided a strong foundation for cable service.

Hollywood Movies on Cable

The notion that consumers would be willing to pay a substantial monthly fee for recent, high-quality, commercial-free movies actually predates satellite cable by at least two decades. What was tried by the various pay-TV enterprises of the 1950s and 1960s would be perfected by HBO, Showtime, and other cable networks in the 1980s and 1990s. But pay-cable networks faced some significant challenges during their early years. While movies present themselves as a popular and ready-made programming source, their acquisition can be at least as difficult as original program production. Sometimes, acquiring movies for cable has meant cable networks' actual involvement (financial and otherwise) in producing movies for theatrical release.

Throughout the 1980s HBO/Cinemax and Showtime/The Movie Channel vied for exclusive pay-TV rights to the approximately 150 major feature films released annually by Hollywood studios. Cable rights to movies were secured in one of several ways: whole or partial ownership in a movie studio, prebuying (i.e., investment in one or more movies), or joint productions. HBO had begun the practice of prebuying in 1976; in 1980 it scored a coup by securing the rights to *On Golden Pond* through a prebuy. The cable network then struck major release deals with Columbia pictures in 1981 and 1982. Also in 1982 it joined with Columbia and CBS Inc. to form Tri-Star Pictures, a major Hollywood studio.

Over the years, HBO has had many other arrangements with Hollywood studios that have allowed it favorable, if not exclusive, cable rights to movies. Trailing only a few paces behind was Showtime, which engaged in some lucrative early exclusivity deals of its own. In December 1983 Showtime signed a $600–700 million deal with Paramount, which guaranteed the pay network 75 movies over five years.[23] Beginning in 1985, it also negotiated several prerelease agreements with studios.[24] In fall 1986 Orion, the last studio to sign an exclusivity deal with cable, signed with Showtime/The Movie Channel.[25]

The competition between these two main pay-cable entities was heated, but for several years no other cable networks had the resources to enter the bidding. In October 1989, however, USA paid Buena Vista Television (Disney's syndication company) $52 million for a package of Disney theatrical features. At the time, USA's president Kay Koplowitz commented that "this marks the first time a basic cable network has preempted the entire syndication market on a major motion picture package. [It] reflects our commitment to acquire the very best, most desirable movie product."[26] Not to be outdone, a few weeks later Lifetime bought a 23-film package from Orion, estimated to have been worth $40-50 million.[27]

Ted Turner superseded both of these efforts with an aggressive acquisitions policy for his growing family of cable networks. Never more than a step ahead of the insurmountable debt that overcame other cable entrepreneurs of the 1980s, Turner had set out to buy as many programming sources as possible. Already the owner of the Atlanta Braves, whose games provided the foundation for his superstation, Turner went on to even bigger ventures in the late 1980s and early 1990s. He bought the MGM film library in 1986, and in the years to follow either started or acquired the following production companies: New Line Cinema, Castle Rock Entertainment, and Hanna-Barbera Productions.[28]

When HBO became part of the giant Time-Warner empire in 1989, it gained access to Warner Bros. movies as well as a massive distribution mechanism for its own productions. In 1989, just a few years after it acquired Showtime, Viacom launched a studio, Viacom Pictures, dedicated to producing lower-budget movies for the pay-cable network.[29] And at the time of its launch, The Disney Channel's lineup contained about 40 percent movies from the Disney film library.[30] These are just a few examples of how media synergy, the elusive goal toward which all media conglomerates strive, has helped cable networks in various ways. Movie deals such as these made during the 1980s continued to fill the pages of the television trade press during the 1990s. This, of course, only fed the merger and acquisition mania that saw the joining of Viacom and Paramount (and later CBS), Disney and ABC, Time, Inc. and Warner Communications (and later America Online), and several others. Clearly, any reluctance on the part of Hollywood studios to test the waters of nonbroadcast television had dissipated. Cable both fed the new media environment and profited from it. And it is because of this that modern cable was able to overcome one of the major obstacles that had plagued earlier forms of pay-TV dating back to the 1950s.

Yet cable was not the only media player vying for prominence during the 1980s and early 1990s. Perhaps the biggest challenge faced by any cable network whose reputation depended on movies during these years was the rise of the videocassette recorder for home movie viewing. In the mid-1980s subscriber numbers for premium cable services began to flatten as viewers took advantage of the ability to select their own movie titles and viewing times. The cable industry tried to tap into the appeal of on-demand movie viewing by introducing pay-per-view (PPV) channels to their systems. Pay-per-view had been lurking on the cable horizon since the early days of pay-TV. Several of the experimental systems of the 1950s and 1960s had tried to offer consumers the ability to pay directly for movies and special events programming through coin boxes, telephone lines, and other devices—all of which were fairly awkward for both operators and consumers. Modern cable technology improved the situation; among other things, it facilitated billing and allowed impulse buys of PPV events. On 25 September 1982 *Star Wars* became the first nationally distributed pay-per-view movie (on cable as well as broadcast pay-TV, which was still viable at the time). Within a few months there was major discussion in the cable industry about the potential impact of pay-per-view on cable networks, especially premium networks. In 1986, studies revealed that basic-only cable subscribers were buying 40 percent more PPV programming than those who subscribed to two or more premium services. Not surprisingly, many PPV customers were former premium channel subscribers.[31]

Of course, a major advantage cable networks continued to hold over home video and PPV was their ability to provide a continuous stream of programming for a flat monthly fee. As competition among new media technologies grew, cable networks—in particular the premium services, which were hit hardest by the new competition—began to claim new territory in the area of high-quality original programming. Cable's growing success in original programming was apparent by July 1988, when cable networks had 318 of the 5000 programs placed in competition for the Emmy Awards. Of these, HBO had 146, Showtime 69, Cinemax 29, USA 20, WTBS 16, A&E 13, CBN 12, Disney 6, MTV 4, and Nickelodeon 2.[32]

Original Cable Movies and Other Made-for-Cable Programming

HBO's early and well-funded entry into the satellite cable programming business already had paid off by the early 1980s—for the network itself and, arguably, for movie and television audiences in general. HBO has been the most pioneering producer of original cable programming over the years. As discussed in Chapter 4, HBO became a presence in the cable industry during the 1970s—giving it a clear advantage of incumbency over subsequently launched networks. Additionally, HBO's wealthy corporate parent, Time Inc. (later Time-Warner), provided resources that allowed it to innovate in programming long before it had recovered its start-up costs. By the 1980s HBO's production efforts were both lavish and prolific when compared with its premium and basic cable counterparts.

The Terry Fox Story, produced by HBO Pictures and first shown on HBO in 1983, was pay-cable's first original movie. During the 1980s the company went on to produce numerous other acclaimed movies such as *The Josephine Baker Story* (1991), the Oscar-winning *Down and Out in America* (1986), and the Emmy-winning *Dear America* (1987). HBO's original movies have been routine contenders for Emmys—due in part to the pay network's ability to take on controversial issues that basic cable, broadcast television, and even Hollywood movie studios have avoided (or at least downplayed). HBO's viewers are self-selected and have been willing to pay $10–20 per month for the pay service; if they were consistently offended by the programming, obviously they would discontinue the service. In the 1990s HBO began to make movies dealing with such problematic topics as abortion (*A Private Matter,* 1992; *If These Walls Could Talk,* 1996), AIDS (*And the Band Played On,* 1992), and institutionalized racism (*Miss Evers' Boys,* 1997; *Rosewood,* 1997).

HBO has also been innovative with specials and original series. The 1982 documentary special *She's Nobody's Baby: American Women in the Twentieth Century* won a Peabody Award. HBO's original series include the 1988 *Turner '88,* a collaboration between political cartoonist Garry Trudeau and film director Robert Altman, designed to coincide with the current presidential campaign. In 1997 HBO would introduce *Oz,* a controversial but critically acclaimed series about daily life in a maximum-security federal penitentiary.

Another indicator of the success of HBO's original productions has been their ability to draw audiences outside of HBO's own core viewership. Many HBO original movies are available for sale or rental. And HBO's series *Dream On* (1990–96) was shown on FOX affiliates while its newer episodes were still in their first-run release on cable. HBO also produced *Montana* (1990) for the basic cable network TNT. This was an adaptation of the Larry McMurtry novel and starred Gena Rowlands and Richard Crenna.

Analysts have noted the ever-growing importance of brand recognition to HBO's long-term success. By the early 1990s, with many popular and profitable cable networks in operation, HBO's early position of incumbency no longer provided a guarantee of success. In more recent years, the network has had to demonstrate repeatedly that it offers movies, series, sports, and entertainment specials not available elsewhere. Like HBO, Showtime has built up a substantial collection of original movies and series.

The original programming seen on pay networks like HBO, Showtime, and others certainly has been worthy of note, and has helped cable as a whole gain a level of respectability within the television programming market overall. Even people who do not wish to pay the steep monthly fees for these networks no doubt have heard about their award-winning programs. What is even more striking is the amount of original programming seen on basic cable networks. Even as early as 1990, some of the more long-standing (or at least well-funded) networks were turning out several original movies and/or series every season.

Unlike most of its basic cable counterparts, Nickelodeon's daytime schedule, as far back as the early 1980s, was all original programming—about half of which was produced in-house. Like the pay networks, Nickelodeon has had wealthy corporate parents to help fund its programming, first Warner-Amex and later Viacom. Nickelodeon has always boasted of its ability to give kids the kinds of programming they want to watch. It built its reputation around such shows as *You Can't Do That on Television,* described as a sort of "*Laugh-In* for children"; *Kids Writes,* in which a cast of five actors performed original material sent in by viewers; and *Livewire,* a talk show focusing on issues of importance to teenagers. Through the 1980s and early 1990s, Nickelodeon's program lineup was augmented and changed, but the focus on children's entertainment remained. Such programs as *Nick News* took an adult genre and made it appealing and appropriate for children. *Ren & Stimpy, Rugrats,* and *Doug* helped fuel the wave of cartoons that flooded television in the early 1990s. One thing that has been especially notable about Nickelodeon's original programming is the network's effort to serve every age group of its young audience—ranging from the Nick Jr. block for preschoolers to teen-oriented shows such as *Clarissa Explains It All.*

During the late 1980s and early 1990s CBN-Cable/The Family Channel also began to make a name for itself in the area of original children's programming. As detailed in promotional materials, some original Family Channel productions included in the 1991 schedule were:

- *Big Brother Jake:* starring Jake Steinfeld as a stuntman who gives up his career in order to return home and help his foster mom raise five kids.

- *Black Stallion:* action/adventure series based on the original Academy Award–winning film. Mickey Rooney reprises his role as the crusty, aged trainer.
- *Maniac Mansion:* (produced with Lucasfilms): a zany comedy starring Joe Flaherty as a fumbling scientist who lives in a mansion with his extended family.
- *Rin Tin Tin K-9 Cop:* action series featuring Rin Tin Tin as both man's best friend and canine crime fighter.
- *The New Zorro:* He's a masked swordsman, a defender of the poor, and a romantic hero.

The Family Channel's ability to produce original material was helped by the network's longevity and the resources of its parent company, CBN. This included access to the video production school at CBN's Regent University.

Most of USA's original programming has been in the area of drama/adventure series and movies. This is in keeping with its target audience of younger, typically male viewers. For example, in spring 1989, USA launched a series of original movies entitled "World Premiere Movies." The focus of the series, which was budgeted at $2.5–3 million, was action. As David Kenin, senior vice president for programming, explained, this was intended to counterprogram the "disease of the week" emphasis of broadcast television's original movies.[33] Hour-long series that have debuted on USA include *The Big Easy, Pacific Blue,* and *Silk Stalkings.*

Throughout the 1980s Turner Broadcasting System produced or coproduced history and nature documentaries for the superstation and later for Turner Network Television (TNT). Among the TBS standards is *National Geographic Explorer,* which has been coproduced with *National Geographic* magazine since the mid-1980s. TBS also introduced the popular children's cartoon *Captain Planet and the Planeteers* (produced by Turner subsidiary Hanna-Barbera) in 1990. TBS began airing original movies in the mid-1990s, often showcasing the work of well-known Hollywood actors, directors, and screenwriters. Some of the best known were *Cold Sassy Tree* (1989) starring Faye Dunaway, who also was executive producer; *Christmas in Connecticut* (1991), Arnold Schwarzenegger's directorial debut; and Ted Turner's "signature" Civil War epic, *Gettysburg* (1993). TNT's original movies and miniseries have been widely publicized and reviewed. Unlike most basic cable networks,

TNT has been able to draw from the resources of the Turner media empire, and later from corporate parent Time-Warner as well. This gave it a major competitive advantage in its early years. At least until the mid-1990s, TNT was the only basic cable network whose original movies could compete with those shown on pay-cable and broadcast networks.

Since the presence of original shows is one of the major ways to "brand" a cable network, these have also been extremely important to most cable networks. Even the more poorly funded networks managed to develop "signature" talk shows, music video shows, or other inexpensive program types during their early years. As will become evident in the following chapter, though, the original programming discussed above has been more the exception than the rule. Enhancing or reconfiguring preexisting program material has been a far more reliable way for most start-up cable networks to distinguish their schedules.

Conclusions

The 1980s were marked by a great deal of experimentation in cable programming, but what should be apparent by this point is that cable's most successful ventures were those that strayed the least from the standards and practices set by broadcast television. Perhaps it is not surprising that the late 1970s, satellite cable's earliest years, saw the rise of cable networks that filled their schedules with reruns, old movies, and sports. After all, there were no regulatory constraints to prevent them from using these economical and popular staples. But what is striking is that these practices continued to be successful into the highly competitive 1980s. Satellite cable pioneers like HBO, CBN-Cable (The Family Channel), and WTCG (Superstation TBS) continued to dominate the market in the 1980s. They were joined either by other general interest networks, like USA and TNT, or by those such as CNN, ESPN, and The Weather Channel that had found a popular broadcast genre to deal with in depth.

It is difficult to gauge the success of very early satellite cable networks using measures established for the broadcast television industry. The A. C. Nielsen Company will only provide its service to networks reaching at least 15 percent of U.S. households. As of late 1983, only seven basic cable networks met Nielsen's criteria: ESPN, WTBS, CBN-Cable, CNN, USA, and MTV.[34] More information was available in 1990, by which time more cable networks qualified for Nielsen ratings; and data about them thus was more precise. Ratings for successful cable networks during the period from 1 January through 2 November were as follows:

Table 4
Nielsen Ratings for Cable Networks in 1990

NETWORK	RATING	NETWORK	RATING
HBO	1.6	Discovery	.5
USA	1.3	Showtime	.5
TBS	1.3	MTV	.5
ESPN	1.2	A&E	.5
Lifetime	1.0	Disney Channel	.4
TNT	.9	CNN Headline News	.2
CNN	.7	BET	.1
Family Channel	.7	Weather Channel	.1
TNN	.6	FNN	.1
Cinemax	.6	VH1	.1
Nickelodeon/Nick at Nite	.5	129 other networks	2.8

Source: Nielsen Television Index (figures cited in Mahler 1990).

In comparison, ratings for broadcast networks and stations during the same 10-month period were as follows:

Table 5
Nielsen Ratings for Broadcast Networks and Independent Stations
in 1990

NETWORK	RATING	NETWORK	RATING
NBC	12.3	FOX	6.2
ABC	11.3	PBS	2.3
CBS	11.0	Independents	5.9

Source: Nielsen Television Index (figures cited in Mahler 1990).

These statistics show that cable networks were still dwarfed by broadcast television in 1990 (as they would continue to be). Yet this is due, at least in part, to the fact that the available audience was spread among so many of them. Clearly, cable as a whole *was* making inroads in the U.S. television programming landscape.

The 1980s had not witnessed the anticipated proliferation of specialty networks, though. As will be discussed in Chapter 6, even those networks that targeted specific audience constituencies (sports enthusiasts, African Americans, etc.) found themselves continually having to broaden their scope so as to capture the largest possible audience—precisely the imperative that has driven commercial broadcast television throughout its entire existence. It is not that the cable industry did not want to develop more narrowly targeted networks. In fact, such networks did begin to develop in the mid-1990s (e.g., the Golf Channel, My Pet TV, Television Food Network/Food Network). But during the 1980s and early 1990s most of these types of networks remained unsustainable.

When envisioning a short-term scenario in which cable would be a narrowcasting supplement to broadcast television, Blue Sky optimists may have failed to account for two important factors: cable networks' need to recover high start-up costs and the television audience's general reluctance to make radical changes in viewing habits. Certainly the early networks economized by filling their schedules with recycled programming. But they never could have succeeded without an audience willing to watch (or at least advertisers who believed there was an audience willing to watch).

In retrospect, though, the 1980s contributed more to making cable a specialized programming medium than was apparent at the time. Left to the forces of open-entry competition, cable could not possibly have shunned the advertiser-driven lowest-common-denominator programming imperative, given the high costs of production. And we can speculate about how the situation might have been different if government regulators had stepped in to guide cable programming in different directions. However, such speculation inevitably rests on an idealism that neglects the conservatism of the television audience, who might claim to want more variety and specialization on television, but in reality will "vote" for traditional fare when actually selecting channels.

It becomes clear when we observe the development of satellite cable programming that there *were* changes taking place—slowly and incrementally. The U.S. television audience has not been entirely unwilling to alter its viewing preferences, but given the number of years in which there was only a very limited selection of television programs, we should not be surprised that this has been a gradual process. One might go so far as to argue that the amount of time it took early cable networks to recover their start-up costs and begin producing original programming is no greater than the amount of time it took the U.S. television audience to make the new viewing options part of their channel "repertoires." Viewed this way, the fledgling cable networks of the 1980s did lay the foundation for the increasingly specialized program choices that developed in the 1990s.

The next chapter will look more closely at how, during the 1980s and early 1990s, cable networks made the sorts of programming and scheduling innovations that allowed them to carve out distinctive territory for themselves in the competitive environment of U.S. commercial television. The reliance on broadcast-type programming material posed a challenge for modern cable networks. They had to devise ways to present the secondhand programming in ways that distinguish their schedules from those of broadcast networks and stations. Some creative—and enduring—strategies resulted. Indeed, many of cable's short-term scheduling and promotional strategies not only remained in place long after cable networks began to make profits; they also have been hallmarks of television programming generally in the 1990s and beyond.

A Scheduling and Programming Innovator, 1980–1995 *PART II*

Today's cable networks unquestionably bear evidence of the medium's historical dependence on broadcast television—certainly more than policymakers of the 1960s and 1970s would have predicted or planned. Yet a consideration of modern cable programming practices also would not be complete without a look at how cable networks have differentiated themselves within the larger world of televised entertainment and information. In the highly competitive open-entry market situation that characterized television in the 1980s and 1990s, cable networks faced the significant challenge of making inexpensive and usually recycled types of programming seem as interesting and worthwhile as what viewers already could watch free of charge on broadcast stations. This was especially true in the case of basic cable networks such as USA, Nick at Nite, Comedy Central, The Family Channel, E! Entertainment Television, Arts & Entertainment, Lifetime, Black Entertainment Television, and others.

Although premium networks have been responsible for significant programming breakthroughs, by the 1980s most of them enjoyed financial advantages not available to the basic networks. Most premium networks had been in existence since the previous decade, so they had begun to recover start-up costs and had more resources to use on original programming. The additional revenues provided by the hefty monthly subscriber fees they charge also helped them in experimenting with longer, more elaborate, and more narrative-driven program genres. As discussed in earlier chapters, premium networks like HBO and Showtime set standards for various areas of original cable programming. In contrast, during the 1980s off-network reruns and subsequent-run movies continued to dominate the schedules of even the more successful basic networks, such as TNT, USA, and The Family Channel. Since basic networks had to develop ways to maximize the potential of inexpensive programming, this was the tier of cable programming in which the greatest number of packaging and scheduling innovations took place.

As discussed in the previous chapter, modern cable networks have developed some economical and inventive strategies for producing original programming, especially in popular genres such as news and sports. They also have explored some alternative sources for acquired programming. Nevertheless, some of cable's greatest programming breakthroughs have been in the areas of scheduling and promotion. Clearly there is no single factor that is responsible for the success or failure of a cable network. Rather, it is how a particular network negotiates its position within the competitive world of commercial television. Creating a "brand" identity to distinguish itself from other channels is one of the key factors in any cable network's success. Joseph Turow (1997) outlines a tripartite strategy that cable networks have employed to create and sustain these identities: (1) the consistent use of logos and other on-screen promotions, (2) a selection of "compatible" reruns, and (3) signature shows. It is in the third of these, Turow explains, that networks zoom in on the precise qualities they desire in their audiences (104–106). But it seems equally apparent that Turow's second item is what draws viewers to a network in the first place. And it is his first item that gives viewers reason to continue watching one particular cable network, as opposed to watching other broadcast or cable networks that show similar reruns.

This chapter looks at how basic cable networks (and some premium networks as well—following the lead of the basic networks) have exploited aesthetic sensibilities including "TV literacy," camp, nostalgia, and postmodernism to draw audiences back to familiar, often overused, program material. It also considers how the economics-driven segmentation, rearrangement, and reconfiguration of programming units have become the stylistic hallmarks of several cable networks. More broadly, this chapter focuses on the ways cable networks have scheduled their programming so as to appear "narrowcast." As will be discussed, the goal of true narrowcasting—that is, offering a schedule of original programs intended for a highly specialized viewership—has not been realized in modern cable. Rather, the appearance of such specialized targeting has resulted from various compromises and innovations: balancing a small amount of truly original programming with a large amount of carefully selected acquired programming, using interstitial material such as bumpers (program lead-ins) and other self-promotional spots to reinforce the chosen identity, and altering acquired programming through the use of voice-overs and image-overs.

While using the foregoing historical argument as a frame of reference, this chapter also draws from theories of television scheduling and viewership, including reception theory, theories of co-optation, and postmodernism. These bodies of theory, when used in conjunction with industrial history, are well equipped to analyze the sorts of program texts and programming strategies brought about by particular economic conditions and regulatory imperatives.

Narrowcasting?

The development of cable's trademark scheduling strategies was a gradual process—and one of trial and error. Few could have predicted that so many cable networks would make their mark simply by recycling broadcast television programming. It had been expected that cable would need a stockpile of originally produced special-interest programming even to enter into competition with broadcast television. And indeed, in some cases, this *was* the strategy that paid off. Some of the earliest successful cable networks included the all-news CNN, the all-sports ESPN, and the all-weather Weather Channel. Many more narrowly focused news and sports networks would be launched successfully in the late 1980s and the 1990s. Other established and popular broadcast genres would be exploited in this way as well.

The case of cable's cultural networks

Still, it is the *combination* of established popularity *and* low production costs that has made genres like news and sports succeed as cable fare. Even long-standing genres cannot survive on cable if their program production or acquisition costs are disproportionately high in relation to the size of the cable viewership they can expect to attain. This point is illustrated well by the fate of some much-anticipated "cultural" networks launched or planned during the early 1980s. CBS Cable, Bravo, ABC-ARTS (Alpha Repertory Television), and The Entertainment Channel all were established to offer opera, theater, symphony, art film, and other programming typically associated with PBS. Since these types of programming were seldom available on commercial broadcast television, it was assumed that they would prove lucrative on cable. Cable entrepreneurs believed that viewers who were frustrated with the formulaic narratives of commercial broadcast television would flock to any cable network providing an intelligent alternative. Things did not go exactly as planned, however. The cultural networks, as they had been designed, were short lived.

Apparently the PBS viewers targeted by the cultural networks had little interest in other television channels. To subscribe to cable would mean paying for a number of unwanted bundled channels in order to receive one or two cultural networks. There appears to have been little reason to do this, though. PBS was widely available over the air, particularly in the urban areas where viewership for the cultural networks was expected to be highest. Cable, on the other hand, was only beginning to make inroads in urban areas at this stage. David Waterman (1986) proposes that whatever small carryover audience existed between PBS and cable was not sufficient to sustain the high production costs of the sorts of original cultural programming that would have distinguished cable's cultural networks from PBS (92–107). Furthermore, as industry analysts observed at the time, the cultural networks had tried to produce their lavish original programming without adequate attention to ancillary markets such as foreign distribution and home video—markets that have been quite advantageous for PBS.[1]

The PBS audience is relatively small to begin with. If PBS had to depend on advertising revenues (instead of federal tax dollars, contributions from viewers, corporate sponsorship, and tie-in products), its chances of survival in the television marketplace would be slim. Yet this is essentially what cable's early cultural networks attempted to do. Moreover, while it is true that PBS has built its reputation on showing the sorts of programs not available from the commercial broadcast networks, its schedule nonetheless has encompassed a wide variety of program genres, and the network has programmed for several different categories of viewers. In addition to its arts programming, PBS has been known for its children's programming, its public affairs programming, and its "how-to" shows. Few of cable's cultural networks made such a concerted effort at scheduling diversity. The cable industry eventually learned the advantages of both ancillary markets and diversified schedules—but not early enough to alter the fate of the cultural networks.

The much-anticipated CBS Cable went out of business shortly after launching, but most of the other cultural networks traded in their initial plans and found ways to adapt to their environment. It is in their development that we can begin to see how cable as a whole was finding ways to become competitive. Most of the cultural networks found a middle ground—between their original programming goals and the types of programming traditionally successful on broadcast television. Those that survived managed to strike a balance between programming that was new or unusual and programming that was familiar and inexpensive to acquire. In so doing, they found both advertisers and the viewing audience to be much more receptive.

Various components of ARTS and The Entertainment Channel were absorbed by a single new network, Arts & Entertainment (A&E). A&E became a standard part of the basic tier and quickly became one of cable's most popular networks.[2] This can be attributed in large part to original programming, such as *Biography* and various historical documentaries, that initially was budgeted carefully and used sparingly. To sustain its original programming, A&E also began to schedule a selection of syndicated programming, including such off-network dramatic series as *Quincy, Columbo,* and *Remington Steele.*

Bravo, for its part, remained viable largely because it avoided building an identity around lavish original productions. It chose instead to select from among relatively low-cost acquired programs, such as independent and foreign films, not offered elsewhere on cable.[3] Bravo cites its ability to "frame" its longer programming (notably movies and stage performances) with shorter contextualizing programs such as interviews and documentaries.[4] Bravo's move away from being a strictly "film and arts" network was aided by the 1994 formation of its premium sister network, The Independent Film Channel, which is better able to cultivate Bravo's original niche following. Given all of these developments, Bravo's mature incarnation could be best characterized as an upscale metaentertainment network, rather than as an arts or culture network.

Narrowcasting redefined

The cultural networks provide the most revealing example of how little expectations for cable programming matched marketplace realities, but they were hardly the only cable networks to find themselves making adjustments during modern cable's early years. In fact, most basic cable networks discovered a need to broaden their coverage—either through the use of programming outside their chosen niches (as A&E had done) or by reassessing which program genres could fit within their market classifications. Even the sports networks ESPN and USA, whose initial reception was favorable overall, had to use this strategy to a certain extent. At first, both had filled large portions of their schedules with obscure sports such as fencing, water polo, and Slo-Pitch softball. They undoubtedly saw this as an inexpensive way to make ends meet without straying from their intended specialty. Eventually, though, the poor marketability of this minor sports coverage became apparent, and both networks began to replace it with sports-oriented talk shows—simple and inexpensive to produce, yet appealing to a wide audience segment (Waters and Wilson 1979, 124). In a different niche-expanding strategy, in fall 1984 CNN introduced the half-hour *Showbiz Today,* an entertainment news show that went after some of the audience for the popular syndicated program *Entertainment Tonight.*

Other networks that had to reconsider how they were defining their market niches were those that had set out to target demographically defined groups. Even with a sizable target audience, a network still may have had to make adjustments to its schedule in order to meet the demands of both cable operators and potential advertisers. Black Entertainment Television (BET) was notable in this regard. A major challenge for BET was convincing both advertisers and cable operators of the buying power of its primarily African American audience. One way BET mollified concerns about its stereotypically low-income population was through an appeal to some "crossover" market segments, especially teenage and young adult white viewers. While this probably was more of a cost-cutting measure than a deliberate attempt to widen its demographic niche, the effect is apparent in the fact that BET is one of the longest-surviving basic cable networks. BET became especially well known for its music video programs, focusing on black musicians and historically black music genres that have been underrepresented on MTV and elsewhere. As will be discussed later in this chapter, the music video has been an economical and popular source of programming for cable. BET also began using reruns of "evergreen" shows such as *I Spy, The Jeffersons,* and *Benson* that feature African Americans. From their original appearance on broadcast television, these programs have been popular across racial lines.[5]

Lifetime also provides a useful, though somewhat more complicated, example of this sort of niche-broadening strategy. Like A&E, Lifetime represents the distillation and reconfiguration of two unsuccessful specialty networks: Daytime and the Cable Health Network. The Cable Health Network had been launched in early 1982, with a 12-hour block of health and "lifestyle" programming targeted toward both medical professionals and the general public. Daytime also had been launched in early 1982—to air talk shows and other daytime genres traditionally aimed at women. Neither network was able to sustain its narrow focus, though, and in 1984 the two pooled their resources. The resulting new network, Lifetime, set out to program for medical professionals on Sundays and for women the rest of the time.[6]

A great deal of attention was paid to daypart segmentation for Lifetime; while women remained the target audience, the network's programmers were aware that women neither have uniform viewing interests nor do they always watch television alone. Thus, early morning and early evening programming was aimed at working women, daytime programming at homemakers, and evening prime-time programming at couples.[7] Clearly this was a move in the right direction, as Lifetime experienced a more than 87 percent viewership increase during its first year.[8] But it was also a move away from fulfilling cable's touted narrowcasting potential. As Carolyn Bronstein (1994–95) explains, even though there have been programs that deal directly and responsibly with women's issues throughout Lifetime's history, the network's primary imperatives are those that have driven virtually every other form of commercial television in the United States. She explains that "Lifetime's evening lineup may be more women-oriented than prime time on the general networks (broadcast and cable), but the programs must remain sufficiently mainstream to attract a large audience of both men and women" (231).

By the early 1990s Lifetime's schedule consisted of a balance between original programming, including made-for-TV movies and series, and syndicated programming, including old movies (both theatrical and made-for-TV) and broadcast series. The variable target audience presumably could be retained only through this programming mix. Lifetime has continued to offer a wide range of originally produced child-care programs, variety shows, and talk shows. In addition, it has scheduled a great deal of off-broadcast melodrama, a popular genre believed to appeal to women somewhat more than to men. For example, some of Lifetime's popular syndicated series have included *thirtysomething, Sisters,* and *Barbara Walters: Interviews.*

Nickelodeon, the popular children's network, employed a different strategy in broadening its audience—a strategy that actually involved creating a bifurcated identity for the network. Nickelodeon had to redefine its programming strategy when it began to program a 24-hour day, since late-evening viewers were not expected to value Nickelodeon's trademark original children's programs. So the network filled its evening and late-night hours with reruns of broadcast sitcoms, recognizing—as so many cable networks have—the enduring popularity of these programs. In fact, the reruns proved to be so popular that Nickelodeon has been able to treat this part of its programming day as an autonomous network called Nick at Nite. As will be discussed later in the chapter, Nick at Nite has gone to great lengths to promote the nostalgia value of the "classic" sitcoms.

The Nashville Network (TNN), which launched in 1983, targeted a niche defined by both demographics and taste. While one might assume, given the network's name, that TNN has focused on country music, this would only be partially correct. TNN set out to draw rural viewers in more general ways—a wise decision, considering the lack of interest broadcast television had shown in this population ever since CBS dropped its "hayseed" sitcoms in the late 1960s. At its debut, TNN boasted several original series, including *Dancin' USA,* which featured music and dance instruction; the half-hour comedy *I-40 Paradise;* a game show called *Fandango; Yesteryear in Nashville,* a documentary; and the variety show *Nashville Now!*[9] Since then, even more program genres have been added to the TNN roster. A major success for TNN has been its all-day Sunday sports programming, introduced in 1986 (primarily motor sports, hunting, and fishing). Weekday programming has generally consisted of a mixture of lifestyle programs (e.g., crafts shows) and off-broadcast reruns, such as *Alice, Dallas,* and *The Waltons,* with particular appeal to rural or southern viewers.

The case of The Family Channel

One of the most complex and intriguing stories of a cable network widening its market niche involves The Family Channel. The Family Channel was launched by the Christian Broadcasting Network in 1977 as CBN-Cable. It had a strong religious identity at the start; but it transformed itself into a "safe but entertaining" general interest network, and thus increased its popularity. As discussed in previous chapters, founder Pat Robertson's practice of surrounding his television pulpit with popular—and revenue-generating—programs can be traced back to the early 1970s, when CBN was a network of affiliated broadcast stations. At that time, this did not seem to preclude Robertson's televangelistic goals; rather, it was a means to an end. Thus, a schedule that combined religious themes with secular entertainment was what had evolved at CBN by the time Robertson took his programming outfit to satellite. Within a few years of starting the satellite network, however, the more religious programming appeared to be draining profits from the cable network, while the so-called filler material continued to draw audiences.

By the mid-1980s CBN was finding that a nonspecific "family" programming identity draws a larger audience than a blatantly religious identity can. Like most other cable networks, CBN was feeling pressures from the television marketplace. But during the late 1980s there were two other factors also pushing CBN toward downplaying the religious affiliation of its popular cable network and giving it a more mainstream identity: scandals involving other televangelists (Jim and Tammy Faye Bakker, Jimmy Swaggart, and Oral Roberts) and Pat Robertson's bid for the 1988 Republican presidential nomination. In September 1988 the Robertsons (Pat and his son Tim) changed the name of their cable network from CBN-Cable to The Family Channel. The new name was accompanied by a new logo, graphics, and music, as well as by some new programming strategies.

From 1988 until its 1996 acquisition by News Corporation, the portion of The Family Channel's schedule taken up by religious programming was not much greater than that of some other cable networks, particularly the superstations. The Family Channel continued to include a variety of religion-oriented paid programs during fringe time.[10] Other than these programs, the only remnant of The Family Channel's religious roots was the continued presence of *The 700 Club* every weeknight during prime time. By the early 1990s The Family Channel was programming primarily for mainstream audiences. It relied on both first-run and off-network syndicated programs (movies, reruns, and game shows), a practice that was helped tremendously when, in 1993, then parent company International Family Entertainment acquired the MTM production company and its valuable syndication library. These rerun programs were complemented by an increasing number of originally produced movies and series, including such programs as *Healthy Baby* for parents and *Big Brother Jake,* a children's sitcom. Publicity materials and spokespersons for the cable network have described this programming as "safe but entertaining." Of course, such a claim is easiest to make when program content is controlled in-house. Nonetheless, the images of acquired programs were discursively manipulated to fit an ideal of family values, often being characterized as parables.

CBN-Cable's evolution into The Family Channel represents an extreme form of adaptation to the economics of the television programming marketplace—and a successful one for its stage in cable history. According to Family Channel sources, annual advertising revenues grew from less than $45 million in 1986 to approximately $80 million in 1990 (Landro 1990). By replacing signifiers of televangelism with those of a nonspecific family entertainment identity, while also continuing to promote itself as a purveyor of morality lessons, The Family Channel managed to retain its Christian fundamentalist viewers while also appealing to more mainstream audiences. Its goal therefore was not narrowcasting, but rather general-interest programming that nonetheless could distinguish itself from what was available on broadcast channels.

It is clear that an awareness of how to balance innovation with economics and audience preferences produced several cable success stories during the 1980s and early 1990s. In all of these areas, one of the more prominent lessons learned was not to specialize too much in any one type of programming. Of course, in the move to broaden their appeal, cable networks did have some misses along with the hits. In 1985, for example, ESPN tried incorporating dramas such as *The Babe,* a one-man performance, and *Lombardi, I Am Not a Legend,* a two-man play, into its schedule. Roger Werner, executive vice president of marketing, told *Broadcasting* that ESPN was "looking into the possibility of scheduling sports movies, biographies, documentaries and other programs with 'a higher human interest content' that relates to sports themes."[11] It seems reasonable to assume the network was trying to draw more female viewers, but a look at the ESPN schedules of the 1990s makes it clear that this strategy did not last. There obviously were more than enough traditional sports fans to create a viable audience for ESPN. So instead of keeping the dramatic programs, the network chose to supplement sports events with more directly sports-related news and talk shows. The challenge for ESPN here was (as it was for most of its cable counterparts) to understand the degree to which the target audience could be expanded without alienating the core viewership.

Framing

The most common and probably most successful methods cable networks have used to expand their market segments have involved the strategic selection and presentation of recycled programming. A known quantity such as a classic broadcast sitcom can draw audiences who probably would not sample an unfamiliar cable network otherwise. Relying so heavily on syndicated product has created a challenge for cable networks, though: how to distinguish their schedules from those of their broadcast competitors—who offer similar programming free of charge. One way they have done this is by using familiar acquired programming as lead-ins or hammock poles for original programming. Another way is by using bumpers, IDs, and other promotional tools to *frame* the syndicated programming within their schedules, cueing viewers to read and understand it in particular ways. Overall, the goal has been to make all of the programs flow together in a way that reinforces the network's chosen identity. As Robert Rosencrans, founder of the USA network, commented in 1981, he and his associates had discovered "that it was important to control the whole day, otherwise your programming lost some of its coordination and meaning, and you couldn't promote it correctly. You almost have to be a coordinative service on a 24-hour basis." [12]

Actually, the framing strategies used by cable networks are grounded in long-standing broadcast scheduling practices. In an analysis of broadcast television's aggregate daily and weekly schedule (or "supertext"), Nick Browne (1987) explains that viewers have been addressed according to particular demographic and consumer categories. The combination and sequence of material in the schedules—programs and commercials—then reinforce those identities, "help[ing to] produce and render 'natural' the logic and rhythm of the social order" (588). Framing not only interpellates or hails desirable audiences, it can be used to assert a narrowcast identity that might not be apparent from the program selection. It also can obscure an undesirable public image. It can invite a particular reading strategy such as nostalgia or camp irony. Above all, it can breathe new life into overused, overly familiar reruns and movies. The following sections look at a variety of framing strategies used by popular cable networks.

Bumpers and IDs

Among the lessons cable networks learned early on was that creating and reinforcing a "brand" identity is essential to success in the competitive and largely undifferentiated television programming marketplace. By its second season of operation, the ABC-ARTS network had realized this, and increased on-air promotions considerably.[13] This lesson seems to have been carried forward when it became part of Arts & Entertainment in 1984. The Family Channel used its program selection to shape and articulate an identity it believed to be marketable. It also used bumpers and ID spots to reinforce that identity—for example, a brief spot instructing viewers about how to prepare economical meals for their families. Lifetime has been known to use promotional bumpers to call attention to features of its off-network reruns that might appeal to women specifically—even going so far as to promote *L.A. Law* as a show featuring "hunky" male lawyers.[14]

This is a common cable programming strategy. In fact, a few cable networks use bumpers and ID spots so extensively and so creatively that these interstitial scheduling components have taken on an entertainment function that sometimes rivals the network's actual programming. MTV and Nick at Nite especially have gone to great effort to design a wide variety of humorous, eye-catching, and memorable bumpers and IDs.

Lauren Rabinovitz has suggested that MTV's 1986 introduction of such ID spots coincided with the cable network's transformation from a largely unsegmented sequence of music videos to a more traditionally structured television schedule. She explains that the "pure flow" of MTV's early years had caused several critics to characterize it as the quintessentially "postmodern" form of television. Its program texts were heterogeneous and juxtaposed at random within an unbounded schedule. MTV's programming was no less commercialism than it was art. The music video production style itself frequently was self-reflexive, and the imagery used was purely stylistic. This hip, new aesthetic characterization quickly became a point of self-identification for MTV, even though the program schedule itself was becoming increasingly similar to broadcast television schedules. In order to continue asserting its trendy "postmodern" identity, the cable network began to fabricate signifiers of a postmodern aesthetic. These took the form of ID spots that, as Rabinovitz (1989) explains, "covered an eclectic range of styles, techniques, and representations, [and] referred neither to unified subject matter nor to shared symbols" (103).

Since their introduction, MTV's IDs and bumpers have become more elaborate, and the promotional campaigns that accompany them more sophisticated. In fact, MTV has created thousands of variations on its familiar logo for use in ID spots. As John Seabrook (1994) describes:

> One of the set pieces in any young producer's or writer's career at MTV is making an MTV promo spot, the basic purpose of which is, as Abby Terkuhle, the head of the department told me, "to make you feel good about watching MTV." . . . The fixed elements in the promo spots are time (usually ten seconds) and the presence of the MTV logo, but you are free to change the shape of the logo, and in terms of the history of logo design that freedom is one of the revolutionary things about MTV. (64)

MTV also has run series of thematic ID bumpers (longer than the spots discussed above). The "Rock the Vote" campaigns run during election years are one example. Another example was the "Art Breaks" campaign of the late 1980s, which featured the work of prominent artists including Robert Longo, Dara Birnbaum, and Jenny Holzer—each of whom had received a small grant from the cable network (Bravin 1990, 2). Associating IDs with campaigns such as these strengthens the cable network's public image; innovative and thought-provoking material is presented to MTV's young audience in a way that is not didactic and does not disrupt the cable network's regular programming format. It also has the more commercially motivated purpose of retaining viewers' attention during commercial breaks.

The use of bumpers and IDs during commercial breaks has been pursued even more aggressively by Nick at Nite, a cable network that promotes a particular reading strategy for the half-hour sitcom reruns that comprise its schedule. As discussed earlier, Nick at Nite began in 1985 as a way to extend Nickelodeon's 13 hours of children's programming. Looking for material that would be both popular and inexpensive, Nickelodeon opted to use only off-network sitcoms for its new evening and overnight schedule. Although Nick at Nite does not alter the original content of its programs, the programs nonetheless are meant to be understood differently in their new context. Nickelodeon programmers believed that the sitcom reruns could be promoted for both their camp and their nostalgia values, thereby drawing viewers from more than one generation (King 1991, 80).

By promoting these two reading strategies, Nick at Nite has invested the timeworn practice of showing reruns with a renewed cultural significance. A camp effect, as Andrew Ross (1989) explains, "is created not simply by a change in the mode of production, but rather when the products of a much earlier mode of production, which has lost its power to dominate cultural meanings, becomes available, in the present, for redefinition according to contemporary codes of taste" (139). The complementary nostalgia value lies in the idea that if we have seen the programs before, we probably are not watching to find out what happens to familiar characters, as we would be with first-run programs. Rather, we are watching familiar characters do familiar and predictable things.

Using clever bumpers, ID spots, and special promotions, Nick at Nite has billed its reruns as "classic TV" and used to refer to itself as "TV Land," the home of familiar sitcom characters (since 1996, TV Land has been the name of a separate network, spun off from Nick at Nite). Many of the IDs are very brief animated spots accompanied by commercial-type jingles. More elaborate bumpers have included tongue-in-cheek "testimonials," such as Brandon Cruz, former child star from *The Courtship of Eddie's Father*, saying (with reference to the series' theme song), "People let me tell *you* about my best friend: Nick at Nite." Other promotional spots have mimicked traditional public service announcements—for example, the "TV psychologist" Dr. Will Miller telling us why we *really* watch *Mr. Ed,* or characters from *The Patty Duke Show* informing us that identical cousins now may file joint tax returns.

Nick at Nite also has used its bumpers to provide "backstory" for featured programs, or to provide more general television trivia. These can be quite elaborate. For example, in a highly stylized music video format, singer Suzanne Vega recounted details about *I Dream of Jeannie* to the tune of her popular and widely parodied 1987 song, "Tom's Diner." Another Nick at Nite promo tells the story of how CBS limited the number of times Mary Tyler Moore was allowed to appear in her trademark "Capri" pants on any given episode of *The Dick Van Dyke Show* (the rest of the time she had to be wearing a skirt). This information might seem trivial, but as Nick at Nite's spokespeople would tell us, it is an essential part of "our precious television heritage." It also is an invitation into a camp reading of a program like *The Dick Van Dyke Show.* Even if the Capri pants anecdote fails to tell the whole story (e.g., what kinds of codes and practices might have led to this form of censorship), it reminds the audience of our cultural distance from *The Dick Van Dyke Show.* Since clever bumpers and IDs such as these are interspersed throughout all of Nick at Nite's commercial breaks, the chosen identity and asserted entertainment value of the cable network penetrate the entire schedule.

The use of bumpers and IDs by cable networks expanded dramatically in the 1990s. One of cable's most memorable promotional campaigns began in 1993, when ESPN hired the Portland advertising firm of Weiden & Kennedy. This was the same firm that had designed the "Just Do It" campaign for Nike and the "Where Do You Want to Go Today?" campaign for Microsoft. The campaign Weiden & Kennedy designed for ESPN was "This Is *SportsCenter,*" which featured bumpers of on-air talent from the popular sports newscast in "off-camera" moments. As described by journalist Michael Freeman (2000):

> The advertiser produced a whimsical spot in which [anchors Keith] Olbermann and [Dan] Patrick carry on in front of a bathroom mirror about the masculinity of hockey fighting, all the while applying make-up. "You need more rouge," Olbermann says to Patrick. "You know, your foundation has looked great recently." (200)

Marathons and theme days

Bumpers and IDs also are essential components of marathons and theme days—promotional strategies dating back to early HBO that are uniquely suited to cable's scheduling flexibility. A marathon features back-to-back episodes of a particular series, and can run for days at a time depending on the number of episodes in the series. Cable networks sometimes run marathons for series they either are introducing or are about to discontinue. Marathons also are used to counterprogram major television events on other channels. On the day of the 1993 Super Bowl, for instance, The Family Channel ran 10 hours of *Bonanza: The Lost Episodes,* Nostalgia Television showed 14 hours of *Family,* and A&E offered 13 hours of *The Jewel in the Crown.* Shorter marathons can simply be used to break up schedule monotony as needed. During the mid-1990s, for example, Nick at Nite began offering "Vertivision," four back-to-back episodes of particular programs, during prime time. The Vertivision selection in summer 1994 ("Block Party Summer") included "Mary Mondays," "Lucy Tuesdays," "Bewitched Bewednesdays," "Jeannie Thursdays," and "Sgt. Joe Fridays." Also, established cable networks occasionally schedule marathons for what are known as "sheltered launches" of spin-off networks. For example, superstation TBS ran several cartoon marathons just prior to the 1992 launch of parent company Turner Entertainment's Cartoon Network. The purpose of a sheltered launch is to expose audiences to the programming of a new cable network. If they like the programming, then presumably they will ask to have the new network added to their channel selections (Weaver 1993, 16–18).

Unlike marathons, theme days feature episodes from different programs that center around selected themes. This practice both increases and flatters viewers' "television literacy," since it highlights recurring character types and story lines from different times in television history. Theme days are a popular Nick at Nite programming strategy because they cultivate an adoration for "classic" television above and beyond the appeal of individual series. In addition to reinforcing the humor in the programs themselves, theme days hold a special appeal for advertisers: the chance to link their products to relevant themes that last an entire evening. In 1992, for example, Nick at Nite ran a special theme sequence called "Men in the Kitchen," with episodes from four different series, all featuring inept husbands or bachelors trying to feed themselves. One promo for this special used a clip from *Dragnet,* one of the featured programs, with the following voice-over:

Slaving over a hot stove . . .
Scrubbing linoleum floors . . .
Preparing glazed *duck* . . .

[Gannon presents duck and says, "Nice, huh?"]
Men in the kitchen will continue on Nick at Nite.

The joke about men's domestic ineptitude made "Men in the Kitchen" an excellent complement for the commercials of the theme day's named sponsor, Ragu Chicken Tonight, a convenience food product.

"Hosted" programs

Most of Nick at Nite's bumpers and IDs are interchangeable; even those created specifically for theme days can be used at any time during the designated block of programs. Another distinct framing strategy, however, uses bumpers to create a secondary diegesis for certain types of programming—a situation known as a *mise-en-abyme,* in which the televised program is about viewers watching another program. These bumpers are sequential and closely tied to particular programs. The most developed example of this is the "hosted" movie program. In parodies of more traditional "film jockeys," Comedy Central, USA, TBS, TNT, and The Movie Channel have used segues into and out of commercial breaks to frame low-budget movies with the irreverent, tongue-in-cheek comments of zany hosts. Comedy Central's *Mystery Science Theater 3000* used commercial breaks to develop the far-fetched backstory of how its hosts—a nerdy janitor and four "robot friends"—were launched into space by his mad scientist boss, and came to be watching the "cheesy" movies featured on the program.[15]

USA's *USA: Up All Night* segued into and out of commercial breaks (known as "wrap-around" segments) consisting of both parodic critiques of the movies and idle chatter. Gilbert Gottfried (in New York) and Rhonda Shear (in Los Angeles) either made derisive remarks about the evening's movies or engaged in inane and unrelated activities. Similarly, on The Movie Channel's *Joe-Bob's Drive-In,* self-styled redneck Joe-Bob Briggs made politically incorrect and otherwise socially unacceptable quips about the evening's featured B movie(s). Several descendants of these original hosted movie programs have appeared on cable networks since the early 1990s.

On hosted movie programs, not only are there commentators to tell us how and where to find camp humor in the movies, the commentators themselves try to be funny. The mediation provided by the hosts is what makes these distinct cable *programs,* as opposed to simply movies shown on cable. Indeed, these cable programs draw from long-standing production practices that distinguish television sound tracks from movie sound tracks. As Rick Altman (1987) explains, because most television viewing is semiattentive (i.e., typically accompanied by other household activities), various audio cues are incorporated into the sound track to draw viewers' attention back to the screen at critical intervals. The use of what Altman calls "internal audiences" is one way television producers accomplish this. For example, a laugh track cues us to the funny moments in sitcoms and on-screen announcers preview important plays (or replays) in sports events (566–584). The hosts of cable shows such as *Mystery Science Theater 3000, USA: Up All Night,* and *Joe-Bob's Drive-In* have a similar function: to cue us to specific readings of B movies. Their banter both previews on-screen action we might wish to view and summarizes what we might have missed.

Cable's parodic movie hosts fill the internal audience role extremely well, since their presence turns what otherwise would be a subversive viewing practice into a new standard for producing commercial television. The camp viewing of low-budget movies—whether in second-run theaters or on late-night television—predates satellite-served cable networks by several decades. However, it was not until the arrival of cable programs like *Mystery Science Theater 3000* that this type of audience behavior actually began to be packaged by programmers along with the actual movies. Among other things, the flippant wrap-arounds give viewers reason to believe the commercial breaks (still taken up primarily by commercials) are an integral part of the program texts. For this reason, the programs represent an exhibition strategy much the opposite of premium cable networks such as HBO and Cinemax, since those networks distinguish themselves from broadcast television by offering commercial-free, uninterrupted movies.[16] Hosted movie programs make the commercial breaks meaningful parts of the viewing experience. This is not the appropriate exhibition venue for anyone wanting to watch these movies *as movies;* however, the second-generation (television program) texts have become extremely popular in and of themselves. Videotaped episodes of *Mystery Science Theater 3000* are even traded by collector-fans—a practice sanctioned by its producers, who eventually began to include the message "Keep circulating the tapes" in the closing credits.

Mystery Science Theater 3000 was particularly successful as a hosted movie program since it took the framing strategy one step further than did the other programs mentioned above. First, its commercial segues were used to build backstory about how the hosts had come to be watching the movies. Rather than limiting their commentary to times before and after commercial breaks, the janitor and the robots appeared as silhouettes in front of the program's featured movies. Their jokes and sarcastic remarks could be heard along with the movies' original dialogue, thus simulating the possible camp viewing behavior of audiences watching at home or in theaters.

Mystery Science Theater is probably the best-known example of the typical Comedy Central strategy of reappropriating televisual material using a voice-over/image-over strategy. But the strategy also has been used in other programs. For example, in 1992 Comedy Central began a tradition of producing, and then altering, live coverage of the Democratic and Republican national conventions and the presidential election returns. This coverage closely resembles that of broadcast networks and CNN, except that Comedy Central's "political commentators" (actually stand-up comics) are seen and heard on top of more straightforward updates and analysis taking place in the background. The Olympics have provided another major event to be reappropriated as comedy material by Comedy Central.

The strategy of placing older program material within an ironic context actually is not limited to Comedy Central's voice-over/image-over programs. MTV's *Beavis and Butt-Head* is an animated program that features two moronic teenagers "watching" and making fun of live-action music videos. The featured videos are no longer (or never were) in heavy rotation elsewhere on MTV, so, like hosted movie programs, *Beavis and Butt-Head* serves as a way to reinvigorate older material. Other reappropriation programs on cable have included HBO's *Dream On,* a sitcom that interspersed clips from old movies and television programs with an originally produced narrative, and E!'s *Talk Soup,* a hosted collection of talk show excerpts.

It should be clear by this point that there have been a number of ways in which cable networks have tried to contextualize their secondhand program material. Sometimes the intervention in the actual program content is minimal—as in the case of Nick at Nite's clever bumpers and ID spots. Nick at Nite does not alter the programs themselves through this framing strategy; it merely suggests ways in which they might be read. Comedy Central's extensive use of voice-overs and image-overs, on the other hand, exemplifies the degree to which a cable network might change actual program content so as to create new meaning. Any original message of the programming is reconfigured, reshaped, and even ridiculed.

Indeed, one might say that some cable networks have adopted a fairly irreverent attitude toward the products of their media predecessors. Cable has also taken liberties with the scheduling conventions of broadcast television—in particular the standard half-hour or hour-long program formats that the "big three" have relied on since the 1950s. Although most cable networks have adhered to traditional scheduling blocks, in many cases this seems merely a matter of convention since the program narratives themselves fit within much smaller units of time. A look at the programming history of MTV will set the stage for a discussion of how cable networks have developed what I call the *video bite* style of programming.

MTV and Programming Innovation

Modern cable networks also have introduced variations on traditional narrative structures as a way of making the programming more flexible and easier to schedule. During the 1980s and 1990s a number of cable networks experimented with small programming units that could be recombined to form longer programs. In most situations, this strategy proved to be successful. The network that pioneered this new programming strategy was, of course, MTV, with its sequences of music video "clips." The music video, one of cable's few truly original program formats, buttressed the notion that audiovisual meaning can be conveyed in much shorter spans of time than the traditional half-hour or hour scheduling slots of broadcast television. This, in turn, has encouraged the use of short program segments to build longer programs—increasing recyclability while creating new meanings.

The institution of music video as an original cable program format resulted from an arrangement beneficial to both its producers and its distributors. Most music videos are produced entirely at the expense of recording companies, giving music video networks a continual supply of popular programming, particularly for the hard-to-reach teen and young adult demographic. As a virtually unsurpassed promotional tool (especially during the 1980s and early 1990s, before widespread penetration of the Internet), the music video has also benefited the recording companies. The earliest music videos featured performers who were not receiving much radio airplay in the United States, and thus helped to boost sales of their music. Music videos have also been valuable for promoting new album or CD releases—much less costly to produce than a concert tour, yet able to reach many more potential music consumers.

Moreover, for both demographic and stylistic reasons, music video has had built-in appeal to traditional television advertisers. MTV's primary audience has been the 18–24 age group, viewer-consumers not sufficiently reached by most other television program outlets. MTV not only has been able to capture this audience; it has shaped it into a self-identifying group—a class of consumers who build their identity around MTV programming and the consumer products associated with it. Media critic John Seabrook (1994) aptly has described this as "the magical process of stamping the MTV brand name on the feeling of youth" (69). Furthermore, the highly stylized "look" of MTV videos has approximated the appearance of many nonmusic commercials, creating a conflation of advertising and entertainment that appeals to the MTV audience. Over the years, advertisers have exploited this program-commercial blurring by using commercials that imitate music video production styles. The soft sell or "primary experience" by which Pat Aufderheide (1986) characterizes music video has been equally apparent in the overwhelming majority of other (i.e., more traditional) commercials on MTV (117).

By the mid-1980s the music video specifically had become a highly desirable program format for programmers, advertisers, and audiences. There were quite a few MTV imitators—successes as well as failures. MTV itself spun off a sister network, MTV2 (subsequently renamed VH1), in summer 1984. The new network targeted the 25–49 age group, an older audience than that of MTV, with soft rock and "classic" hits. Also in 1984, Ted Turner launched his Cable Music Channel; this was intended as direct competition for MTV, but failed after only two months (its assets were bought out by MTV). A similar network, Discovery Music Network, was also proposed in 1984—though it was never actually launched. In 1985 Odyssey, a music video network similar in format to VH1, launched specifically for the purpose of filling late-night programming hours on both cable networks and broadcast stations.[17]

Perhaps more telling of the appeal of the new music video programming format, though, is the number of established basic cable networks (as well as broadcast network affiliates and independent broadcast stations) that began to feature music video shows as *part of* their program days. Music videos served as foundation programming for such niche networks as The Nashville Network and Black Entertainment Television. The format was believed to attract coveted crossover audiences. USA also added music video blocks to its schedule during the mid-1980s, even replacing some of its established drama and variety programming.

Still, television advertisers, accustomed to demographically segmented broadcast network schedules, did not find the "pure flow" of

MTV's early years accommodating to their efforts at targeting specific audience/consumer groups. Even a brief 1985 shift to the familiar Top 40 radio format of heavy hit rotation did little to alleviate this problem; a steady drop in ratings made it very clear that MTV could not be programmed in the same way as radio. When parent company Warner-Amex sold MTV to Viacom in 1986, the new owners immediately began to segment MTV's programming day based on the same kinds of demographic research and ratings data that broadcast television networks have used since the 1950s. Since the late 1980s MTV's entire program day has been divided into hour or half-hour programs, featuring thematic music "blocks" such as *Yo! MTV Raps, MTV Unplugged* (acoustic), and *120 Minutes* (college/alternative).

In spite of the new segmentation, textual fragmentation and random juxtaposition have continued to define MTV's schedule—a point overlooked by Rabinovitz in her assertion that the ID spots have been the only lasting signifiers of the cable network's postmodern identity. These attributes have continued to characterize MTV's VJ-mediated blocks, which, in many cases, are categorically delimited versions of "pure flow." They also have pervaded the cable network's nonmusic (or not exclusively music) program formats, though in more subtle ways. The popular and controversial *Beavis and Butt-Head* provides a case in point. While each episode of this half-hour program is loosely premised on a comic situation, the story itself offers little reward to viewers who follow it through to its conclusion. A channel surfer might derive more pleasure by tuning in to the program for only one of the animated characters' moronic one-liners or one of the campy video clips that complement the dialogue. *Dead at 21,* a half-hour adventure drama, was another bite-able MTV offering during the early 1990s. As with *Beavis and Butt-Head,* the story in any given episode of *Dead at 21* existed primarily to showcase the program's "look" (or "attitude") and the featured music. Its production style mirrored that of music videos and MTV's other programming: rapid cutting, dance sequences, and genre pastiche. Many of the scenes in *Dead at 21* appeared to be aesthetically, rather than causally, motivated. Also, the narrative structure was serial, much like a soap opera (a genre known to appeal to intermittent attention spans)—making it easy to tune in and out of the program without losing track of the story. In effect, *Dead at 21* was an action-adventure program in the same sense that *Beavis and Butt-Head* is a sitcom: a viewer tuned in to *Dead at 21* for only one dance sequence, like a viewer with time to laugh at only one of *Beavis and Butt-Head's* stupid pranks, would not have missed the point of the program—or its overall entertainment value.

It is clear from these examples that the music video's narrative structure and scheduling flexibility have been combined with more traditional television program structures to invest a varied program schedule with MTV's trademark look and feel. Even though, by the mid-1990s, there was no longer any part of MTV's schedule not captioned by a specific program title, the three- to four-minute program segment has continued to be its defining characteristic. Thus, MTV's history has not been about a failure to break away from broadcast television's conventions. Rather, it has shown how—given a viable funding structure, a desirable target audience, and a flexible narrative structure—a new program format can subtly alter long-standing television programming practices. In fact, MTV's success with this new music video–based program format, a "video bite," has had a powerful impact on the programming and scheduling strategies of many cable program networks.

Video Bites

Basically, video bites are self-contained programming units that range from a few seconds to a few minutes in duration. Some types of video bites are produced individually, while others are segments of longer programs. In addition to music videos, video bites can be news segments, portions of stand-up comedy routines, weather bulletins, or product pitches on home shopping shows—to name a few of the more obvious examples. Video bites can be combined in an infinite variety of sequences to form longer programs. Often, moderators introduce the video bites and assert particular themes under which these segments are meant to cohere, as in comedy showcases, music video blocks, home shopping programs, and so on. Thus, while they typically are fit into traditional television time slots, video bite programs cannot be understood as simply reproducing the conventions of older, more traditional television genres. Instead, they represent a negotiation between very short, self-contained narratives (measured in seconds or minutes instead of half hours or hours) and traditional program structures (that *are* measured in half hours or hours). The result is a schedule of standard-length programs that nonetheless are composed of very brief individual entertainment and information messages.

Since its debut in 1982 CNN Headline News has been an ideal example of video bite programming. The programming day of Headline

News is divided into half-hour news blocks, with fixed categories of news (international, entertainment, etc.), each relatively autonomous within the overall newscast. Because Headline News cycles through a complete newscast every half hour, each video bite within these blocks can be updated as needed without necessarily changing the rest of the newscast. The Weather Channel similarly cycles through various categories of video bite weather reports (local, ski conditions, international, etc.). Other Weather Channel miniprograms give background information on particular weather phenomena.[18] Several other information-based cable networks have contributed to the video bite–permeated program environment without actually using the abbreviated format as the foundation for their programming. A cable network such as CNN or C-SPAN, with programs that lack traditional narrative closure, encourages viewers to determine for themselves the amount of time to spend watching.

Providing another prominent example of cable's video bite strategy are the various home shopping networks. Clearly, practically all developments in cable programming have involved either the use of actual broadcast programming or the imitation of successful broadcast genres. Any significant break from existing television programming and scheduling conventions would be extremely difficult to accomplish, since it would require a reliable means of funding programming and a flexible program format. Arguably, though, the home shopping format does represent such a break with television conventions.

Even though its roots can be traced back to the various Popeil family ventures of the 1960s and 1970s,[19] the cable version of televised shopping began in October 1982, when Group W's Manhattan cable system aired the show *Access to Shop the World,* in which categories of products were featured in four- to six-minute segments, with detailed individual product descriptions and a toll-free number for ordering. Similar shows were to follow, sometimes as scheduling components for existing cable networks.[20] The idea of cable networks devoted exclusively to direct marketing came about when Roy Speer started Home Shopping Network (HSN) in 1985.

HSN, its competitor QVC (launched in 1986), and their successors had little difficulty finding a home on many cable systems. Typically cable operators pay a per-sub fee to the basic networks whose programs they carry. A network's fee ranges from a few cents to a few dollars, based mostly on its popularity and operating expenditures, so an operator must weigh the added subscribership potentially generated by a particular network against the cost of carrying it. Home shopping networks, in contrast, split their revenues with operators, allowing systems actually to make money from carrying them. In 1987 home shopping generated $1.1 billion in revenues, about 10 percent of cable's total for that year.[21] Its popularity only continued to grow during the early 1990s.

Like the information-based cable networks discussed above, home shopping networks are not tied to clearly delimited viewing times. Because programming is continuous and not defined by traditional narrative structures, viewers can watch as little as a single sales pitch or as much as an entire day of sales programs. For this reason, home shopping has contributed significantly to cable's redefinition of television programming conventions. However, it is with entertainment programming that cable networks have been the most innovative in the use of video bite programming. Both presegmented programming and programming that can be dissected into textual components or signifiers are well suited to the comedy "showcases" and "best of . . ." programs that populate so many cable schedules. A program's original entertainment value can be enhanced or renewed when characteristic portions of it are excerpted and juxtaposed with other video bite material—as shown in the following two case studies.

Short Attention Span Theater

The strategic importance of video bites within a cable network's supertext became apparent in the late 1980s, when two separate basic cable comedy networks emerged: HBO's spin-off, The Comedy Channel, and Viacom's HA. The Comedy Channel essentially was intended to be an all-video-bite channel with clips from current movies, stand-up performances, and classic TV shows brought together in comedy "showcases." HA, in contrast, focused on longer-format programs such as movies and syndicated sitcoms. It is not surprising that the two networks merged in 1990 to form Comedy Central, which remains a basic cable favorite—especially among teenage and young adult males. It also is not surprising that the new network combined the longer and shorter program formats, using the longer programs to cultivate sustained viewership and the shorter program excerpts (along with originally produced bumpers and IDs) to capture flagging attention spans and reinforce network identity.

Comedy Central has mixed and recycled video bite excerpts in a variety of programs to maximize programming resources. As with MTV, a distinct programming style that draws upon narrative economy and program interchangeability runs throughout Comedy Central's entire schedule. Both sketch and stand-up comedy, the dominant program formats, make ideal sources of video bites since isolated portions of either can be as entertaining as a whole programs. Sketch comedy (as seen in programs such as *Saturday Night Live* and *SCTV*) is produced in short, self-contained segments—providing ready-made video bites. And, since most stand-up comedy routines lack clear starting or ending points, their boundaries—like those of television in general—are arbitrary. Comedy Central has been known to excerpt various other program types, including sitcoms, movies, and even commercials.

Short Attention Span Theater, a Comedy Central program that ran during the early 1990s, offers an excellent example of this network's creative use of video bites. *Short Attention Span Theater* was a mediated program that featured clips from a variety of different sources, segmented according to themes. At the beginning of each episode and after commercial breaks, stand-up comic hosts would chat casually with each other, perform brief monologues, and introduce the episode's featured themes. On 27 November 1992, for example, hosts Joe Bolster and Ted Blumberg opened the program by announcing some celebrity birthdays. They also announced—in an obvious parody of broadcast variety programs ranging from *The Today Show* to *Late Night with David Letterman*—that it was Kids' Day in Edina, Minnesota; Swine Time in Climax, Georgia; The Great Alaska Shoot-Out in Anchorage; and the Festival of Carols in Topeka, Kansas. The first set of clips was a collection of five excerpted stand-up routines centering on the theme of grocery shopping.

Following a commercial break, Comedy Central bumpers, and another hosted segment, a series of clips featuring comedian Gilbert Gottfried was introduced. This portion of the program included a promotional clip from the recently released Disney film *Aladdin,* in which Gottfried played the voice of Iago the parrot; a clip from *Look Who's Talking, Too* (then in its first television run on Showtime), in which Gottfried played a supporting role; a skit from *Saturday Night Live;* and a stand-up monologue. A third segment of the *Short Attention Span Theater* episode was called "Comedy Update," and presented more comedy clips (from current movies, TV, and theater) in broadcast news style. Another segment of the program included two "classic" television clips: from *The Best of Groucho* and *Sergeant Bilko.* The remainder of the hour-long program featured similar stand-up themes (hotel and motel jokes, pizza jokes), material by comic Mojo Nixon, and assorted other comedy material.

The only new material featured on *Short Attention Span Theater* consisted of the economically produced in-studio host segments that bound together all of the secondhand material. Thus the start-up cable network was able to put its limited programming resources to good use. Another advantage this program offered Comedy Central was its function as a laboratory for new program development. Even though *Short Attention Span Theater* itself was discontinued, program concepts originally tested on it—including *Dr. Katz: Professional Therapist*—went on to become full-length programs.

Talk Soup

Whereas *Short Attention Span Theater* drew from a mélange of different comedy genres, E! Entertainment Television's *Talk Soup* (still in production as of 2002) focuses exclusively on talk shows from other channels. *Talk Soup* is a half hour– or hour-long "summary" of a given day's talk shows that reinterprets their literal meanings through a mocking or camp sensibility. A stand-up comic host/moderator outlines the topic of each featured talk show episode, and this summary is followed by a clip from the original program. Each clip is three or four minutes long, beginning with the original program's title, airtime, and topic captioned in the lower left corner of the screen—notably similar to music video credits. A single mid-1990s episode of *Talk Soup*, for example, might have featured clips from such daytime talk shows as *Montel Williams, Bertice Berry, Vicki!, Ricki Lake, Jerry Springer,* and *The Today Show,* with such topics as "Married Couples/Hot Sex" and "Lyle, the Effeminate Heterosexual."

Between the featured clips, the comedian-host mimics the words and gestures of the talk show guests, occasionally with the help of studio effects such as slow-motion replay and a blue-screen matte sequence. *Talk Soup* takes a great deal of license in editing and editorializing the clips it uses. The video bites on *Talk Soup* feature terse, attention-grabbing dialogue and rely heavily on reaction shots. In fact, facial expressions are so important to *Talk Soup's* sensationalism that a split screen often is used to derive the most irony from a single brief excerpt—capturing expressions from two of the contentious parties simultaneously. Particularly shocking dialogue typically is used without context or follow-up.

The narrative structures of *Short Attention Span Theater* and *Talk Soup* are strikingly similar. The hosts introduce all of the clips, addressing the audience directly with commentary and information about the sources from which the clips have been taken. Each program features a barrage of sound and images, with no clip lasting longer than the average commercial break (or another video bite program). All clips include music video–style credits captioned in the lower left corner of the screen. Both *Short Attention Span Theater* and *Talk Soup* have filled entire hours using inexpensive program material, making them ideal for networks such as E! and Comedy Central that were starting out during the early 1990s. As these two programs demonstrate, a major advantage of a video bite strategy has been to allow programmers of cable networks to maximize limited programming resources. Since cable networks often have to differentiate inexpensive and overused acquired programming from the newer programming of more resource-laden broadcast competitors, the idea of program material that either comes in segments or is easily segmented—material that can be recombined endlessly to create "new" programs—is especially appealing.

Furthermore, since a typical video bite program segment is about the same length as a commercial break, video bite programs accommodate the presumed short attention spans and frequent channel-changing of modern cable audiences. Viewers seem to appreciate this since it gives them more control over the types of programs they can watch, as well as the amounts of time they need to spend watching those programs. This also is advantageous to advertisers, since video bite programming strategies make it easy to conflate program and commercial texts; they become ready substitutes for each other and meld the commercial and entertainment functions of television in the minds of viewers. MTV and other cable networks have even been known to obscure the boundaries between programs and commercials deliberately, trying to make as many commercials as possible reflect the "look" of their trademark programming. Nick at Nite has even gone so far as to suggest that its advertisers unearth old commercials to run alongside its off-network reruns—a practice in use since the mid-1990s (Goldman 1993).

Of course, there were some generic and narrative precedents for modern cable's use of video bites in earlier broadcast television programming. Although variety shows, nightly newscasts, and children's programs like *Sesame Street* have hardly ever recombined or recycled their component segments (at least not until cable networks began doing it for them), the potential to do so has always been there. To go a step further, it could even be argued that the very nature of U.S. commercial television has made the widespread use of video bites an inevitable stage of its development. Mimi White (1986) characterizes the television text cultivated both directly and indirectly on American commercial television for several decades as a single, endlessly self-referential diegesis or a self-enclosed "world" of television. Television characters frequently "leave" their own programs temporarily to make guest appearances on other programs, drawing their loyal audiences along with them. Or popular secondary characters leave their original series permanently to become the lead characters in spin-off series. And popular actors (either in or out of character) have themselves appeared in commercials (60–61).

It is not difficult to understand how modern cable's video bite programming practices fit within larger economic patterns in television history, as well. Scheduling flexibility is a characteristic of broadcast television that predates satellite cable by several decades. An important precedent for the video bite programming strategy actually was introduced to broadcast television in the 1950s, when the "magazine" format of sponsorship began to replace the single-sponsor format television had inherited from radio. The magazine format has allowed program production costs to be shared among several different sponsors. It also has allowed advertisers to use the same commercials during many different programs, thus maximizing the return on their production costs. The magazine format rapidly became the standard for commercial television, and the parceling out of commercial time has proven so successful over the years that commercials progressively have become shorter and their messages more compact—allowing ever greater numbers of advertisers to participate in the sponsorship of a program. Furthermore, since the introduction of off-network syndication, also in the 1950s, entire television programs have taken on interchangeability attributes similar to those of commercials. After being removed from their original schedules and becoming reruns, programs' original scheduling contexts become irrelevant.

Video bite programs like *Short Attention Span Theater* and *Talk Soup* indicate that the notion of interchangeability is no longer limited to commercials and standard-length programs. Interchangeability is so pervasive that even small portions of programs can become meaningful scheduling components. One might argue that video bite–driven programs, like those discussed above, make up only a small fraction of what is available on cable. This may be true in the sense that most cable programs continue to adhere to the standard half hour– and hour-long program formats (including such standard cable genres as documentaries, how-to shows, and cartoons), but we can see that even these programs have been subjected to a new scheduling logic. They tend to be repeated at intervals throughout the day, they are often excerpted at length for use in network promotions (a contrast to the brief sight gag clips still used in broadcast network promotions), and they are sometimes subjected to cable's trademark dissecting and recombining.

In this context, it also should be noted that the distinctions between cable programming and scheduling strategies and those of broadcast television are becoming fewer and are harder to discern. Cable programming strategies designed for a multichannel, remote control–mediated television environment have also been adopted by broadcast television in recent decades. Broadcast networks and stations have been no less concerned than cable networks about competing for viewers. Television executives and programmers have felt uncertain of their ability to orchestrate the program-commercial "flow" in a multichannel television environment that is mediated by remote control devices and rapid programming flow. So they have had good reason to make programs and commercials as indistinguishable from one another as possible— thereby making even schedules of viewers' own construction into viable vehicles for pitching consumer products or consumption in general.

Conclusions

The formal exchanges between cable and broadcast television programming would continue into the 1990s and beyond, with cable gaining a much more solid position in the television marketplace. The amount of original cable programming increased and the "look" of that programming improved. By the early 1990s many basic cable networks were operating at a profit, receiving widespread carriage, and selling time to major advertisers. In fact, by this point the more popular basic cable networks were in a position to compete with broadcast stations for the best syndicated programming. Additionally, some—including TNT, A&E, and Lifetime—had begun to receive high acclaim for their original movies and series, which frequently feature well-known directors and actors. CNN, ESPN, the Weather Channel, and various other networks had set benchmarks for programming within their respective genres. Even newer networks such as The History Channel, The Cartoon Network, and Sci-Fi Channel were able to offer fairly polished original programming in their early years, owing in large part to the success of networks previously launched by their corporate parents.

Nonetheless, an intriguing legacy of both the CATV era and satellite cable's resource-starved early years can be seen in the persistence of recycled programming on cable and in the endurance of programming strategies that were developed to reinvigorate it. Long after they began to make a profit, cable networks continued to use framing and video bite strategies, often increasing the production values of existing programs instead of replacing old programs with new ones. For example, some of the resources that Comedy Central might have put into developing new programs instead went toward increasing the production values of *Mystery Science Theater 3000*. Even though *Mystery Science Theater* continued to be one of the most economically produced series on television, the cost per episode increased tenfold between the program's initial airing on independent broadcast station KTMA in 1986 and its final run on Comedy Central a decade later (Brauer 1991). This was due both to increased revenues for its production company, Best Brains, and to increased revenues and carriage for Comedy Central.

One can only speculate about how modern cable's programming strategies and imperatives might have been different if more structured policies had been developed—and adhered to—in response to the Blue Sky proposals. What we can be certain of, though, is that modern cable did not begin with a blank slate at the time satellite transmission became a reality. More than two decades of operating as an enhanced retransmission medium for broadcast television set precedents for modern cable that would have been difficult to dislodge even with clearly structured policy guidelines. As it was, no such guidelines ever were put in place. It is little wonder, then, that modern cable networks have opted to fill their schedules with known quantities that also hold the advantage of being economical to obtain. Indeed, it could be considered quite remarkable that, given the lack of policy guidance or oversight, cable networks have made as many programming innovations as they have.

Every year dozens of new cable (or now direct broadcast satellite) networks are planned, many of which appear to meet the narrowcasting intentions articulated during the Blue Sky era. Yet, contrary to what had been anticipated during the late 1960s and early 1970s, most of these have been, and will continue to be, steeped in the economics of open-entry competition—needing to recycle programming and combine original programs with syndicated fare, and striving to keep pace with shifting viewing practices and new technologies. Two decades of adopting and adapting available programming conditioned the cable industry to program for this environment.

The legacy of satellite cable's first two decades has been far-reaching. In the process of struggling to make ends meet—to make inexpensive and low-budget programming seem appealing to television audiences—

cable networks developed many of the innovative new programming strategies that would come to define television in the digital age. The converging of new media technologies, ranging from VCRs to the Internet, has changed television viewing behaviors and expectations. Audiences have grown accustomed to a rapid and fragmented flow of information and entertainment (not to mention an increasing bombardment of commercials). Cable's flexible programming units and scheduling strategies accommodate this environment well—and should continue to do so, even as the medium of cable itself evolves into newer and more technologically sophisticated means of transmission.

Cable Television's Past, Present, and Future

Cable Programming's Historical Imperative

In spite of its many promotion and scheduling innovations, U.S. cable programming sometimes has been perceived as a failure or, perhaps, a series of compromises. In large part, this is due to the tremendous optimism and idealism generated during the late 1960s and early 1970s, the period in cable history known as "Blue Sky." At that time, cable began to be understood as more than a simple retransmission medium, and many proposals envisioned ways in which it might expand, or even reinvent, television programming. The following statement, which appears near the beginning of the well-known 1971 Sloan Commission report, *On the Cable: The Television of Abundance,* is representative of the mind-set that guided those proposals:

> Cable television today is at a stage where the general exercise of choice is still possible. If for no better reason than that there is a history of government regulation in the field of television, it remains possible by government action to prohibit it, to permit it, or to promote it almost by fiat. Citizens may still take a hand in shaping cable television's growth and institutions in a fashion that will bend it to society's will and society's best intentions. It is not as yet encumbered by massive vested interests, although that day may be no longer remote. It is not as yet so fixed a part of the national scene, as for example conventional television is, that it appears almost quixotic to attempt to redirect its energies. There is, in short, still time. (3)

The Sloan Commission, as well as many other individuals and groups researching and writing about cable television during the Blue Sky years, expressed optimism that policy might be instituted to guide cable away from its strong dependence on broadcast television. Like other Blue Sky studies, the Sloan Commission report included detailed recommendations for policymakers. Also like other Blue Sky studies, it warned that the time for altering cable's trajectory was rapidly running out.

The scenarios about which the Blue Sky visionaries cautioned policymakers and the general public did come to pass. By the mid-1970s cable programming was controlled almost entirely by big business. And since that time its content has not diverged significantly from that of broadcast television. In fact, cable has maintained such close ties to broadcasting that some of its most popular program services have been actual broadcast stations—in the form of retransmitted signals from nearby stations, as well as in the form of cable "superstations." This ongoing relationship should not be surprising to anyone familiar with cable's history. Throughout that history the television audience habitually has supported the sorts of mass-appeal programming that characterize broadcast network television. And policymakers have repeatedly supported a cable environment in which these sorts of programs can flourish.

An enduring precedent for cable's reliance on broadcast programming was set at the time of its "invention" in the late 1940s: as community antenna television (CATV), cable was to be a retransmission medium for broadcast television signals. Even after microwave relays had been enlisted to enhance, and sometimes substitute for, the capabilities of community antennas, the medium still was known almost exclusively for its ability to provide broadcast programming. The attempts of a few isolated CATV operators to introduce locally originated programming to their subscribers hardly constituted a standard practice for their industry during the 1950s. And while the concurrently developing pay-TV industry was exploring several nonbroadcast sources of television programming, at that point pay-TV was mired in regulatory controversy and its associations with cable remained extremely tenuous.

Throughout the 1960s, the CATV/cable industry demonstrated both more willingness and more ability to develop non-broadcast-derived programming than it had in the previous decade—including possible joint ventures with pay-TV companies. However, during the 1960s restrictive federal guidelines were instituted for cable, and these slowed the medium's growth considerably. Though the restrictions eventually would be lifted, for several years cable was virtually banned from entering communities served by broadcast television. Pay-television also remained in regulatory limbo during the 1960s. Some pay-TV operations had been waiting more than a decade for permission to move beyond limited trials. Regulators' stated purpose both in instituting strict cable regulations and in delaying the licensing of pay-TV was to protect broadcasters, a goal they understood as being synonymous with their mandate of guarding the public interest.

During cable's second decade of existence, it was in larger, broadcast-served communities that operators might have found the critical mass of subscribers necessary for introducing nonbroadcast programming options. Indeed, it seems as though providing more than simply retransmitted broadcast signals would have been *essential* to the successful marketing of cable service in broadcast-served communities. The development of local origination and public access programming in Manhattan (where cable systems had been franchised prior to passage of the rules) demonstrates that cable operators were open to the idea of using special-interest and community-oriented types of programming as ways to draw additional subscribers. One can only speculate about what sorts of programming might have developed elsewhere.

Yet aside from Manhattan and a handful of other cities, during most of the 1960s cable was able to develop only in rural areas, where it was not economically feasible for most operators to provide more than a selection of retransmitted broadcast signals and possibly some channels of automated programming. Few were offering local programming, and hardly any were experimenting with pay-TV. Moreover, even though barely any prohibitions had been placed on rural cable systems, their operators still were concerned about the unstable regulatory climate. It was extremely uncertain which aspects of cable and pay-TV might be banned in the future. So, of course, many of these small-town entrepreneurs were reluctant to experiment with, and invest in, elaborate new programming schemes. As of the late 1960s, two decades after the medium's first uses, cable still was being used almost exclusively for the retransmission of broadcast signals. Outside of a few pioneering local origination schemes, no distinct cable programming existed.

The regulatory tide turned abruptly for both cable and pay-TV in the late 1960s and early 1970s, initiating a significant reconceptualization of the functions of both forms of television. First, pay-TV officially was permitted in 1969—prompting a proliferation of pay-cable services that offered movies and sports. Even more significantly, because of the Blue Sky and other protechnology discourses circulating at the time, government policymakers began to make rules forcing the rapid implementation of non-broadcast-derived programming. As the result of two critical bodies of regulation, cable operators were required first to initiate local programming operations and then to maintain public access facilities for their communities. It is clear, then, that the official position on cable had changed drastically within an extremely brief period of time. Attitudes toward cable moved from a perception that it would threaten the public interest to an expectation that it would restore localism and democracy to television service. In effect, policymakers were suggesting that cable become an entirely new medium, and this represented an abrupt shift for the growing cable industry as well as for a television audience accustomed to the programming of commercial broadcast networks.

Some cable operators did make efforts to introduce local programming. Among these, many were independently owned systems with ties to the communities they served. And for a few years the cable trade press was filled with local origination success stories and suggestions for prospective producers. Nonetheless, the cable industry as a whole—an industry increasingly dominated by powerful MSOs—opposed the rules on the grounds that they imposed too great a technological and financial burden. Regulators responded by lifting the local origination and access requirements, one by one, throughout the 1970s. The rules that were not repealed by the FCC itself were struck down in federal courts. In the meantime, the cable industry was given more and more latitude as to the amounts and types of broadcast-derived programming it was permitted to use. By 1980 almost no regulatory controls existed for cable programming.

The arrival of a presidential administration that strongly favored big business had been a major factor in regulators' increasingly lenient treatment of cable. The same (Nixon) administration was responsible for the deregulation of the domestic satellite industry. Indeed, the deregulation of cable and the deregulation of satellite communications complemented each other to ensure that early satellite cable would be almost entirely dependent on the programming conventions, frequently the actual programs, of broadcast television. By the time of Blue Sky, a great many independent cable systems were being bought out by MSOs. These large corporations enjoyed economies of scale due to centralized management of the cable systems, and these economies logically were extended into cable programming as soon as widespread distribution technologies became available.

By the mid-1970s, when the cable industry began using satellites for program distribution, there were no regulatory mechanisms in place to ensure subsidies for special-interest programming. Nor were there any federal regulations requiring cable operators to continue providing locally oriented programming once they were able to offer their subscribers a selection of satellite networks. Nearly the only parties able to launch satellite networks were those with preexisting television programming operations and strong financial backing. These parties also were interested in drawing large audiences at the lowest possible cost—which generally meant filling schedules with broadcast-type programming such as off-network reruns, movies, and sports. Even in the early twenty-first century, cable program schedules are driven by corporate competition more than by a concerted plan to offer a diverse and comprehensive range of program choices.

Modern Cable Programming: Compromise or Innovation?

In retrospect, it seems that policymakers abandoned the goals of Blue Sky no less hastily than they had tried to implement those goals in the first place. In the postsatellite era there have been no federal-level incentives for cable operators to make production facilities available to members of their communities. And there have been no mechanisms in place by which to subsidize niche-interest programming for nationwide audiences. The major defect usually cited regarding the early 1970s cable and telecommunications policies is that these policies limited the possible number of cable programming producers. For the most part, only large, well-financed entertainment corporations have had the resources necessary to program for cable. Democratic participation in the modern cable scenario thus has been severely limited since, as Robert W. McChesney (1996) points out, "the market is not predicated on one-person, one-vote, as in democratic theory, but rather upon one-dollar, one-vote" (105).

Had any of the Blue Sky plans been instituted successfully, though, could cable have changed the public's uses and expectations for television programming? Audience preferences and established uses of television both need to be taken into account when answering this question. By the late 1960s a set of programming practices clearly had developed within the broadcast network system that defined American television in the minds of its audience—regardless of whether that audience received programming over the air or by cable. Furthermore, no precedent exists in U.S. history for government policymakers to play a strict role in governing the use of a mass communication medium.

By the time of Blue Sky, the entire U.S. television audience had had two decades in which to become accustomed to the programming fare of broadcast networks; CATV/cable had only helped spread the popularity of that programming. Regardless of how much certain idealists in sisted that the U.S. television system needed reform, people had built expectations for future programming on past experiences with mass-appeal forms of broadcast media. The programming that was developed by and for broadcast network television during that medium's early years was supported by national advertising revenues. Thus, it naturally boasted much higher production values than any form of locally produced cable programming could have done. Any locally produced cable programming would have been at a tremendous competitive disadvantage in terms of audience expectations.

Basic laws of supply and demand make it seem clear that local and niche-interest programming would have required extensive subsidies at the outset, and even then could not have drawn more than a negligible share of the cable audience. This is not to say that alternative programming has not developed at all in the years since Blue Sky. The continued presence of public access facilities in many communities (often required by local franchising processes) suggests that the public can find uses for certain types of local and special-interest cable programming. But access programming remains marginal at best, and hardly defines modern cable as a medium distinct from broadcast television. And small inroads made by innovators like Bravo and Home Box Office—showing movies too controversial to be shown elsewhere, picking up series canceled by broadcast networks, and so on—have not reshaped the image of cable programming as a whole.

Still, the major purpose of this study has not been to lament the lack of diversity in modern cable programming. It is difficult to define precisely what might have constituted a diverse cable scenario had a more stringent regulatory framework for cable programming been instituted. Many of the Blue Sky planners seem to have envisioned an environment in which some sort of enlightened cable programming would supersede the lowest-common-denominator fare that had developed on broadcast television. But their expectations for cable might inadvertently have been premised on a notion that all spheres of social, professional, educational, and political activity could productively be reproduced on the small screen. Not only would this have meant rearticulating existing uses and expectations for television's small screen, it also might have implied retrofitting television to the ideals of elite society. After all, policymakers hardly represent a cross section of the American populace.

This does not mean that cable programming in the post-satellite era has been without innovation. As this study has shown, modern cable networks have devised a number of different ways to promote and schedule broadcast-type programming so as to distinguish it from what is available on actual broadcast channels. They have created programming that is not constrained to traditional half hour or hour blocks of time. They have used commercial bumpers and other interstitial material to assert unique identities that encompass entire program schedules. They have created new programs by rearranging segments of older, recycled programming. They have created new programming that pokes fun nostalgically at outdated production conventions and, at the same time, creates and reinforces a canon of "classic" television. And they have updated the ways in which traditional broadcast genres such as news and children's programs are produced and exhibited. Many of the strategies cable networks have enlisted as ways of making do in the short term were so successful that they actually became hallmarks of television programming overall during satellite cable's first two decades. The influence of the "video bite" style of programming, for instance, now can be seen not only on MTV but also on many other cable networks, as well as on established broadcast networks. Clearly, by the mid-1990s cable had found its own programming styles. If it still retained connections with broadcast television, this was at least as much a matter of preference as of necessity.

Cable for a New Millennium

I chose to end this study in the mid-1990s because I believe cable programming has entered a new phase in recent years. By the middle of the decade satellite cable had reached a stage of maturity in that the first wave of networks had recovered their start-up costs and were able to be much more selective in their programming choices. Also, advertisers, once skittish in their support of cable programming, had become a reliable source of income for the medium. By 2000 cable's ties to broadcast television were only slightly greater than its ties to other media, including computers and telephones. Both converging technologies (e.g., the ability to transmit moving images over the Internet) and corporate mergers (e.g., between TCI and AT&T that created the largest cable MSO in the United States) have ensured that cable programming will become increasingly harder to separate from other sources of entertainment and information.

In recent years cable networks have been using increasing amounts of non-broadcast-derived programming. And more specialized networks are being launched every year. Cable and related television technologies now possess the bandwidth needed to carry hundreds of channels of programming, so limited shelf space is no longer the deterrent it was in the past. Furthermore, cable MSOs and other entertainment corporations have both the resources and infrastructures necessary to subsidize more specialized programming and networks. Audiences also have grown more accustomed to multiple channel choices—perhaps even looking to television to fulfill some of the entertainment and information needs once met by magazines. One could say that by the year 2000 the vision of cable as a narrowcast medium was being realized.

Digital compression technologies have allowed ever more channels to be carried by cable and satellite systems, and the Internet has provided the interactivity cable was never able to achieve. As these and related technologies have come together, the electronic entertainment and information scene looks more and more like the scenarios described by Ralph Lee Smith, the Sloan Commission, and others from cable's Blue Sky period. Just as in the 1980s and early 1990s competition from cable helped to shape the direction of broadcast television, now the presence of the Internet is helping to shape the direction of cable. Specialty cable networks, with coordinated websites, have begun catering to a range of consumer tastes and interests including cooking, travel, pet care, home improvement, fitness, and even aviation. The roster of original programs is impressive.

Those who advocated free-market competition as the most expeditious way for cable to achieve its public service potential might well claim a victory; after all, cable networks needed a decade or so to recover their start-up costs before going on to produce specialized and original programming. It seems more likely, though, that other factors are driving the specialization of cable's programming selection. Given the reality that satellite cable has been very much under the control of advertisers, we must be cautious when comparing an increasingly niche-driven cable programming environment that began in the 1990s with those scenarios put forth in the late 1960s and early 1970s.

Recent cable narrowcasting trends clearly have been an outcome of the deregulatory policies and programming practices initiated in the 1970s—not a revolutionary move away from them. There was a market-driven logic to satellite cable's early programming practices, even if this logic was not well understood at the time. As fledgling networks set up schedules packed with reruns and other easily acquired fare, they were careful to "brand" themselves using frequently repeated promotional material. As soon as finances allowed, the networks added "signature" shows to the mix. Signature shows are originally produced programs with a direct appeal to both target audience and core advertisers.[1] Sometimes these shows even have old-style single sponsors—typically major retailers whose products are featured regularly. For example, The Home Depot has been the single or primary sponsor of programs on Discovery Home & Leisure.

Signature shows, when combined with more familiar offerings, have allowed viewers to become acclimated to the notion of specialized programming. In some instances, networks will start out with a broad focus—including inexpensive acquired programs as a way to economize and at the same time meet the expectations of broadcast-conditioned audiences—and then gradually adopt a more specialized niche through the inclusion of more original shows. To some extent this strategy can be seen in the development of networks such as BET and Lifetime. In other situations, popular general-interest networks will introduce more specialized original programs as a sheltered launch for new networks begun by their parent companies. This strategy has been pursued by A&E in launching The History Channel and by Discovery Networks in launching a plethora of specialty networks including Discovery Home & Leisure, Discovery Wings, and the Discovery Travel Channel.

Still, any claim that narrowcasting characterizes U.S. cable's most recent incarnation calls for some qualification. On the one hand, the recent proliferation of signature shows on cable channels represents a new degree of specialization. On the other hand, however, few of them stray far from traditional television genres. While never a staple of prime-time network television, gourmet cooking, home improvement, and animal shows have always had a place among syndication and public television offerings. What is new about cable's recent narrowcast emphasis is not the types of programs, but rather the concentration of particular program types throughout the schedules of individual networks. This has called more for a change in audience viewing and consumption habits than for a change in actual program tastes.

Specialized cable channels, combined with the Internet and recent retailing and target-marketing trends, have encouraged viewers to select programs according to how they fit particular lifestyles rather than where they fit individuals' daily or weekly schedules. Where cooking programs were once the daytime domain of housewives, these programs are now available around the clock—and to the widest possible spectrum of viewers. Rather than waiting for a PBS affiliate's daily or weekly showing of *This Old House,* home-repair enthusiasts can now tune in to Home & Garden Television (HGTV) or Discovery Home & Leisure 24 hours a day.

The categories of specialized cable programming available today represent a set of consumer-oriented categories designed to intersect a variety of media and retail outlets. This is part of a more widespread set of marketing trends, as Turow (1997) explains:

> The ultimate aim of [the] new wave of marketing is to reach different groups with specific messages about how certain products tie into their lifestyles. Target-minded media firms are helping advertisers do that by building *primary media communities.* These are formed when viewers or readers feel that a magazine, TV channel, newspaper, radio station or other medium reaches people like them, resonates with their personal beliefs, and helps them chart their position in the larger world. For advertisers, tying into those communities means gaining consumer loyalties that are nearly impossible to establish in today's mass market. (4)

I would suggest, in addition to this, that there has been a push to create these sorts of media communities where they had not existed previously. In some situations, this has meant compiling and redirecting existing cultural practices; in other situations, it has meant generating entirely new fads.

New pastimes are being cultivated among the highly sought-after upscale adult consumers, who perceive themselves as too busy with work and family to participate in traditional hobbies. Cash-hungry activities such as home improvement, cooking, travel, fitness, and pet care—which already are part of most people's daily or weekly routines to some extent—allow for varying degrees of participation. Consumption can be encouraged through a carefully coordinated combination of how-to shows, informational websites, and retail superstores. As cable offers an increasingly diverse and interactive array of lifestyle programs along with traditional television entertainment, and as it makes this programming available throughout the day and week, it could be said to be achieving the nebulous goal of "something for everyone."

One might even argue that the convergence of cable, the Internet, and other new media technologies *eventually will* approach the degree of specialization once envisioned by cable television's Blue Sky planners. Yet it seems unlikely that a media driven by corporate profits can—or would even strive to—uphold the time-honored goals of democratic participation or replace activities traditionally carried out in public spaces. The private space of the suburban shopping mall never truly replaced the town square; so too the currently developing "medium of the future" cannot do more than obliquely signify the cultural practices that it has assimilated. But then again the cultural practices themselves have not disappeared—nor are they in danger of disappearing as long as consumers recognize that watching television of any variety is only one activity among many.

It seems clear that the history of cable programming in the United States has been one of mismatched goals and unplanned outcomes. There have been a variety of social goals underlying plans for the medium's development, yet the real driving forces have always ended up being the imperatives of a free-market economy. This is not surprising given the history of mass media in the United States generally; the nation is grounded in a notion of hands-off oversight of the media. Nor should it *necessarily* be viewed negatively that cable television programming has been guided more by market forces than by a concerted developmental plan. It is easy to forget that most new media are introduced with little more than the expectation that they will improve upon the functions served by existing media. It is only after some exposure to these media that visionaries enter the picture—as they inevitably do—and develop grandiose schemes. History has shown time and again that by the time of its mature phase, a particular medium's primary functions represent a compromise between what was intended for it initially and the hopes and expectations later set for it. A lot of original programming has been added to cable as a whole in recent years, including new genres and genre hybrids. Surely this was true of U.S. cable by the mid-1990s; it was still retransmitting broadcast signals, as it had done since the late 1940s, but it had also introduced many new types of programming and programming strategies.

In fact, there has been a great deal of innovation in cable over the years. It could be argued, though, that rather than allowing radical new programming plans to stagnate as fickle audiences retreated to older media forms, the free-market approach allowed innovations to be added gradually and subtly. Surely if we were to compare today's cable offerings to those of the 1980s we would notice a dramatic difference in program selection. It also seems likely that we would notice cable viewers increasingly relying on specialized networks for specific types of entertainment and information. Whether today's cable programming selection reflects the needs and interests of a broad cross section of the population—as opposed to merely those perceived to be good consumers—is another question, of course.

It is impossible to determine if cable could have developed differently had policy initiatives followed different paths. Perhaps if federal regulators had developed, and adhered to, more structured cable programming plans, cable's intervention in the evolution of media content might have been different. Audiences might indeed have come to understand television in a more expanded sense than broadcast channels alone could define. Still, in retrospect it seems unlikely that cable could have brought about high levels of audience engagement or more democratic forms of program production and distribution, since no precedents were in place for these uses of television. Blue Sky planners seem to have been blissfully neglectful of the fact that the passive viewing habits engendered by commercial broadcast television had been in place for decades by the time satellite cable entered the scene. And they probably did not take enough account of the many precedents for free-market competition within the U.S. media industries generally—dating back at least to the rise of the telegraph in the mid-1800s.[2]

It is equally impossible to know the extent to which cable's convergence with the Internet and other new technologies can lead to the development of an even more specialized medium for the future. New media technologies almost seem to be introduced to the public on a daily basis. But their adoption and eventual uses are no more predictable than were those of past media. It does seem likely that the purely technological aspects of modern cable, many of which date back to the medium's founding in the 1940s, will give way to more sophisticated means of program delivery. Still, as this study contends, it has been forces other than the purely technological that have guided the nature and variety of cable programming over the years. Just as broadcast television altered the conventions of radio programming in the 1950s, so cable altered the conventions of broadcast television programming in the 1980s and 1990s. The medium of the future, as we can already see, will not have begun with a blank slate—but rather with the conventions and innovations that cable television developed in response to a combination of audience tastes, market forces, and creative inspiration.

Preface

1. See, for example, Linder 1999 and *Public Access, Everyone's Channel* (video recording) 1990.
2. Note that these listings reflect these individuals' affiliations at the time they were consulted.

Chapter One

1. Statistics from Waterman and Grant 1991, 179–188.
2. See, for example, Williams 1981; Bibb 1993; and Goldberg and Goldberg 1995.
3. See Horwitz 1989 for a more detailed discussion.
4. See, for example, McChesney 1996.
5. See, for example, McChesney 1997, 1999; Herman and McChesney 1998; Solomon 1999; and Aufderheide 2000.
6. See, for example, Waterman 1986; Waterman and Grant 1991; and Grant 1994.
7. In related studies, Morse (1986), Frith (1989), Grossberg (1993), and several other scholars have looked at the effects of the new televisual context on traditional pop music promotion. Fry and Fry (1986), Aufderheide (1986), and Savan (1993) all focus work specifically on the aesthetic and economic relationships between music videos and traditional commercials. Rabinovitz (1989) focuses a study on MTV's animated ID logos, asserting that as the cable service has grown progressively more constrained by the demands of traditional television advertisers, its "postmodern" identity has become more of a promotional tool than an accurate aesthetic characterization.
8. See, for example, Stout and Burda 1989 and several studies anthologized in Heeter and Greenberg 1988.

Chapter Two

1. *The 1948 Radio Annual* (New York: Radio Daily, 1948).
2. For an extensive discussion of this regulatory dilemma and its implications for cable television, see LeDuc 1973, Chaps. 3 and 4.
3. A booster station amplifies and retransmits the signal of a broadcast station. A translator rebroadcasts a station's signal on a different frequency. Boosters and translators generally appeared in sparsely populated, mountainous western states such as Colorado and Montana. At first these stations were prohibited by the FCC; and almost without exception, they were built without the consent of the station whose signal was being retransmitted.
4. Others have laid claim to this accomplishment, including John Walson Sr. of Mahanoy City, Pennsylvania. However, Parsons's claim is the most easily verified. Many of these very early systems were located in Pennsylvania—a state where virtually all communities lay within 150 miles of one or more broadcast television markets, yet where many nonetheless had poor over-the-air signal reception due to the mountainous terrain. Other early systems were located in New York and Maryland.
5. See Phillips 1972 for details of the NCTA's formation.
6. John Walson, oral history interview by Mary Alice Mayer, August 1987, interview transcript, National Cable Television Center and Museum, Penn State University, University Park, Pa., 9, 22–23 (hereafter cited as Cable Center). For discussion of the debate surrounding Walson's claims, see Parsons 1996.
7. "Biggest Community Antenna System . . . ," *Television Digest* 9, no. 9 (28 February 1953): 7.
8. *NCTA Membership Bulletin,* 15 August 1953, 2 (cited as *NCTA Monthly Bulletin* in Phillips 1972, 43).
9. Modern satellite transmissions also use microwave frequencies.
10. See, for example, Seiden 1972.
11. "Pendleton Picture Improves as Microwave Service Begins," *NCTA Membership Bulletin* 3, no. 39 (1 October 1956): 225.
12. "Community Video Service Is on Its Way to Oneonta," *Oneonta Star,* 17 November 1954, 14; "Oneonta Video Co. Brings Television in Variety to TV Set Owners in Oneonta," *Oneonta Star,* 28 January 1956.
13. Albert Bagnardi, telephone interview by author, 6 November 1994. It is worth noting that Western Microwave was begun by Robert Magness, who, until shortly before his death in 1996, was chairman of the board of cable MSO Tele-Communications, Inc. (TCI).
14. "Direct 'Wave' to New York: TV Service to Expand," *Oneonta Star,* 18 October 1962, 3. Available sources do not indicate any reasons for the delay between the announcement of plans to build the microwave relays during the mid-1950s and the actual appearance of the stations in 1962.

15. "Microwave for Dubuque," *NCTA Membership Bulletin* 4, no. 3 (19 January 1962): 24.
16. See Schatz 1990, 127.
17. "Why San Diego Stations Worry about CATV," *Broadcasting*, 2 August 1965, 54. In most areas of San Diego, viewers also were able to receive Los Angeles signals off the air. However, when polled, only a very small percentage of CATV nonsubscribers reported watching Los Angeles channels the most. U.S. FCC 1966.
18. "Wild Escalation in CATV Fight," *Broadcasting*, 21 February 1966, 25–28.
19. Most of the limited number of VHF stations had been purchased during the 1940s by radio station owners, who already had affiliations with one of the major networks (CBS or NBC). In contrast, a number of the approximately 140 UHF stations operating in 1954 were affiliated exclusively with either ABC or DuMont (16 and 10, respectively), more than 60 carried multiple affiliations (almost always including ABC, DuMont, or both), and 25 carried no affiliation. *Radio Annual and Television Yearbook* (New York: Radio Daily, 1954).
20. "Pennsylvania Broadcaster Compiles Brochure Showing CATV 'Plus' Coverage," *NCTA Membership Bulletin* 2, no. 48 (5 December 1955): 4.
21. "WDAU's CATV Shepherdess," *Broadcasting*, 30 June 1958, 84.
22. "FCC Ought to Rope, Brand CATV, Western TV Operators Tell Hill," *Broadcasting*, 2 June 1958, 60.
23. "Freedom of Competition for NCTA—Doerfer," *Broadcasting-Telecasting*, 13 June 1955, 69–70.
24. *The Television Inquiry: The Problem of Television Service in Smaller Communities*, prepared by Kenneth A. Cox (Washington, D.C.: GPO, 1959; cited in Phillips 1972, 53).
25. 32 FCC 459, 1962. The Commission's decision was affirmed by the U.S. Court of Appeals (321 F2d 359), and the Supreme Court refused to review the case (cert. denied 375 US 951).
26. For detailed discussion of *Carter Mountain* and its effects, see Seiden 1965, 41. In addition to the common carrier companies, there were numerous microwave relays licensed either as Business Radio or CARS (Community Antenna Relay Service) built to serve single CATV systems.
27. Predicted grade A contour is defined as the line representing the service area in which a good picture is computed to be available 90 percent of the time at 70 percent of the receiver locations. Predicted grade B contour is defined as the concentric area marking a television station's service area in which a good picture is computed to be available 90 percent of the time at 50 percent of the receiver locations.
28. See Seiden 1972, Chap. 8, for a summary and analysis of the *First* and *Second Report and Order* on CATV. See also "FCC Closes Fist around CATV," *Broadcasting*, 14 March 1966, 48–50, for a short-term analysis of the 1966 rules.

29. "CATV Universe Still Expanding, Even in Major Markets," *Broadcasting,* 17 October 1966, 45.
30. As of 1964, H&B also owned relays in Washington, Montana, and Alabama.
31. Philips 1972, 43; E. Stratford Smith, interview by author, 16 March 1995, Penn State University, University Park, Pa. At the time, Dage cameras were sold primarily to small broadcast stations.
32. *NCTA Membership Bulletin* 1 (15 August 1953): 2 (cited in Phillips 1972, 43; see note 8 above).
33. "Cable TV Thriving in Hills," *Broadcasting,* 19 March 1962, 77–78.
34. "Other Program Gear for CATV's," *Broadcasting,* 26 July 1965, 55.
35. AP intended to charge CATV systems rates comparable to the rates it charged television stations for its service, based on market size and subscriber numbers. "Now Visual News for CATV's," *Broadcasting,* 26 July 1965, 54–55; *NCTA Membership Bulletin* 7, no. 40 (29 October 1965): 354; "New CATV News Service Makes Debut in Manhattan," *Broadcasting,* 20 November 1967, 59.
36. "UPI to Provide News for CATV Systems," *Broadcasting,* 17 January 1966, 66.
37. "Community TV Plans Come to a Boil," *Broadcasting-Telecasting,* 1 June 1953, 43.
38. "Md. Community TV Seeks Advertising," *Broadcasting-Telecasting,* 22 August 1955, 94.
39. "All Channels Lead to Cumberland," *Broadcasting,* 16 June 1958, 78.
40. "Cumberland System Announces Huge Expansion," *NCTA Membership Bulletin* 3, no. 29 (29 September 1961): 188.
41. Smith interview by author. See also "Long-Planned 'Commprovision' Closed Circuit Gets Under Way," *NCTA Membership Bulletin* 3, no. 10 (12 March 1956): 70–71.
42. "CATV Originators Run Feature Films," *Broadcasting,* 3 July 1967, 58–59.
43. Smith interview by author.
44. *Teleprompter Corp. v. CBS, Inc.,* 415 US 395 (1974).
45. "Skiatron Subscription-TV System," *Television Digest* 9, no. 23 (6 June 1953): 15; "FCC Squares Off to Face Subscription TV Dilemma," *Broadcasting-Telecasting,* 15 November 1954, 31–32.
46. "Community TV: Palm Springs Under Way," *Broadcasting-Telecasting,* 14 April 1952, 74; Thomas M. Pryor, "Hollywood Ready for Test with TV," *New York Times,* 14 September 1953; Joe Schoenfeld, "Telemeter's Preem Film-Grid Show 'Works' but B.O. Potential a Poser," *Variety,* 2 December 1953, 1; "Pay-TV to Get New Paramount Movies," *Broadcasting-Telecasting,* 7 December 1953, 40; "CATV Lures Telemeter Back," *Broadcasting,* 25 May 1967, 40.
47. Fred Hift, "Telemeter to Invade Two Cities; Exhib Coin in Closed-Circuit Runs," *Variety,* 4 May 1955, 1.
48. Ibid.; "Home-Toll and Advertising, Too," *Variety,* 14 August 1957, 5; "Paramount Pitch Attacks Free TV," *Broadcasting-Telecasting,* 19 August 1957,

92–93; Paul MacNamara, "Plans of International Telemeter Corporation for Subscription and Cable Theater Operations," supplement to *NCTA Membership Bulletin* 4, no. 46 (18 November 1957).

49. HR-586, introduced by Rep. Owen Harris (D-Alaska), would impose a $10,000 fine on anyone charging a fee for television programs. S-2268, introduced by Sen. Strom Thurmond (D-S.C.), proposed similar penalties. During the 1950s pay-TV's most outspoken opponent in Congress was Rep. Emanuel Celler (D-N.Y.). "Five Bills Pend in Congress to Ban Tollvision from American Waves," *Variety,* 5 February 1958; Pay Television, report prepared for Batten, Barton, Durstine and Osborn, 2 January 1958, archived at Hagley Museum and Library, Wilmington, Del., accession #1803, box 22, folder 30 (courtesy of Cynthia Meyers).

50. E. Stratford Smith, original research, communication with the author 1 April 1994.

51. There were plans eventually to include "a music-news-weather audio program, a Muzak-type music channel and a live pickup circuit." "Benchmark in Bartlesville," *Broadcasting-Telecasting,* 9 September 1957, 32.

52. Smith, original research.

53. Ibid.

54. "Movies-in-the-Home Are on Verge of Failing," *Broadcasting,* 12 May 1958, 34–35; "Home Cable Theatre Committee Report," *NCTA Membership Bulletin* 5, no. 11 (17 March 1958): 59; "Suspension of Bartlesville Trial No Surprise to N.Y. Execs; Taught Pay-See Showmen Some Essentials," *Variety,* 28 May 1958, 23.

55. Ibid.

56. "KLRD-TV Asks Permit for Wired Toll TV," *Broadcasting-Telecasting,* 8 April 1957, 68–69.

57. Martin F. Malarkey, oral history interview by Kathleen B. Hom, August 1985, interview transcript, Cable Center, 54–55.

58. MacNamara, "Plans of International Telemeter Corporation."

59. "Support Growing for Pay-TV," *Broadcasting,* 7 March 1960, 76.

60. "What They Pay for Pay-TV in Canada," *Broadcasting,* 7 November 1960, 62–63.

61. "Hockey-on-Tour A Tollvision Coup," *Variety,* 25 October 1961, 22.

62. "Pay-TV Set for Canadian Start," *Broadcasting,* 22 June 1959, 122–124.

63. *NCTA Membership Bulletin* 6, no. 29 (31 July 1964): 1; "Commercials on Atlanta Pay-TV?" *Broadcasting,* 10 August 1964, 67–68.

64. "FCC Gets Pay-TV Pleas," *Broadcasting,* 10 October, 1966, 47. The comparable Home Theatres of Georgia and Florida Home Theatres Corp. also had been started as of mid-1964. While franchises were granted to these companies in several cities throughout the South and Southwest, no Home Theatres systems ever actually launched.

65. "CATV Lures Telemeter Back," *Broadcasting,* 29 May 1967, 40.

66. Ibid.

67. "On-Air Toll-TV Test Is Underway," *Broadcasting,* 2 July 1962, 45.

68. At this point, Phonevision reported 4,800 subscribers out of approximately 200,000 Hartford TV households. Thus, the audience share was 2 for the fight, 1.6 for the movie, and 1.1 for the Kingston Trio special. "Pay-TV: On Air or On Wire?" *Broadcasting,* 20 July 1964, 23–26.

69. "Hartford Revisited: Will Pay-TV Work?" *Broadcasting,* 21 January 1963, 68–70.

70. "Pay-TV Showdown in the Making," *Broadcasting,* 15 March 1965, 33–36.

71. "West Coast Getting New Pay-TV Venture," *Broadcasting,* 26 August 1963, 32.

72. Fox died shortly before STV was due to launch.

73. Shortly prior to Weaver's accepting the position, STV had been considering either CBS president James Aubrey or advertising executive Rod Erickson for the position. "Pay-TV: Aubrey vs. Erickson?" *Variety,* 4 September 1963, 25.

74. "The Beginning or the End?" *Broadcasting,* 20 July 1964, 26–27.

75. See Whiteside 1985 (part I), 49–58, for a discussion of the STV operation and its defeat.

76. See Anderson 1997.

77. Ibid. See also White 1990, 145–163.

78. One of its founders was Robert Rosencrans, subsequently the founder of both UA-Columbia Cablevision (a large cable company) and the USA cable network. Other founders included William Rosensohn and Hollywood producer Walter Wanger.

79. "Robert Rosencrans: Nurturing a Cable MSO from Infancy," *Broadcasting,* 3 July 1978, 89; "Sheraton Hotel Chain Enters Closed Circuit TV Business," *Wall Street Journal,* 6 June 1955; Robert Rosencrans, oral history interview by E. Stratford Smith, May 1992, interview transcript (draft), Cable Center, 5–11.

80. Irving Berlin Kahn, oral history interview by Marlowe Froke, July and October 1987, interview transcript, Cable Center, 158–159.

81. Ibid., 158.

82. "Pay-TV Moves Close to Showdown," *Broadcasting,* 27 June 1960, 78–82.

83. The systems carrying the fight included TelePrompTer's own systems in Liberal, Kansas; Farmington and Silver City, New Mexico; and Rawlins, Wyoming; as well as systems in Aberdeen, Washington; Alexandria-Pineville, Louisiana; and Snowflake, Page, Holbrook, Morenci, Safford, Winslow, and Miami, Arizona. "Was the Big Fight a Little Start for Wired Toll TV?" *Broadcasting,* 27 June 1960, 79.

84. Kahn interview, 159.

85. "CATV into Pay-TV? Not So Easy," *Broadcasting,* 13 July 1964, 27–30.

86. See also Balio 1990a, 31.

87. "Special Report: Spanish-Language Market," *Broadcasting,* 25 May 1964, 77–95.

88. Ibid., 79.

89. See Barnouw 1990, 140–142.
90. "ETV Opportunities Boom for CATV," *NCTA Membership Bulletin* 3, no. 21 (31 July 1961): 128.
91. "FCC Lifts CATV Freeze if ETV Is Sought," *Broadcasting,* 1 April 1963, 81.
92. *Television and Cable Factbook* (Washington, D.C.: Warren Publishing, annual); *Radio Annual and Television Yearbook* (New York: Radio Daily, 1960).
93. See Litman 1990, 115–144.
94. See, for example, Lachenbruch 1965; Warren 1966, 1967; Hastings 1967; Johnson 1967; and Smith 1968.

Chapter Three

1. See Barnouw 1990, 396–399 and 454–455.
2. See Balio 1990b, 292. The networks still were permitted to syndicate their own programs overseas.
3. See, for example, Warren 1966, 90, and "The Four Letters That Have Rocked *Broadcasting,*" *TV Guide,* 29 July 1967, 4–7.
4. "Nick Johnson Splits on CATV," *Broadcasting,* 9 October 1967, 65.
5. Here Smith is referring to time-saving services that would reduce or eliminate the need for business travel and small errands.
6. "Task-Force Plan: Air Plus Cable," *Broadcasting,* 9 September 1968, 27–30.
7. U.S. President's Task Force on Communications Policy, Final Report (The Rostow Report), 1968, 10 (Chap. 7).
8. As Stephen White, one of the foundation's vice presidents, explained, "It dawned on us that the government was speaking only for the broadcast interests and the cable interests." "Hands Off for Healthy Cable Growth—Sloan," *Broadcasting,* 13 December 1971, 40–41.
9. "Ford Grant Backs Cable-TV Study," *Broadcasting,* 30 June 1969, 65–66.
10. "Barking Back at Rand Report," *Broadcasting,* 9 February 1970, 42–43. The Rand studies included Walter S. Baer, *Interactive Television: Prospects for Two-Way Services on Cable,* Rand Memo. R-888-MF (Santa Monica: Rand Corporation, 1971); Leland L. Johnson, *The Future of Cable Television: Some Problems of Federal Regulation,* Rand Memo. RM-6199-FF (Santa Monica: Rand Corporation, 1970); and Rolla E. Park, *Potential Impact of Cable Growth on Television Broadcasting,* Rand Memo. R-587-FF (Santa Monica: Rand Corporation, 1970).
11. "Special Feature on Cable Television," *NEA Journal–Today's Education,* November 1971, 52–59.
12. Although challenged in court and temporarily extended, this deadline was affirmed in 1972 in *United States v. Midwest Video Corp.* (*Midwest Video I*), 406 US 649.
13. "Programming Called Key to Cable Future," *Broadcasting,* 4 May 1970, 25; "CATV Headed for Ad-Supported Network?" *Broadcasting,* 4 May 1970, 23–24.

14. This applied to all new systems. Existing systems had until 1977 to expand.
15. "585 Systems Turning Out Local Fare," *Broadcasting*, 10 September 1973, 58–59.
16. By the time Woodard's book had been published, the FCC's 1972 *Cable Television Report and Order* had been passed, and all new cable systems were required to have at least 20 channels.
17. Lon Cantor, "Pennsylvania System Gets Lots of Volunteer Help," *TV Communications*, July 1971, 94–100.
18. Waldo T. Boyd, "Santa Rosa CableVision: Origination Success Story," *TV Communications*, November 1971, 40–50.
19. "CATV Headed for Ad-Supported Network?" For more details on the Pittsfield system, see Don Andersson, "Experienced Perspective On the Origination 'Bug'," *TV Communications*, March 1971, 44–51.
20. "CATV Headed for Ad-Supported Network?"; "A Syndicator Eyes the Big CATV Market," *Broadcasting*, 2 March 1970, 54–55.
21. This is a loose-leaf book containing descriptions of locally produced cable programming, as well as information about syndication packages for use on cable systems.
22. Thomas C. Dowden, "Cox Origination Experiments Reveal Economic Facts of Life," *TV Communications*, May 1971, 39.
23. Bonnie Molitor, "Well, It Looks Like You Can Make It in Color with Cable Too!" *TV Communications*, August 1972, 56–60; John Rather and Christopher Burnett, "Local 'O' in San Francisco Gets an 'E' for Excellent," *TV Communications*, April 1973, 60–62.
24. "New York Wired TV System in Expansion," *Broadcasting*, 20 April 1964, 102–103.
25. "Decision on New York CATV Delayed Month," *Broadcasting*, 26 October 1964, 76–77.
26. "New York City Gives Three CATV Grants," *Broadcasting*, 6 December 1965, 47–49.
27. "New York Reviews CATV's Status," *Broadcasting*, 31 July 1967, 34–35.
28. "NY Cables Get OK to Originate," *Broadcasting*, 23 December 1968, 24–25.
29. Kathleen Collins, "Subscriber Promotion: How It's Done in New York City," *TV Communications*, May 1969, 42–45.
30. "NY Cables Get OK."
31. "No Access Crunch on New York CATV's," *Broadcasting*, 12 July 1971, 48.
32. Paul S. Maxwell, "Say the Magic Words—You're on the Cable," *TV Communications*, October 1972, 33.
33. On 30 September 1969—in a ruling against the National Association of Theater Owners and the Joint Committee Against Toll TV—the U.S. Circuit Court of Appeals for the District of Columbia affirmed the FCC's authority to license pay-TV systems. 34 FR 15370, 1969 (cited in Howard and Carroll 1980, 36).

34. Similar restrictions applied to over-the-air systems.
35. Other systems also existed at this time, but had not yet been licensed.
36. Alan Greenstadt (representing Optical Systems), "Optical Systems," *TV Communications,* November 1972, 54–56; Ruth Steinberg, "Channel 100 in Here!" *TV Communications,* August 1973, 40–47; Lachenbruch 1973, 29–34.
37. Dore Schary (representing TheatreVisioN, Inc.), "TheatreVisioN," *TV Communications,* November 1972, 43; Lachenbruch 1973.
38. Richard Lubic (representing Home Theater Network), "Home Theater," *TV Communications,* November 1972, 43–46; Ruth Steinberg, "Step Right Up Ladies and Gentlemen, For Just Three Dollars, You Will Get . . . ," *TV Communications,* February 1973, 36–39.
39. Richard K. Doan, "Will You Pay for TV?" *TV Guide,* 17 November 1973, 6–8; Richard K. Doan, "Pay-TV: Poised for a Giant Leap?" *TV Guide,* 26 July 1975, 2–7; Baer and Pilnick 1974, 28.
40. "Can Programming Pay on CATV?" *Broadcasting,* 15 June 1970.
41. See Owen 1985, 46, and "AT&T's Telstar Ushers in Global TV Age," *Broadcasting,* 16 July 1962, 38–41.
42. "Domestic Satellite around the Corner," *Broadcasting,* 18 April 1966, 61–62; "Is Satellite Act Ambiguous?" *Broadcasting,* 8 August 1966, 66–73.
43. Ibid.; Magnant 1977, 106.
44. "Whitehead Flexes OTP's Muscle," *Broadcasting,* 17 April 1972, 23–24.
45. Certain restrictions applied to AT&T as well as to COMSAT (in which AT&T held a 29 percent interest).

Chapter Four

1. "Hard Decision FCC Faces Now on Pay-Cable," *Broadcasting,* 12 November 1973, 23–25.
2. Copyright Revision Act, 17 USCA Sec. 1, *et seq.* The act became enforceable on 1 January 1978.
3. "Armed with New Copyright Bill, NCTA Will Seek a Fresh Look at FCC's Rules on Signal Carriage," *Broadcasting,* 11 October 1976, 48.
4. "Senate Starts Probe of CATV Copyright Issue," *Broadcasting,* 8 August 1966, 82; "Another Investigation of CATV," *Broadcasting,* 17 January 1966, 70.
5. Of course, the new rule cut into cable interests' profits. For their part, broadcasters and professional sports leagues felt that the imposed blackout zone did not cover the entire market within which a sports event draws its audience and therefore offered inadequate protection from cable competition. "Sports-Carriage Rules for Cable to Stand," *Broadcasting,* 10 November 1975, 52–53.
6. "Cable Opts for Networking Role," *Broadcasting,* 30 June 1969, 71–72.

7. "Teleprompter Considering Satellites?" *NCTA Membership Bulletin* 7, no. 47 (22 December 1965): 1–2.

8. "How Teleprompter Figures to Weave a Cable Network," *Broadcasting,* 19 March 1973, 114–116.

9. Teleprompter Corporation, application for domestic communication satellite receive-only earth stations (1971). Cable Center, accession #94-IK-1118, 3.

10. Ibid., 9–10.

11. "Cable-Satellite Group Is Off the Launch Pad," *Broadcasting,* 3 September 1973, 27.

12. Jacqueline B. Morse, "Captain Video May Blast Off Again—and This Time Spin into Orbit as the New Captain Cable," *TV Communications,* November 1972, 36. This statement was based on the 1969 feasibility study that Teleprompter completed in conjunction with Hughes Aircraft.

13. Frank Cooper, oral history interview by E. Stratford Smith, June 1990, interview transcript, Cable Center, 29.

14. Actually it was not until October 1974 that HBO finally began serving the subscribers of Manhattan Cable. By that point, the pay service already was available via 36 cable systems in four states and claimed to be serving 300,000 subscribers. "Pay-cable Makes It into Manhattan," *Broadcasting,* 21 October 1974, 29.

15. "HBO: Off the Ground, but Flying Low," *Broadcasting,* 4 February 1974, 47.

16. In fact, a large portion of this network was owned by Eastern Microwave, the company that had been started for the purpose of carrying New York independent stations to rural CATV systems in the early 1960s.

17. Statistics from "HBO: The First Twenty Years" 1992.

18. This effort was extended in the late 1970s, when Time Inc. actually subsidized the cost of receiving dishes for a number of cable systems.

19. "HBO Buys BBC Series for Pay-Cable Showing," *Broadcasting,* 27 October 1975, 51. *The Pallisers* was a coproduction with Time-Life, the series' U.S. distributor.

20. "'Beacon Hill' Draws Round of Applause from Pay-Cable Audience," *Broadcasting,* 5 July 1976, 34.

21. "HBO Makes Deals for Movies, Cable System," *Broadcasting,* 28 June 1976, 55–56.

22. See Hilmes 1990, 304–305.

23. See Frank Beerman, "Premiere Plans to Go Dark," *Variety,* 7 January 1981, 27; Brown 1980b; Tony Schwartz, "Court Halts Pay-TV Network," *New York Times,* 1 January 1981 (Lexis-Nexis).

24. For a discussion of this series of changes, see Schatz 1993, 8–36.

25. "Viacom Becomes Second By-Satellite Pay-Cable Network," *Broadcasting,* 31 October 1977, 45; "Cox Deal Boosts HBO's Prospects," *Broadcasting,* 6 November 1978, 62.

26. WWHT slogan from personal memory. Additional stations were launched in Los Angeles, Boston, Detroit, Phoenix, Fort Lauderdale, and Cincinnati.

27. "Subscription TV Entrepreneurs Say Medium Has More Long-Term Potential than Pay-Cable," *Television/Radio Age,* 26 February 1982, 82 (cited in Howard and Carroll 1980, 52).

28. *Pay TV Newsletter,* 14 February 1980 (cited in Howard and Carroll 1980, 142).

29. In addition to Bibb, see Williams 1981, Goldberg and Goldberg 1995, and Whittemore 1990.

30. Note that several of the passive superstations have since affiliated with newer broadcast networks such as UPN and WB.

31. "TV Throws a Punch at Cable Superstations," *Business Week,* 30 April 1979, 29.

32. "Television's Fragmented Future," *Business Week,* 17 December 1979 (Lexis-Nexis).

33. By this point, Eastern Microwave was headquartered in Syracuse and was part of the large Newhouse media empire.

34. CBN also included some radio stations, both in the United States and overseas. Comprehensive histories of CBN and the Robertson empire include Dabney 1980, Donovan 1988, Hadden and Shupe 1988, and Taylor 1994.

35. Robertson asked for 700 members of his television congregation each to pledge $10 a month—the money to be applied to the station's operating expenses.

36. Robertson takes credit for saving many of these stations from bankruptcy. Donovan 1988, 100–101.

37. Following the scandal in the late 1980s, several books have been written documenting the history of PTL. See, for example, Barnhart 1988.

38. In 1990 the Bakkers' former assets, including the Inspirational Network as well as the Heritage USA theme park, were purchased by Morris Cerullo World Evangelism, an organization that already was distributing religious programming worldwide via broadcast stations and satellite. At the time, the PTL satellite reached some 800 cable systems and an estimated 7 million subscribers. "Morris Cerullo World Evangelism" 1990.

39. The network was renamed Univision in 1987, following its acquisition by Hallmark Cards. Its founder, Emilio Azcarraga, has since regained control, though the Univision name has remained.

40. "Hispanic Broadcasting Comes of Age," *Broadcasting,* 3 April 1989 (Lexis-Nexis).

41. Or, as one 1982 analysis put it, "So far Qube's main accomplishment has been to help nail down franchises for Warner Amex by wowing municipalities with its bells and whistles." O'Donnell and Gissen 1982, 109.

42. For details of QUBE's progressive demise, see Sally Bedell Smith, "Two-Way Cable T.V. Falters," *New York Times,* 28 March 1984 (Lexis-Nexis).

43. In 1985 each of these services moved to its own transponder, at which point The Movie Channel began programming entire days, and Nickelodeon spun off Nick at Nite.
44. "Warner to Offer Children's Channel," *TV Communications,* 15 December 1978, 33.
45. Kathleen Murray, "Tuned In to Kids, She Takes Nickelodeon to the Top," *New York Times,* 14 March 1993.
46. "Reviews of Major Cable Services Available in the Tristate Area: Sports on Cable," *New York Times,* 12 July 1981.
47. Cited in Waters and Wilson 1979, 124.
48. Les Brown, "Garden Cable Network Is Going Beyond Sports," *New York Times,* 7 April 1978; "Time Inc. to Buy 50% of Firm That Provides Cable TV Programs," *Wall Street Journal,* 28 August 1981; Golden 1980.
49. BET moved to its own transponder in 1982.
50. Robert Rosencrans, oral history interview by E. Stratford Smith, May 1992, interview transcript (draft), Cable Center, 69–72.
51. The House Speaker's control of C-SPAN's coverage probably was most apparent in 1983 when some Republican congressmen were using the "Special Orders" period at the conclusion of the House's business day to make inflammatory speeches in front of C-SPAN cameras—and an otherwise empty chamber. Upon becoming aware of this deception to the television audience, O'Neil ordered that cameras regularly pan the (often empty) rows of seats. Krolik 1992, 94.
52. For detailed discussions of C-SPAN's development, see Krolik 1992, Meyer 1992, and Lardner 1994.

Chapter Five

1. Prior to their 1989 merger, both Time Inc. and Warner Communications were heavily invested in cable.
2. "Rising Price of Independents," *Broadcasting,* 27 June 1983, 63.
3. For several MSO representatives' comments on this issue, see "The Superstations: Between a Rock and a Hard Place and Doing Just Fine," *Broadcasting,* 30 November 1987, 47 (Lexis-Nexis).
4. "Making WTBS 'blackout-free,'" *Broadcasting,* 31 July 1989, 40–41.
5. United Video promotional brochure, 1995.
6. It is worth noting, though, that by the mid-1990s, most passive superstations had affiliated with either UPN or WB. These start-up "mini-networks" no doubt appreciated the additional viewership afforded by satellite distribution to cable systems.
7. "Chief of WGN-TV Dennis FitzSimmons Is Independent Force," *Electronic Media,* 23 January 1989, 148 (Lexis-Nexis).

8. Meg LaVigne and Lee Kinberg, interview by author, WSBK-TV38, Boston, 22 July 1994.
9. "Turner Talking TNT," *Broadcasting*, 29 February 1988, 40–41.
10. "Turner Takes TNT to Madison Avenue," *Broadcasting*, 4 July 1988, 44–45.
11. John Dempsey, "Vintage TV Hours Ripen on Cable Vine," *Variety*, 24 March 1996, 31 (Lexis-Nexis).
12. "C-SPAN: Documenting a Decade of Public Affairs," *Broadcasting*, 3 April 1989, 63.
13. This phenomenon has not been lost on programmers of national cable networks looking for comedy material. In the early 1990s Comedy Central even ran a program called *Access America*, which featured a selection of the most outrageous access fare from across the nation. For more details, see John Stark, "Combing a Nation for the Weirdest in Cable Fare," *New York Times*, 29 March 1992.
14. "Bristol-Myers to Produce Health Shows on Cable," *New York Times*, 18 February 1981; "Why Advertisers Are Rushing to Cable TV," *Business Week*, 2 November 1981, 96; "Bristol-Myers to Furnish Series to USA Network," *Broadcasting*, 23 February 1981, 67–68.
15. Sharon D. Mostovi, "Lifetime Finds Niche in Advertiser Co-production," *Broadcasting and Cable*, 22 March 1993, 42 (cited in Bronstein 1994–95, 219–220).
16. Ibid.; Maureen McFadden, "What's New in Advertising," *New York Times*, 10 June 1984; Hickey 1982, 37–42.
17. See Laurie Halpern Benenson, "Part Inside Look and Paid Promotion: 'The Making of . . . ,'" *New York Times*, 7 August 1994.
18. For a detailed report on the status of regional sports networks as of the mid-1980s, see "The Uncertain World of Regional Cable Sports Networks," *Broadcasting*, 25 March 1985, 42ff.
19. "ESPN Scores with NFL Football," *Broadcasting*, 4 January 1988, 98; "ESPN Gets to 'Play Ball' for $400 Million," *Broadcasting*, 9 January 1989, 93ff.
20. For an extensive account of ESPN's programming and expansion efforts throughout its history, see Freeman 2000.
21. See, for example, Whittemore 1990.
22. FNN was begun primarily to provide financial news to broadcast stations. However, since it was distributed by satellite, a number of cable systems chose to carry it for their subscribers as well.
23. "Showtime/Movie Channel and Paramount: Power through Partnership," *Broadcasting*, 2 January 1984, 38–39.
24. "Showtime/TMC: 10 Years Old and Moving toward the Future," *Broadcasting*, 7 July 1986, 75–80.
25. "Deal Struck," *Broadcasting*, 6 October 1986, 14.
26. "USA Goes for Movies in a Big Way," *Broadcasting*, 9 October 1989, 78–79.

27. "Lifetime Buys Film Package from Orion," *Broadcasting,* 30 October 1989, 39.
28. Turner's multifaceted media holdings not surprisingly made his empire a desirable takeover target for larger conglomerates. In 1995 both Time-Warner and General Electric vied to acquire Turner Enterprises, with Time-Warner ultimately winning.
29. "It's Showtime for Viacom," *Broadcasting,* 24 June 1989, 70–71.
30. "Disney Deal," *Broadcasting,* 15 August 1983.
31. "PPV Revelations," *Broadcasting,* 28 July 1986, 10.
32. "Looking for an Emmy," *Broadcasting,* 18 July 1988, 78.
33. "USA to Launch Made-for-Cable Movie Series," *Broadcasting,* 25 July 1988, 74–75.
34. For discussion of early efforts to rate cable networks, see "The Rush to Cable TV Is Now Turning into a Retreat," *Business Week,* 17 October 1983, 135ff. (Lexis-Nexis).

Chapter Six

1. "Sifting through the Fallout of CBS Cable, Disney," *Broadcasting,* 20 September 1982, 27–29.
2. See NCTA's *Cable Television Developments* for annual figures on the top cable networks.
3. Bravo did not show commercials until 1998, though it did accept corporate underwriting. It is currently offered as a basic network, but has been offered as a premium network in the past.
4. Bravo promotional video, 1996.
5. For a discussion of BET's early challenges, see "BET: Still Small but Determined," *Broadcasting,* 18 February 1985, 67–69.
6. The medical programming was discontinued.
7. "Lifetime: Cable Service Aims for Power through Partnership," *Broadcasting,* 13 February 1984, 174.
8. "Almost One Year Old," *Broadcasting,* 31 January 1983, 15.
9. "Nashville Goes Cross-Country," *Broadcasting,* 14 March 1983, 146–147.
10. According to statistics provided by the cable network in 1991, "inspirational" programming accounted for 13.4 percent (22.5 hours) of the weekly schedule. There was another 15.5 percent (26 hours) of "paid" programming, which included some religious programs. Therefore, by this stage, about one quarter of The Family Channel's schedule was filled with the types of programming for which Pat Robertson had started the Christian Broadcasting Network in 1960.
11. "What to Look Forward to on Cable, *Broadcasting,* 10 June 1985, 92–97.
12. Quoted in "State of the Industry: Part II: The Cable Perspective according to Robert Rosencrans," *Broadcasting,* 30 November 1981, 38ff.

13. "ARTS in the Evolving Cultural Medium," *Broadcasting,* 15 March 1982, 162.
14. Sara Rimer, "Television That's Just for Women . . . and Men," *New York Times,* 11 November 1991.
15. This program actually began in 1986 as a way for Minneapolis independent station KTMA to differentiate cheap movies ($500 to screen the average low-budget movie) from those of other independent stations and cable services. The program was bought by Comedy Central's predecessor, The Comedy Channel, in 1988. Brauer 1991, 40.
16. The commercial-free movies shown on American Movie Classics (AMC) also might be included in this category. AMC's scheduling and promotion practices, while not parodic, do represent the framing that typifies basic cable services. AMC uses both expert hosts and programs about movie-making to frame its actual movies.
17. "The Part-Time Network," *Broadcasting,* 21 January 1985, 10.
18. For details on the Weather Channel's "program wheel," see Stuart Elliott, "The Media Business: Advertising: Defying the Skeptics, the Weather Channel Finds a Silver Lining in Mother Nature's Mood Swings." *New York Times,* 9 June 1993.
19. See Thomas 1989.
20. "Shopping via Cable," *Broadcasting,* 11 October 1982, 82.
21. "Home Shopping Comes into Its Own," *Broadcasting,* 9 May 1988, 40–41.

Chapter Seven

1. See Turow 1997, 104–106.
2. See Czitrom 1982.

Adler, Richard, and Walter S. Baer, eds. 1974. *The Electronic Box Office: Humanities and the Arts on the Cable.* New York: Praeger.

Adorno, Theodor, and Max Horkheimer. 1972. "The Culture Industry: Enlightenment as Mass Deception." In *Dialectic of Enlightenment*, trans. John Cumming, 120–167. New York: Herder and Herder.

Altman, Rick. 1987. "Television Sound." In *Television: The Critical View.* 4th ed. Edited by Horace Newcomb, 566–584. New York: Oxford University Press.

Anderson, Christopher. 1997. "Television and Hollywood in the 1940s." In *Boom and Bust: The American Cinema in the 1940s,* ed. Thomas Schatz. New York: Scribner's.

Aufderheide, Patricia. 1986. "The Look of the Sound." In *Watching Television,* ed. Todd Gitlin, 111–135. New York: Pantheon.

———. 2000. *The Daily Planet: A Critic on the Capitalist Culture Beat.* Minneapolis: University of Minnesota Press.

Baer, Walter S., and Carl Pilnick. 1974. "Pay-Television at the Crossroads." In *The Electronic Box Office: Humanities and the Arts on Cable,* ed. Richard Adler and Walter S. Baer, 19–48. New York: Praeger.

Balio, Tino. 1990a. "Introduction to Part I." In *Hollywood in the Age of Television,* ed. Tino Balio, 3–40. Boston: Unwin Hyman.

———. 1990b. "Introduction to Part II." In *Hollywood in the Age of Television,* ed. Tino Balio, 259–296. Boston: Unwin Hyman.

———, ed. 1990c. *Hollywood in the Age of Television.* Boston: Unwin Hyman.

Barnhart, Joe E. 1988. *Jim and Tammy: Charismatic Intrigue Inside PTL.* Buffalo: Prometheus Books.

Barnouw, Erik. 1990. *Tube of Plenty: The Evolution of American Television.* 2d ed. New York: Oxford University Press.

Bibb, Porter. 1993. *It Ain't as Easy as It Looks: Ted Turner's Amazing Story.* New York: Crown.

Brauer, David. 1991. "The Million-Dollar Sight Gag." *Corporate Report Minnesota* (April): 40. Lexis-Nexis.

Bravin, Jess. 1990. "Why You Want Your MTV." *Los Angeles Times,* 22 July. TV Times.

Broadcasting and Cable Yearbook 2001. New Providence, N.J.: R. R. Bowker.

Bronstein, Carolyn. 1994–1995. "Mission Accomplished? Profits and Programming at the Network for Women." *Camera Obscura* 33\34 (May–September–January): 213–242.

Brown, Merrill. 1980a. "FCC Expands Cable TV's Programming; Substantial Deregulation of the Industry." *Washington Post,* 23 July. Lexis-Nexis.

———. 1980b. "Justice Department Files Antitrust Suit on Pay-Television System." *Washington Post,* 5 August. Lexis-Nexis.

Browne, Nick. 1987. "The Political Economy of the Television (Super)Text." In *Television: The Critical View.* 4th ed. Edited by Horace Newcomb, 585–599. New York: Oxford University Press.

Cablecasting Guidebook: A Collection of Ideas and Aids for the Cablecaster. 1973. Washington, D.C.: National Cable Television Association.

Cable Television Developments. Annual. Washington, D.C.: National Cable Television Association (NCTA).

Carey, James W. 1989. *Communication as Culture: Essays on Media and Society.* New York: Routledge.

Collins, Jim. 1992. "Television and Postmodernism." In *Channels of Discourse, Reassembled,* ed. Robert C. Allen, 227–253. Chapel Hill: University of North Carolina Press.

Czitrom, Daniel J. 1982. *Media and the American Mind: From Morse to McLuhan.* Chapel Hill: University of North Carolina Press.

Dabney, Dick. 1980. "God's Own Network," *Harper's* (August): 33–52.

Denisoff, R. Serge. 1988. *Inside MTV.* New Brunswick, N.J.: Transaction.

Director, Roger. 1982. "Are Cable Sportscasters as Good as the Networks?" *TV Guide,* 13 February, 31–33.

Doan, Richard K. 1973. "Will You Pay for TV?" *TV Guide,* 17 November, 6–8.

———. 1975. "Pay-TV: Poised for a Giant Leap?" *TV Guide,* 26 July, 2–7.

Donovan, John B. 1988. *Pat Robertson: The Authorized Biography.* New York: Macmillan.

Douglas, Susan J. 1987. *Inventing American Broadcasting, 1899–1922.* Baltimore: Johns Hopkins University Press.

Downing, John. 1990. "The Political Economy of U.S. Television." *Monthly Review* (May): 30. Lexis-Nexis.

Ellis, John. *Visible Fictions.* 1992. New York: Routledge.

Final Report: Satellite Interconnection Feasibility Study, prepared by Booz, Allen and Hamilton Inc. for Cable Satellite Access Entity, Norfolk, Va. 1974 (1 August). Irving Kahn papers, National Cable Television Center and Museum, Penn State University, University Park, Pa.

Fiske, John, and John Hartley. 1978. *Reading Television.* New York: Methuen and Co.

Freeman, Michael. 2000. *ESPN: The Uncensored History*. Dallas: Taylor Publishing.

Friendly, Fred W. 1970. "Asleep at the Switch of the Wired City." *Saturday Review,* 10 October, 58–60.

Frith, Simon. 1989. "Video Pop: Picking Up the Pieces." In *Facing the Music,* ed. Simon Frith, 88–130. New York: Pantheon.

Fry, Virginia H., and Donald L. Fry. 1986. "MTV and the Politics of Postmodern Pop." *Journal of Communication Inquiry* 10, no. 1 (winter): 29–33.

Gans, Herbert J. 1980. *Deciding What's News*. New York: Vintage.

Garnham, Nicholas. 1992. "The Media and the Public Sphere." In *Habermas and the Public Sphere,* ed. Craig Calhoun, 359–376. Cambridge: MIT Press.

Goldberg, Robert, and Gerald Jay Goldberg. 1995. *Citizen Turner: The Wild Rise of an American Tycoon*. New York: Harcourt Brace and Company.

Golden, Pamela. 1980. "Conversation with Kay Koplovitz." *Videography* (June): 49–57.

Goldman, Kevin. 1993. "Classic Spots to Tempt Nick at Nite Viewers." *Wall Street Journal,* 6 August.

Goodwin, Andrew. 1992. *Dancing in the Distraction Factory: Music Television and Popular Culture*. Minneapolis: University of Minnesota Press.

Graff, Gerald. "Co-optation." 1989. In *The New Historicism,* ed. H. Aram Veeser, 168–181. New York: Routledge.

Grant, August E. 1994. "The Promise Fulfilled? An Empirical Analysis of Program Diversity on Television." *Journal of Media Economics* 7, no. 1, 51–64.

Grossberg, Lawrence. 1993. "The Media Economy of Rock Culture: Cinema, Postmodernity, and Authenticity." In *Sound and Vision: The Music Video Reader,* ed. Simon Frith, Andrew Goodwin, and Lawrence Grossberg, 185–219. New York: Routledge.

Grover, Ronald, and Susan Duffy. 1990. "The Fourth Network." *Business Week,* 17 September, 114. Lexis-Nexis.

Habermas, Jürgen. 1989. *The Structural Transformation of the Public Sphere: An Inquiry into a Category of Bourgeois Society*, trans. Thomas Burger. Cambridge, Mass.: MIT Press.

Hadden, Jeffrey K., and Anson Shupe. 1988. *Televangelism: Power and Politics on God's Frontier*. New York: Henry Holt.

Harrington, Stephanie. 1973. "What's All This on TV?" *New York Times Magazine,* 27 May, 9.

Hastings, Jerry E. 1967. "CATV: Past, Present, and Future." *Electronics World* (August): 23–26.

"HBO: The First Twenty Years." 1992. Published by the Human Resources department of Home Box Office, a division of Time-Warner Entertainment Company.

Heath, Stephen. 1990. "Representing Television." In *Logics of Television,* ed. Patricia Mellencamp, 267–302. Bloomington: Indiana University Press.

Hebdige, Dick. 1979. *Subculture: The Meaning of Style*. New York: Routledge.

Heeter, Carrie, and Bradley S. Greenberg, eds. 1988. *Cableviewing*. Norwood, N.J.: Ablex.

Herman, Ed, and Robert McChesney. 1998. *The Global Media: The Missionaries of Global Capitalism*. London: Cassell Academic.

Hickey, Neil. 1982. "In Search of the 100% Zap-Proof Commercial." *TV Guide*, 8 May, 37–42.

Hilmes, Michele. 1990. *Hollywood and Broadcasting: From Radio to Cable*. Urbana: University of Illinois Press.

———. 1991. "Pay-Television: Breaking the Broadcast Bottleneck." In *Hollywood in the Age of Television*, ed. Tino Balio, 297–318. Boston: Unwin Hyman.

Horwitz, Robert Britt. 1989. *The Irony of Regulatory Reform*. New York: Oxford University Press.

Howard, H. H., and S. L. Carroll. 1980. *Subscription Television: History, Current Status, and Economic Projections*. Knoxville: University of Tennessee.

Huyssen, Andreas. 1986. *After the Great Divide: Modernism, Mass Culture, Postmodernism*. Bloomington: Indiana University Press.

Jenkins, Henry. 1992. *Textual Poachers: Television Fans and Participatory Culture*. New York: Routledge.

Johnson, Nicholas. 1967. "CATV: Promise and Peril." *Saturday Review*, 11 November, 87–88.

Katz, Richard. 1993. "The Syndication Conundrum." *Cablevision*, 25 January, 28–31.

Keating, Stephen. 1999. *Cutthroat: High Stakes and Killer Moves on the Electronic Frontier*. Boulder, Colo.: Johnson Books.

King, Susan. 1991. "Child by Day, Vintage Hip by Night." *Los Angeles Times*, 13 January. TV Times.

Kleir, Glenn E. 1973. "Cable." *Writer's Digest* (August): 31–32.

Krolik, Richard. 1992. "Everything You Wanted to Know about C-SPAN and Were Afraid to Ask." *Television Quarterly* 25, no. 4, 91–100.

Lachenbruch, David. 1965. "He Plants His Antennas in Every Corner of the Nation." *TV Guide*, 24 April, 15–19.

———. 1973. "Little Black Boxes and Self-Destructing Tickets." *TV Guide*, 3 March, 29–34.

Landro, Laura. 1990. "Family Cable Channel Switches Signals from Religious to Entertainment Fare." *Wall Street Journal*, 24 July.

Lardner, James. 1994. "The Anti-Network." *New Yorker*, 14 March, 48–55.

LeDuc, Don R. 1987. *Beyond Broadcasting: Patterns in Policy and Law*. New York: Longman.

———. 1973. *Cable Television and the FCC: A Crisis in Media Control*. Philadelphia: Temple University Press.

Linder, Laura R. 1999. *Public Access Television: America's Electronic Soapbox.* Westport, Conn.: Praeger.

Litman, Barry. 1990. "Network Oligopoly Power: An Economic Analysis." In *Hollywood in the Age of Television,* ed. Tino Balio, 115–144. Boston: Unwin Hyman.

Lyotard, Jean-François. 1991. *The Postmodern Condition: A Report on Knowledge.* Translated by Geoff Bennington and Brian Massumi. Minneapolis: University of Minnesota Press.

Magnant, Robert S. 1977. *Domestic Satellite: An FCC Giant Step.* Boulder, Colo.: Westview Press.

Mahler, Richard. 1990. "Despite Cable's Growth, Networks Remain Mr. Big," *Los Angeles Times,* 11 November, Calendar section, 7. Lexis-Nexis.

Mair, George. 1988. *Inside HBO.* New York: Dodd, Mead and Co.

McChesney, Robert W. 1993. *Telecommunications, Mass Media, and Democracy: The Battle for the Control of U.S. Broadcasting, 1928–1935.* New York: Oxford University Press.

———. 1996. "The Internet and U.S. Communication Policy-Making," *Journal of Communication* 46, no. 1 (winter): 98–124.

———. 1997. *Corporate Media and the Threat to Democracy.* New York: Seven Stories Press.

———. 1999. *Rich Media, Poor Democracy: Communication Politics in Dubious Times.* Urbana: University of Illinois Press.

McLuhan, Marshall. 1964. *Understanding Media.* New York: Mentor.

Meyer, Thomas J. 1992. "No Sound Bites Here." *New York Times Magazine,* 15 March, 46.

Meyrowitz, Joshua. 1985. *No Sense of Place: The Impact of Electronic Media on Social Behavior.* New York: Oxford University Press.

"Morris Cerullo World Evangelism Confirms Offer to Purchase Inspirational Television Network." 1990. PR Newswire, 4 June. Lexis-Nexis.

Morse, Margaret. "Postsynchronising Rock Music and Television." *Journal of Communication Inquiry* 10, no. 1 (winter 1986): 15–28.

Newcomb, Horace, and Paul M. Hirsch. 1987. "Television as a Cultural Forum." In *Television: The Critical View.* 4th ed. Edited by Horace Newcomb, 455–470. New York: Oxford University Press.

O'Donnell, Thomas, and Jay Gissen. 1982. "A Vaster Wasteland?" *Forbes,* 24 May, 109. Lexis-Nexis.

Oppenheim, Jerrold N. 1974. "The Unfulfilled Promise of Cable TV." *The Progressive* (February): 49–52.

Ostling, Richard N. 1986. "Power, Glory—and Politics." *Time,* 17 February, 62. Lexis-Nexis.

Owen, David. 1985. "Satellite Television." *Atlantic Monthly* (June): 45–62.

Parsons, Patrick. 1996. "Two Tales of a City: John Walson, Sr., Mahanoy City and the 'Founding' of Cable TV." *Journal of Broadcasting and Electronic Media* 40, no. 3, (summer): 354–365.

Penley, Constance. 1991. "Brownian Motion: Women, Tactics, and Technology." In *Technoculture,* ed. Constance Penley and Andrew Ross, 135–161. Minneapolis: University of Minnesota Press.

Phillips, Mary Alice Mayer. 1972. *CATV: A History of Community Antenna Television.* Evanston, Ill.: Northwestern University Press.

Price, Monroe, and John Wicklein. 1972. *Cable Television: A Guide for Citizen Action.* Philadelphia: United Church Press.

Public Access, Everyone's Channel (video recording). 1990. Producer-Director-Writer, David Shulman. New Decade Productions in association with Channel Four Television.

Rabinovitz, Lauren. 1989. "Animation, Postmodernism, and MTV." *Velvet Light Trap* 24 (fall): 99–112.

Ross, Andrew. 1989. *No Respect: Intellectuals and Popular Culture.* New York: Routledge.

Savan, Leslie. 1993. "Commercials Go Rock." In *Sound and Vision: The Music Video Reader,* ed. Simon Frith, Andrew Goodwin, and Lawrence Grossberg, 85–90. New York: Routledge.

Schatz, Thomas. 1990."Desilu, *I Love Lucy,* and the Rise of Network TV." In *Making Television: Authorship and the Production Process,* ed. Robert J. Thompson and Gary Burns, 117–135. New York: Praeger.

———. 1993. "The New Hollywood." In *Film Theory Goes to the Movies,* ed. Jim Collins, Hilary Radner, and Ava Preacher Collins, 8–36. New York: Routledge.

Seabrook, John. 1994. "Rocking in Shangri-la." *New Yorker,* 10 October, 64–78.

Seiden, Martin H. 1965. *An Economic Analysis of Community Antenna Television Systems and the Television Broadcasting Industry.* Washington, D.C.: GPO.

———. 1972. *Cable Television U.S.A.: An Analysis of Government Policy.* New York: Praeger.

Shales, Tom. 1979. "Beyond 'Benson': Black-Oriented Channel from a Cable Pioneer." *Washington Post,* 30 November. Lexis-Nexis.

Sloan Commission on Cable Communications. 1971. *On the Cable: The Television of Abundance.* New York: McGraw-Hill.

Smith, Ralph Lee. 1968. "Deadlier than a Western: The Battle over Cable TV." *New York Times Magazine,* 26 May, 34–44.

———. 1972. *The Wired Nation.* New York: Harper-Colophon.

Solomon, Norman. *The Habits of Highly Deceptive Media: Decoding Spin and Lies in Mainstream News.* Monroe, Maine: Common Courage Press, 1999.

"Special Feature on Cable Television." 1971. *NEA Journal–Today's Education* (November): 52–59.

Stout, Patricia A., and Benedicta L. Burda. 1989. "Zipped Commercials: Are They Effective?" *Journal of Advertising* 18, no. 4, 23–32.

Streeter, Thomas. 1987. "The Cable Fable Revisited: Discourse, Policy, and the

Making of Cable Television." *Critical Studies in Mass Communication* 4, 174–200.

————. 1996. *Selling the Air: A Critique of the Policy of Commercial Broadcasting in the United States.* Chicago: University of Chicago Press.

Taylor, John. 1994. "Pat Robertson's God, Inc." *Esquire* (November): 76–83.

TelePrompTer Corporation, application for domestic communication satellite receive-only earth stations. 1971. National Cable Television Center and Museum, Penn State University, University Park, Pa. Accession #94-IK-1118.

Television and Cable Factbook. Annual. Washington, D.C.: Warren Publishing.

Thomas, Clarence W. 1989. "It Chops, It Slices, It Dices: Television Marketing and the Rise and Fall of the Popeil Family Business." *Journal of Popular Film and Television* 17, no. 2 (summer): 67–73.

"Time Inc. to Buy 50% of Firm That Provides Cable TV Programs." 1981. *Wall Street Journal,* 28 August.

Traub, James. 1985. "CBN Counts Its Ble$$ings." *Channels* (May–June): 31.

Turow, Joseph. 1997. *Breaking Up America: Advertisers and the New Media World.* Chicago: University of Chicago Press.

U.S. Federal Communications Commission (FCC). 1959. *Report and Order.* Inquiry into the Impact of Community Antenna Systems, Translators, TV Satellite Stations and TV "Repeaters" on the Orderly Development of Television Broadcasting. Washington, D.C.: GPO.

————. 1965. *First Report and Order.* Washington, D.C.: GPO.

————. 1966. *Second Report and Order.* Washington, D.C.: GPO.

————. 1968a. *Fourth Report and Order.* Washington, D.C.: GPO.

————. 1968b. *Notice of Proposed Rulemaking and Notice of Inquiry.* Washington, D.C.: GPO.

————.1969. *First Report and Order.* Washington, D.C.: GPO.

————. 1972. *Cable Television Report and Order.* Washington, D.C.: GPO.

————. 1976. *Rules and Regulations with Respect to Selection of Television Signals for Cable Television Carriage.* Washington, D.C.: GPO.

————. 1980. *Report and Order on Cable Television Syndicated Exclusivity Rules.* Washington, D.C.: GPO.

Vaughan, Roger. 1978. "Ted Turner's True Talent." *Esquire,* 10 October, 35–48.

Warren, Albert. 1966. "The Coming Cable TV War." *Saturday Review,* 11 June, 90, 93, 101.

————. 1967. "The Four Letters That Have Rocked Broadcasting." *TV Guide,* 29 July, 4–7.

Waterman, David. 1986. "The Failure of Cultural Programming on Cable TV: An Economic Interpretation." *Journal of Communication* 36, no. 3 (summer): 92–107.

Waterman, David, and August Grant. 1991. "Cable Television as an Aftermarket." *Journal of Broadcasting and Electronic Media* 35, no. 2 (spring): 179–188.

Waters, Harry F., and Cynthia H. Wilson. 1979. "An All-Sports TV Network." *Newsweek,* 12 November, 124.

Weaver, Jane. 1993. "Marathon Mania." *Cablevision,* 8 March, 16–18.

White, Mimi. 1986. "Crossing Wavelengths: The Diegetic and Referential Imaginary of American Commercial Television," *Cinema Journal* 25 (winter): 51–64.

———. 1989. "Television: A Narrative—a History." *Cultural Studies* 3, no. 3 (October): 282–300.

White, Timothy R. 1990. "Hollywood's Attempt at Appropriating Television: The Case of Paramount Pictures." In *Hollywood in the Age of Television,* ed. Tino Balio, 145–163. Boston: Unwin Hyman.

Whiteside, Thomas. 1985. "Onward and Upward with the Arts: Cable I–III," *New Yorker,* 20 May, 45–85; 27 May, 43–73; 3 June, 82–105.

Whittemore, Hank. 1990. *CNN: The Inside Story.* Boston: Little, Brown.

"Why Advertisers Are Rushing to Cable TV." 1981. *Business Week,* 2 November, 96.

Williams, Christian. 1981. *Lead, Follow, or Get Out of the Way.* New York: Times Books.

Williams, Raymond. 1974. *Television: Technology and Cultural Form.* New York: Schocken Books.

Woodard, Charles C., Jr. 1974. *Cable Television: Acquisition and Operation of CATV Systems.* New York: McGraw-Hill.

Trade Press

The following business publications have been cited multiple times. Full citations are included in the notes. *Broadcasting, Business Week, Cablevision, NCTA Membership Bulletin, New York Times, TV Communications, Variety,* and *Wall Street Journal.* Only select longer periodical articles are included in the References.

Oral History Transcripts

The following transcripts were accessed at the National Cable Television Center and Museum, Penn State University, University Park, Pa., most of which are currently archived at the National Cable Television Center and Museum, Denver, Colo.

Frank Cooper, interviewed by E. Stratford Smith, June 1990.
Irving Berlin Kahn, interviewed by Marlowe Froke, July and October 1987.
Martin F. Malarkey, interviewed by Kathleen B. Hom, August 1985.
Robert Rosencrans, interviewed by E. Stratford Smith, May 1992 (draft version).

E. Stratford Smith, interviewed by Patrick R. Parsons, March–April 1986.
John Walson, interviewed by Mary Alice Mayer, August 1987.

Interviews by the Author

Albert Bagnardi, by telephone, 6 November 1994, Oneonta, New York.
Meg LaVigne and Lee Kinberg, 22 July 1994, WSBK-TV38, Boston.
E. Stratford Smith, 16 March 1995, National Cable Television Center and
    Museum.